EUROPEA: ETHNOMUSICOLOGIES AND MODERNITIES
Series Editors: Philip V. Bohlman and Martin Stokes

1. *Celtic Modern: Music at the Global Fringe*, edited by Martin Stokes and Philip V. Bohlman. 2003.
2. *Albanian Urban Lyric Song in the 1930s*, by Eno Koço. 2004.

D1552790

Europea: Ethnomusicologies and Modernities
Series Editors: Philip V. Bohlman & Martin Stokes

The new millennium challenges ethnomusicologists, dedicated to studying the music of the world, to examine anew the Western musics they have treated as "traditional," and to forge new approaches to world musics that are often overlooked because of their deceptive familiarity. As the modern discipline of ethnomusicology expanded during the second half of the twentieth century, influenced significantly by ethnographic methods in the social sciences, ethnomusicology's "field" increasingly shifted to the exoticized Other. The comparative methodologies previously generated by Europeanist scholars to study and privilege Western musics were deliberately discarded. Europe as a cultural area was banished to historical musicology, and European vernacular musics became the spoils left to folk-music and, later, popular-music studies.

Europea challenges ethnomusicology to return to Europe and to encounter its disciplinary past afresh, and the present is a timely moment to do so. European unity nervously but insistently asserts itself through the political and cultural agendas of the European Union, causing Europeans to reflect on a bitterly and violently fragmented past and its ongoing repercussions in the present, and to confront new challenges and opportunities for integration. There is also an intellectual moment to be seized as Europeans reformulate the history of the present, an opportunity to move beyond the fragmentation and atomism the later twentieth century has bequeathed and to enter into broader social, cultural, and political relationships.

Europea is not simply a reflection of and on the current state of research. Rather, the volumes in this series move in new directions and experiment with diverse approaches. The series establishes a forum that can engage scholars, musicians, and other interlocutors in debates and discussions crucial to understanding the present historical juncture. This dialogue, grounded in ethnomusicology's interdisciplinarity, will be animated by reflexive attention to the specific social configurations of knowledge of and scholarship on the musics of Europe. Such knowledge and its circulation as ethnomusicological scholarship are by no means dependent on professional academics, but rather are conditioned, as elsewhere, by complex interactions between universities, museums, amateur organizations, state agencies, and markets. Both the broader view to which ethnomusicology aspires and the critical edge necessary to understanding the present moment are served by broadening the base on which "academic" discussion proceeds.

"Europe" will emerge from the volumes as a space for critical dialogue, embracing competing and often antagonistic voices from across the continent, across the Atlantic, across the Mediterranean and the Black Sea, and across a world altered ineluctably by European colonialism and globalization. The diverse subjects and interdisciplinary approaches in individual volumes capture something of—and, in a small way, become part of—the jangling polyphony through which the "New Europe" has explosively taken musical shape in public discourse, in expressive culture, and, increasingly, in political form. Europea: Ethnomusicologies and Modernities aims to provide a critical framework necessary to capture something of the turbulent dynamics of music performance, engaging the forces that inform and deform, contest and mediate the senses of identity, selfhood, belonging, and progress that shape "European" musical experience in Europe and across the world.

Celtic Modern

Music at the Global Fringe

Edited by
Martin Stokes
Philip V. Bohlman

Europea: Ethnomusicologies and Modernities,
No. 1

The Scarecrow Press, Inc.
Lanham, Maryland, and Oxford
2003

SCARECROW PRESS, INC.

Published in the United States of America
by Scarecrow Press, Inc.
A wholly owned subsidiary of
The Rowman & Littlefield Publishing Group, Inc.
4501 Forbes Boulevard, Suite 200, Lanham, Maryland 20706
www.scarecrowpress.com

PO Box 317
Oxford
OX2 9RU, UK

British Cataloging in Publication Information Available

Library of Congress Cataloging-in-Publication Data
Celtic modern : music at the global fringe / edited by Martin Stokes,
Philip V. Bohlman.
        p. cm. — (Europea ; no. 1)
    Includes bibliographical references and index.
    ISBN 0-8108-4780-9 (alk. paper) — ISBN 0-8108-4781-7 (pbk. : alk. paper)
        1. Celtic music—History and criticism. 2. Ethnomusicology. I. Stokes,
Martin. II. Bohlman, Philip Vilas. III. Series.

ML3580.C36 2003
780'.89'916—dc21

                                                                    2003045637

♾™ The paper used in this publication meets the minimum requirements
of American National Standard for Information Sciences—Permanence of
Paper for Printed Library Materials, ANSI/NISO Z39.48-1992.
Manufactured in the United States of America.

Contents

Acknowledgments

Neither Europea, nor this book, the first in the series, would have been possible without the unstinting support and encouragement of Bruce Phillips, and the skillful mediations of the Scarecrow Press editorial team, particularly Jeff Wolf, Melissa Ray, and Andrew Yoder. We would also like to thank the contributors to this volume, whose patience and good humor during the long period in which both series and volume gestated have been very much appreciated. Tim Taylor agreed to write an afterword at short notice, and gamely submitted to more or less impossible deadlines. Chapter six was originally published in *Welsh Music History*: thanks are due to the Centre for Advanced Welsh Music studies at University College Bangor for their permission to reprint.

Philip Bohlman: There are more than a few Bohlmans who would like to think the name is Irish. It's not, but that has never prevented Celtic music from serving the whole family as wish fulfillment. Why else would my siblings, John and Mary Alice, gather annually at that bastion along the global fringe, Milwaukee's Irish Fest? As fine fiddlers, my children, Andrea and Benjamin, weave folk music of many traditions into the mix, where Christine orchestrates it for the whole lot of us. Thanks, as always, for making so much music possible.

Martin Stokes: Betty Thompson-McCausland has, over the long years, nourished my own interest in the world of academic Celticism with a constant supply of books and family anecdotes. I am deeply indebted.

Introduction

Martin Stokes and Philip V. Bohlman

> In the dress of the fool, the two colours that have tormented me,
> English and Gaelic, black and red, the court of injustice, the rea-
> son for my anger, and that fine rain from the mountains and these
> grievous storms from my mind streaming the two colours to-
> gether so that I will go with poor sight in the one colour that is so
> odd that the King himself will not understand my conversation.
>
> —Iain Crichton Smith/Iain Mac a'Ghobhainn 1992, 196

The title of this volume speaks of engagement rather than aboriginality, and of the conversations that have flowed, never easily, across
terrain marked by Crichton Smith's disorderly binarism, the black
and the red. The term "Celticism," as opposed to "Gaelicism," carries with it a certain baggage, notably a tradition of predominantly
English-language scholarship and other forms of cultural production carried out by Anglophone and Francophone elites on the Celtic
fringe. For nationalist scholars, it evokes an anglocentric and politically neutered aestheticism. The Gaelic movement in Ireland, for example, was quite opposed in ideological orientation and aesthetic
disposition to the Celtic Revival. It appealed to the relatively immediate worlds of language, sport, religion, and later, music. Gaelicism
fueled both the Irish and Scottish national imaginary in ways that
the Celtic revival simply could not.[1] Postcolonial critics, for whom
aesthetic Celticism has marked the continuity of colonial cultural
dependence and great house hegemony, by and large, would agree
(Eagleton 1995; Cairns and Richards 1998).

Our intention is partly critique and partly reappraisal, but also a
certain curiosity as to what this difficult term might generate in

relation to a discussion of music. It has certain merits, notably in providing a broader frame of reference than that of the British and Irish archipelago alone. This enables us to consider in this volume the circulation of the Celtic imaginary across Europe, North America, and Australia (see Bithell, Trew, and Smith in this volume, respectively), the location of the Celtic within global cultural flows (see Cadden, Reiss, Griffiths, and Vallely), and national and regional responses on the part of administrators, educationalists, and political activists (see Wilkinson and Symon) to a transnational phenomenon. These are steps that have not yet been taken in the study of Irish, Scottish, Welsh, Manx, and Breton musics individually, and we feel that the effort to bring these diverse perspectives together in this volume has been productive.

The term provides other vantage points, perhaps of a more abstract order. The earliest scholars of Celtic philology pointed out that the term *Keltoi* simply meant *foreigner* or *enemy*.[2] The term itself thus introduces us to a domain of relativities, of the peripheries as seen from centers of power and power-laden classificatory schemes. The point has been taken up, insistently, by a number of anthropologists of a deconstructive frame of mind over the last two decades.[3] Contrary to the appeals to deep Gaelic history on the part of cultural nationalists, and a more sophisticated and critical intellectual apparatus for determining counternational continuities,[4] such continuities do exist, as Edwin Ardener and his students assert, and are a matter of structure rather than content. As Malcolm Chapman puts it: "The 'continuity' of Celts comes from a meeting between a self-consciously civilising, powerful, centralizing culture which produces written records, and a much less powerful culture which leaves no or few written records" (1992, 3). Though scholars working in this tradition are inclined to say little about why such historically abstract structures should continue to produce such intensity of feeling (beyond expressing a kind of frustrated puzzlement), it has the distinct advantage of situating us firmly in a world of structured and structuring relativities, in which "centers" and "peripheries" are not separate social and cultural facts, whose violent coming together is to be understood not simply as a collision of abstracted political and cultural entities driven together by colonialism, or nation-states formation, but interwoven and mutually constituting processes. "Celtic" meanings can thus never be reduced to matters of ethnic property and aboriginal meaning, or to the simple functionalism of domination or subversion, hegemony, or counterhegemony.

A variety of different tropologies of center and periphery piles up on the Celtic fringe. The British Isles context of encounter between Celt and Saxon has been primary. The Tudor monarchy in England was the first symbolically to elaborate the idea of a British polity embracing Celt and Anglo-Saxon, following the fifteenth-century Wars of the Roses. Four centuries later Matthew Arnold (who established the first chair in Celtic studies at Oxford) looked to Celtic culture for the rejuvenation of an Arthurian Britain, which he and others were already anxiously seeking to define in opposition to a Teutonic Europe.[5] But Europe had its own symbolic investment in the Celt. Since Herder's formative encounter with MacPherson's Ossianic myth cycle, European nation builders in the nineteenth century looked in an almost instinctive reflex action to the Celtic fringe.[6] The habit persists today, as Bithell's account of Corsican nationalism in this volume reminds us, much aided by Hollywood (viz. *Braveheart* and others) and other potent global myth makers.

The motor force of the metropolitan imaginary is important to bear in mind. This is not to say that the others that it defines are passive onlookers in the process, but simply to stress that they have to deal with its consequences. Difference on the peripheries can only meaningfully be established according to terms set down by the center, an irony that postcolonial struggle elsewhere has long attested to and that continues to plague the nationalist intelligentsia with its most intractable problems. A convoluted and only partially repressed anglocentrism among the revolutionary nationalist intelligentsia on the Celtic fringe has often been noted (see, for example, English 1996). The architects of Welsh, Scottish, and Irish cultural nationalism in the mid- to late-nineteenth century spoke primarily to an audience in London, in a language that the metropolitan intelligentsia could understand and that was, to a large extent, controlled by them (see, for example, Humphreys 1983; Davies 1989; Chapman 1992).

An emphasis on what we are referring to, for simplicity's sake, as the "metropolitan imaginary" helps us understand an emerging experience gap between metropolitan and local concerns, as a restless and energetic language of realism began to inform Celtic cultural worlds. This took shape, increasingly, as the language of science, progress, and realism framed the intellectual horizons of an emerging local bourgeoisie. To take some brief examples, Thomas Stephens, a

chemist and nonconformist from Merthyr, contested the Madoc legends (concerning the Welsh discovery of America in the twelfth century) and the genteel fictions of the Anglo-Welsh bourgeoisie bound
up with this in public at the Llangollen *eisteddfod* in 1858, initiating fu-
rious debate (Humphreys 1983, 145). And, as another, the *Irish Builder*
remarked in 1901, with heavy sarcasm, "let our young men and maid-
ens compose mystic verses savoring of Bhudism and converse in
what we have no manner of doubt is execrably bad Irish . . . and there
is Ireland regenerated" (quoted in Sheehy 1980, 102). From the outset,
the Celtic Revival had its vociferous local critics. The *Irish Builder*'s
evocation of "Bhudism"[7] points to the by-then well-entrenched part-
ing of the ways of a Celtic imaginary framed by a secular, modernist
internationalism and a Gaelic imaginary framed by a localized and re-
ligiously phrased nationalism, a separation that was itself the product
of formative rifts between city and countryside, between great house,
rural yeomanry, and urban petty bourgeoisie.

Characteristically, this separation turned on the problem of "realism," expressed in the language of Stephen's "scientific" literary
criticism, and the *Irish Builder*'s perception of the "execrably bad
Irish" of the Celtic revivalists.[8] Always expressed as "a problem" in
nationalist scholarship, realism was, in truth, its major legitimating
trope. For the nationalist scholar, the problem with the folk-song collecting of Bunting, or Petrie, or Stanford was precisely its failure to
grasp "the real," its failure to represent things "as they really are."
The Victorian collector, by contrast, subordinated the act of collecting to the imperatives of domestication (that is, adaptation for performance on the piano), academic theoreticism, and sexual and political prudery, in various combinations.[9]

In fact one could plausibly argue the earliest Anglo-Celticists were
on the button as far as "scientific" ethnography was concerned, at
least, as conceived at that time, and in some important respects,
since. During the British Association expedition to Inishmore on the
Aran Isles in 1857, motivated as it was by a fashionable concern with
"antiquities" (see Sheehy 1980; Camille in Edelstein 1992), George
Petrie and Eugene O'Curry traveled from island to island during the
course of two weeks of intense fieldwork. Petrie learned the tunes he
heard in convivial domestic sessions by playing them on his violin
and then transcribing them; O'Curry transcribed the words, later
translated by Whitley Stokes. And, as Hugh Shields's work on James
Goodman, an exemplary "Victorian" collector, has recently shown,

some were able to collect instrumental music in a systematic and organized way, quite uninhibited by the kind of editorial concerns with matters of politics and sexuality that are usually considered to be typical of the period (Shields 1998).

Nonetheless, the paradigmatic "problem" of collecting on the Celtic fringe has invariably been diagnosed as one of realism, transparency, and legibility. All of these are bound up with the emergence of the nation itself, since it is the task of the cultural nationalist to reveal "the real," actively misrepresented by colonial scholarship. It is realism that allows the nation, long spoken for, to speak for itself. It is realism that legitimates a certain methodological reflexivity, through which the colonial meddling of the Anglo-Victorians is shown for what it is. It is realism that, as a literary trope, discursively organizes the smooth movement from opacity to transparency (the revealing, so to speak, of Corkery's *Hidden Ireland*).[10] Petrie and O'Neill, in the Irish context, would stand at roughly opposite ends of this process (note Breathnach 1971; Carolan 1997). There is a restless cultural logic at work here, which continues to separate "the real" from "fakelore"[11] long after the nationalist moment that initially invested the process with such urgency. The institutions and agencies of cultural nationalism continually fall victim to the very rhetoric that was instrumental in their coming into existence. They too are subsequently deemed to speak an elite and politically invested (i.e., "nonreal") language. They too are seen to live in a world of fabrication and artifice, cripplingly dependent upon what they define themselves against; the quest for the real must, therefore, go on.

To critique in this vein is, of course, to enter the process and ultimately endorse precisely what is criticized: the search for a hitherto misapprehended "real" coupled with a (less explicit) demand for its institutional habilitation remain unshaken ideological components in thinking and writing about music on the Celtic fringe. While Ciaran Carson's literary tour-de-force *Last Night's Fun* (Carson 1996) might be read as a point-by-point rejection of the institutionalized musical values of an earlier generation of Irish cultural nationalists, it remains engagingly dependent upon most of its central tropes: the gritty reality of working-class life, the apprehension of "the hidden" in memory and peripheral vision, the follies of academia, the establishment of authoritative counterlineages and countercanons, and so forth. The demand for attention from a "high-culture" orientated (in

this case, literary) intelligentsia and enhanced institutional habilitation continues to revolve around a realist problematic, a matter of
separating what is real from what is not and of separating those who
have been taken in by the fantasies and fictions of an earlier generation and those who have not. And this, in turn, is rooted in the per-
sistently dichotomous ethnic reckoning that has articulated Britain's
industrial expansion and subsequent decline, and a century of nationalist response on its peripheries.[12]

PRAISING THE WORLD'S EDGES

Moli bum ymylau byd, Malu son, melys ennyd; I praised the world's
edges, milling sounds for a brief sweet moment.

—Guto'r Glyn, late fifteenth century, cited in Humphreys 1983, 39

The strategic alliance between subordinated nationalities and black
expressive culture is, for many contemporary theorists, diagnostic of
the postnational (and by extension, postmodern) moment.[13] It in-
vests local struggles with cultural breadth and historical depth; it
transforms national minorities into postnational majorities; it transforms commodity production and exchange into progressive consciousness and radical social movement. But academic and literary
Celticists in the late nineteenth century had little difficulty in making common cause with others on the "world's edge," at least, as
this "edge" has been variously perceived over time. Musicians on
the Celtic fringe build on long traditions of transnational exchange
and dialogue with, often, remote and unlikely others.[14]

Organizers of national festival traditions (*fleadh, eisteddfod, fest-
noz,* pl., respectively *fleadhanna, eisteddfodau, festau-noz*) have a pan-
Celtic field of vision, in the varying and complex ways many of the
contributors to this volume identify (see in particular Reiss, Wilkinson, Vallely). Invitees from other Celtic nations and the Diaspora,
along with traveling enthusiasts, form an important part of any such
event. A certain kind of pragmatism is at work here. Musical activity can form a focus for sociability, communication, and exchange in
ways that the spoken Gaelic languages cannot, despite the best efforts of Welsh, Scottish, Irish, Cornish, Manx, and Breton linguistic
elites (see Chapman 1994; McDonald 1989). The session has, indeed,
relatively recently emerged as the ideal type of informal musicking

across most of western Europe (note Vallely's chapter in this volume), and has grafted itself onto indigenous forms of musical sociality in many parts of North America and Australia (see Trew and Smith, respectively, in this volume). Irish traditional dance music constitutes the dominant medium of exchange, but other forms of music can easily be grafted on and coexist with it. What matters is not what is played but how it is played, along with the observance of a certain social *modus operandi*, certain simple rules of etiquette.[15] This also pertains to the more formal staged presentations. Where language often divides (but shouldn't), musicians, many of whom are experienced hands in the cross-cultural and multilingual worlds of the *fleadh*, the *fest-noz*, and the *eisteddfod*, are often the only people able to shape a shared aesthetic space.

Those involved in the organization of Celtic world festivals have often sought a symbolic language in which the fragmented world of Celtdom could be reunited, and the modern festival bears many of the marks of its Celticist forebears. A strong metropolitan imagination, as always, was at work here. The Abergavenny *eisteddfodau* in the early to middle years of the nineteenth century were, to paraphrase Emyr Humphreys, veritable showcases of a certain kind of bourgeois Welsh worthiness.[16] The 1838 *eisteddfod* was marked by the participation of a Breton deputation, headed by Count Theodore Hersart de la Villemarque, who was initiated into the Bardic order, and celebrated the event with a composition of his own, in "Breton spiced with Welsh" (Humphreys 1983, 133). It was a formative moment for La Villemarque. His *Barsaz Breiz*, published in 1839, a Breton counterpart of MacPherson's Ossianic poems and Charlotte Guest's English translation of *The Mabinogion*, was directly inspired by his *eisteddfod* experience. But it was also a formative moment in the history of the *eisteddfodau*, linking Welsh industry, Anglican Celticists, and highly placed deputations from neighboring states to an elaborate ceremonial stressing the unity of the Celts and the continuity of the Arthurian tradition in the Celtic lands. The subsequent history of the *eisteddfodau* is one, to be sure, in which this legacy has been explicitly rejected, and in which linguocentric notions of a more localized Celtic nationalism have been stressed. But a current of pan-Celtic and largely nonlinguistic ceremonial runs through these events; musicians are active and important participants.

New forms of ceremonial continually come into play, shaped decisively by the modern world (the leisured consumption of "culture,"

tourism, electronic media), but appealing to a deep past. Pilgrimage is
a particularly crucial trope in the contemporary Celticist imaginary, its
appeal, once again, primarily to a leisured class of outsiders. A European frame of reference prevails, connecting the language of Celtic
pilgrimage with a symbolic geography expressed in other heavily
mythologized figures of travel and movement. It was the perception
of similarities between *sean-nós* and Middle Eastern vocal ornament
that lead Bob Quinn to imagine his Atlantean civilization, linking
North Africa and the Celtic fringe in maritime cultural exchange.
Quinn's Atlantean might be considered a published and film docu-
mentary version of a widespread west coast of Ireland folklore, bringing together a popularized *Kulturkreis* ethnology with historical fantasy imagined in terms of epic battles and migrations. One version
stresses Armada survivors, perhaps Moorish galley slaves, who
struggled ashore to impart Mediterranean good looks, some fancy
footwork, and a predilection for microtones to the local population.
Another, with similar consequences, particularly for the supposed
"microtonal" content of *sean-nós* singing, stresses wandering "gyp-
sies." On the Celtic fringe, as elsewhere in Europe, Roma has a vital
symbolic role to play in knitting together the fragments and detritus
of the European "periphery." Roma and Travellers constitute one of
the most important and widespread images of otherness in Europe.
The landscapes of Traveller songs, veritable songlines, often resemble
those forged in the idiom of Celtic pilgrimage, and this is hardly for-
tuitous.[17]

Celticist imaginary landscapes positively demand of those who
would encounter them that they travel, indeed, that they traverse
the intersecting and contradictory planes of geography and history.
These different planes yield what Nigel Pennick calls the "inner and
outer landscapes" of Celtic religion, whereby he distinguishes between the sacred object and the "symbolic qualities, mythic traditions" it contains (Pennick 1996, 9). There are, to put the case more
directly, sacred landscapes we see and those we do not see, particularly in those lands where the present masks the past. If a larger
Celtic spiritual imaginary is to emerge, then journey is necessary as
a means of humanly connecting one sacred landscape to another.
The historical dilemma of Celticist sacred geography is that the idealized stability of its inner landscapes has rarely survived in the
"outer" landscapes, shaped by dispersal and diaspora. In order to
experience the totality of the Celtic sacred landscape, it is necessary

to journey between and among its parts, in the process, transforming journeys into pilgrimages giving meaning to the multiple levels of the Celticist geographical and historical imaginary.

We travel with music. Pilgrimage, especially European Christian pilgrimage, has historically depended on complex processes of colportage: the material culture of broadsides, prayerbooks, and, in the twentieth century, recordings, that have prepared the pilgrim for entrance into the communitas of sacred journey and the pilgrimage itself, providing a musical text for each stage of the journey (Bohlman 2000). Modern "Celtic" pilgrimage is no different. The specific landscapes of Celtic pilgrimage and the specific nature of its semiotic system intensify the functions of musical colportage even more. The visual and sonic imagery of Celtic pilgrimage, therefore, lends itself to widespread commodification and dissemination through the colportage of cassettes and CDs. Cassette culture and colportage converge in a postmodern bricolage, in which historical and geographical journey converge. The trope of pilgrimage organizes a number of recent recordings; Loreena McKennitt's *The Mask and the Mirror* (1994) and The Chieftain's *Santiago* (1996) are striking examples. Like most recorded pilgrimage anthologies, *Santiago* uses sound examples to construct the path of pilgrimage itself. Pilgrimage recordings characteristically begin in a rather undifferentiated landscape, an amalgam of the many and distinct everyday worlds from which pilgrims begin their journeys. Most pilgrimages allow one to begin in different places, but by journey's end there is only a single sacred site. The musical bricolage at the beginning collapses into the intense sonic experience of sacred time at journey's end.

For The Chieftains, the task of performing and recording Europe's Celtic fringe was nothing new (cf. *Celtic Wedding*, "set" in Brittany); indeed, a huge transnational audience, for whom The Chieftains have represented Celtic music writ large for several decades, expects nothing less. In Paddy Moloney's words,

> We recorded as we travelled, deriving inspiration for our musical movements from the places we visited along the traditional pilgrims route to the enchanted cathedral of Santiago de Compostela. Christians hold the site sacred and believe it to be the final resting place of St. James the Apostle. Older legends dating back to ancient Celtic times speak of another pilgrimage that followed the stars of the Milky Way to Lands End. . . . Transcending its own mysterious origins, the

Pilgrimage continues to draw countless thousands from around the
world to this faraway land." (Moloney 1996, 1–2)

But Santiago goes farther, moving to related sites of Catholic pilgrimage and, in effect, musically Celticizing them. The most obvious
resignification is the inclusion of Linda Ronstadt and Los Lobos on
the CD, performing a song called "Guadalupe," the major pilgrimage site in Mexico. But for the Chieftains, the leap from recording as
they traveled to adding fellow musicians to the CD-as-pilgrimage
that draws on "countless thousands around the world" is minimal
indeed. The idiom of the session brings all together. The CD ends at,
or with, an electronic "session" at a pub in Vigo called "Dublin,"
making its end also its beginning, and collapsing sacred site into secular practice.

Celticism thrives, as pilgrimage, in the context of New Age spirituality, post–Cold War religious revivalism, and a mass-mediated
"postmodern" syncretic multiculturalism. One might briefly consider three different sets of musical practice from the 1990s in which
Celticisms are asserted. The first of these might be characterized as
multicultural and multireligious repertories of world music, especially those that mark the boundary regions historically troubled by
religious conflict (cf. Loreena McKennitt's *The Mask and the Mirror*).
The second might be characterized, broadly, as New Age music, an
amalgam of globalized peripheries, medievalist fantasy, and other
plays with and on "deep" past (cf. Anuna's *Omnis*). A third might be
characterized as the revival of "traditional" forms of worship in the
Catholic church in Europe. As different as these three domains are
from each other, they also demonstrate a remarkable degree of unity
and continuity in their use of symbols drawn from a Celticist imaginary, indicating a globalized resurgence of a Celticism expressed in
a religious idiom (cf. King 1997; Wallace 1998; Meek 2000).

LOOKING WEST

Say it loud: I'm black, and I'm proud.

—James Brown/Roddy Doyle, *The Commitments*

If, over the course of a century and more, those animated by the
Celticist imaginary have made insistent efforts to connect with oth-

ers "at the world's edges," it is the new world that has provided the most persistent point of reference. Emigration transformed one myth of aboriginality, biblical in origin (positing the Irish as ancient Milesians, Welsh as offspring of Noah), into another. Native Americans were considered by some to be the descendants of earlier wanderers from the Celtic shores, and it was here, and not in the British Isles, that Celts could most properly and appropriately be Celts. The appropriation of American, and specifically African American, expressive forms by musicians from the Celtic fringe should be understood, certainly, in a general context of globalization and ingrained cultural habits of looking West.[18] A great many musicians have, indeed, moved from the industrial cities of the Celtic fringe into African American–dominated popular musical worlds. The movement is retrospectively given a Celtic patina through various forms of acknowledgment, some explicit and verbal, others cryptic and indirect, of "home's" formative and enduring influences. Van Morrison, Tom Jones, Shirley Bassey, John Cale, and Sinead O Connor spring to mind (see Dai Griffith's chapter in this volume; see also Negus 1997 on Sinead O Connor).

But other, and more explicit, forms of strategic (following Spivak 1995) connections have been forged between "Celtic" and "black" expressive forms, which link contemporary developments with older myths of Celtic aboriginality. The semiotic modalities of this are various. Some, such as *Riverdance*, foreground black (and others) against a Celtic background. In others, such as the Afro-Celt Sound System (on which, see Smith, Vallely, and Reiss in this volume) and a number of Gaelic-language rappers, the reverse is the case: "Celt," expressed either as the Gaelic language itself or as a set of distinct musical figures and textures is set against a black (sound system) background. Their social dynamics are similarly complex and varied. *Riverdance*, as is now well known, has spawned "riverdancing" in Irish clubs and cultural centers across the United States and Europe and has set new and, for most, unattainable standards of professional packaging, marketing, and publicity for aspiring traditional music bands across Ireland and elsewhere. Hip-hop has articulated a Gaelic-speaking subcultural scene in a number of Irish, Scottish, and Welsh cities.

In other contexts, the process of connecting Celtic with black musics has followed the contours of New Age sociability, mentioned earlier, as Smith illustrates in this volume. The *didjeridu* appeared in

New Age circles in the British Isles in the 1980s, used in a variety of forms of therapy and hypnosis, and in forms of hip-hop, trip hop, rave, and other electronic sound contexts not long after, by musicians such as Shaun Farrenden, Cyrung, Ianto Thorbner, Sozo, and Graeme Wiggins. The convergence of the *didjeridu*, Irish traditional music, and Celtic "deep history" takes a particularly engaging form in the work of Simon O Dwyer, who has applied *didjeridu* techniques to reconstructions of a number of Bronze Age Irish horns, discovered by archaeologists in the mid-eighteenth century. The vocal technique of "lilting" in Irish traditional music, a technique that verbally represents the rhythms and melodies of instrumental performance, can be applied (not unproblematically) to the circular breathing and vocalizations involved in *didjeridu* performance. Lilting connects the Australian instrument with the Bronze Age horn and the contemporary performance of Irish traditional music, and the *didjeridu* has been a conspicuous presence among New Age–inspired traditional music performers in Ireland over the course of the last decade (see also Casey 1994; Magowan 1997).

The hopes expressed by Lipsitz and other subculturalists that globalized black expressive forms can translate into progressive critical consciousness require substantial nuancing on the Celtic fringe. The New Age communities that have adopted the *didjeridu* across the British Isles and Ireland have been consistently proenvironment and proindigenous peoples, but their apprehension of "black" is one quite removed from that of the subculturalists[19]: "indigenous" rather than African American, otherworldly and self-renouncing rather than this-worldly and pleasure affirming, ultimately brought into juxtaposition with Western music only to reveal its essential distance and mystique. The use of indigenous musics in New Age recordings (take *Deep Forest* as an example) speaks, arguably, of a politics not of radical connection and inclusion, as Lipsitz would hope (i.e., "we're all 'black'"), but of distanciation and paternalistic preservation, whose neocolonial overtones are hard to ignore.[20] Its Celtic fringe manifestation also speaks of the enduring legacy of eighteenth-century aboriginalist fantasies in contemporary musical practice.

Perhaps one of the best known discussions of black culture in an Irish context has been provided by Roddy Doyle's novel, and Alan Parker's film, about a Dublin R&B band, *The Commitments*. The subculturalist script is given an unexpected twist. The band collapses in acrimony, Wilson Pickett drives off in the opposite direction, and most of the film's best laughs occur at moments of misfit and mis-recognition. The Motown soundtrack plays against the backdrop of drab Dublin tenements; the saxophone player tells mystified street kids "I'm black and I'm proud"; Andrew Strong, as bus conductor, belts out "Mustang Sally" to an audience of embarrassed girls on their way to first communion while he dispenses tickets. The novel/film plays on a different mythology, of wild and (necessarily) unfulfilled male dreams, of fatally undisciplined sparks of creative imagination as the very stuff of a contemporary Irish folk wisdom (the nostalgic message at the heart of all of Roddy Doyle's novels). But it also cleverly mediates the social ramifications of two separate but intertwined myths. Where the subculturalists insisted on the in-evitable appropriateness of black expressive forms in the white sub-cultural struggle for urban space, Doyle/Parker's musicians fail to bridge the gap. Merely wanting to be black is not enough to change things. And where the Celticist intelligentsia have continued to dream of "milling sounds on the world's edges," of a radical process of connecting black and Celtic aboriginality, the ways in which lan-guages of inclusion and romantic connection feed on (and do noth-ing to ameliorate) social processes of exclusion and alienation are all too striking.

Away from thinking-class negritude, it is white America, undoubt-edly, which has played the more significant role in articulating musi-cal life on the Celtic fringe. The American and Irish road west share a common moral topography that converge on surely the most wide-spread and most popular musical practice in rural Ireland: country and western/country and Irish. This is a genre that musicians have adapted to a wide range of more or less indigenous lyric song, in-cluding Gaelic-language *sean-nós* in some parts of the rural Irish west, white gospel classics (as in Nashville), Victorian parlor and music hall songs, and, in the north, political "party" songs. The last category ex-cluded, the repertory of Daniel O Donnell incorporates practically every element. As this short list illustrates, it embraces powerful ten-sions and contradictions, particularly in its superimposition of Amer-ican and Irish moral geographies. The American western can certainly be interpreted as a puritanical allegory of liberal individualism, ani-mated by the solitary, violent, emotionally withdrawn outsider who rides off, alone, into the sunset. By contrast, the Irish myth of the west, as configured by (predominantly Protestant) writers and thinkers

associated with the Celtic Revival, saw the Irish west as a point of relief and escape from the claustrophobic modernism of the Gaelic
League and the Roman Catholic Devotional Revival, a moral space
untainted by industrialism and material progress, and the home of a
passionate and sensual *Gemeinschaft* collectivity (Gibbons 1988). Gibbons's distinction is thought provoking.

But the contrast can be overdrawn. Nashville's country and western, as a musical genre, counterpoints the movie image of the emotionally withdrawn gunman with the figure of the man who is vul-
nerable, tearful, and emotionally demanding. Country and western
in rural Ireland thus draws coherently on two congruent expressive
registers, one "American" and the other "Irish," although, given a
century or more of migration across the Atlantic and the active involvement of Irish writers, musicians, and entrepreneurs in Hollywood and Nashville, it hardly makes sense to speak of the two as
separate entities. The connection of rural Irish socializing with the
intimate "other" of country and western speaks strikingly of the im-
brication of local experience and global form, well documented in a
variety of other contexts. Country and western is perfectly adapted
for performance in small ballrooms and dance floors in rural bars,
perfectly adapted for genteel cross-generational socializing, bringing together families separated by work and residence in Britain, Ireland, and the United States on summer weekends, to reconnect and
forge new alliances through courtship and marriage. It speaks, reassuringly, of the congruity of national and transnational experience,
of tradition and modernity, addressing the trauma of separation and
feelings of powerlessness experienced by those who stay behind,
and the guilt of those who go. It is white, rather than black, America
that has provided the most consequential point of musical connection between Celtic and new worlds.[21]

CELTICISM AND COMMERCE

[These artifacts] show the taste with which the simplest domestic
utensils of the Irish were adorned.

—Margaret Stokes, *Early Christian Art in Ireland*, n.d. (c. 1903), 111

It was in the applied arts, rather than the more sober fine arts, that
popular Irish symbolism was used in its most exuberant fashion.

Stone carvers, stuccodores, makers of furniture and souvenirs in
bog oak, jewellers, producing reproductions of Celtic ornaments
were much less inhibited than their brethren in the Academies.

—Sheehy 1980, 71

Joanne Sheehy poses an interesting question: Why were the "more
sober" fine arts "inhibited" when it came to making serious artistic
use of Celtic symbolism? The frame of reference is that of the visual
arts, and not literature, although music could certainly be included.
It was less inhibition, perhaps, than irrelevance. The Celtic revivalists had an eye on the European avant-garde, whose relevant others
were signaled through coded and conventional points of reference
rather than engaged with through mutually informing cultural
processes.[22] Ossianism took Mendelssohn to the Hebrides, and the
Celtic Twilight took Bax to Donegal; in neither case did the music
they (may have) heard impinge even slightly on their compositional
modus operandi.[23] Nineteenth- and early twentieth-century sym-
phonists approached the Celtic world primarily as a linguistic and
secondarily as a literary phenomenon, and in this respect they embodied the key dispositions of their milieu. The refusal of the Celticist avant-garde to use their Irishness, Scottishness, or Welshness to
good effect is of concern to Sheehy, anxious to explain an absence
and, presumably, maintain the possibility that a properly "high cultural" Celticism might yet emerge. But it also serves as useful reminder that Celticism as commodity form has certainly done more
to shape contemporary Celtic imaginaries than Celticism as writerly
academic endeavor.

Celticism as commodity form rode on the back of a lively trade in
decorative art, initiated by the British arts and crafts movement and
merchandized in an innovative and energetic fashion by Liberty and
Co. of London. This merchandizing, in turn, was bound up with
world fairs, in which Celtic crafts thrived. The Columbian Exposi-
tion in Chicago in 1893, held on the Midway Plaisance, a stone's
throw away from where we write this introduction, was the show-
case for two entire Irish "villages." Alice Hart's "Donegal Castle,"
and "The Countess of Aberdeen's Village" were both shop-fronts for
arts and crafts organizations that were seen by their managers as
stimulants to regional economic regeneration. Beyond articulating a
fascination with "the real" and the authentic in the imagination of
colonized others at the hubs of global capitalism (see Mitchell 1988),

such fairs, particularly toward the end of the century, were particularly important in globalizing bourgeois tastes in ethnic jewelry and home decor. This was, as is well known, far from irrelevant to the twentieth-century avant-garde. Japanese prints and Javanese gamelan, to name but two significant forms of world fair exotica, provided important alternatives to the dominant realism of the visual arts and the symphonicism of nineteenth-century musical aesthetics. But toward the end of the century, home decor had come to assume a particularly important place in the world fairs.

Liberty had hit on the marketability of Celtic ware sometime after the discovery of the Tara brooch, which was displayed at the London world fair in 1851.[24] A replica of it was, apparently, sold to Queen Victoria, a point that was unlikely to have been wasted on Liberty's marketing department. From this moment on there was a lively connection between archaeology, the jewelry trade, and publishing (transformed in this period by new reproduction processes that made possible, for example, the detailed illustrations in Margaret Stokes's *Early Christian Art in Ireland* and a popular how-to literature on Celtic design). The commerce in Celtic craft undoubtedly benefited from some skilled practitioners. One of Liberty's first master designers in the 1890s was Archibald Knox from the Isle of Man. His Celtic-inspired metalwork and design were enormous successes (especially his "Tudric" and "Cymric" ranges), which Liberty exploited to the full, using the latest techniques in casting and mass reproduction. Liberty's commercial and technical *nous*-inspired Celtic jewelry and design ventures elsewhere at around the turn of the century: Charles Rennie Mackintosh in Glasgow, the Irish Arts and Crafts movement, the Dun Emer guild, Cuala Industries, Thomas O Shaughnessy at Marshall Fields in Chicago. Decorative Celticism blended easily with other "non-Western" visual aesthetics, then also in vogue (notably Arab and Japanese), which also rejected depth in favor of exuberant surface. That a Celtic design should have been chosen to decorate Dankmar Adler and Louis Sullivan's Anshe Ma'ariv synagogue on Chicago's north shore (of 1887–1889) merits only passing comment. The use of Celtic design in the decorative adornment of decidedly modern places and spaces counterbalanced the shock of the new with the reassuringly generalized and abstracted continuities of exotic tradition.

Metropolitan marketing and mass production for domestic consumption bear heavily on Celtic musics. The construction of a pan-

Celtic market in music recording and publishing has a long history. The earliest recordings of Irish musicians, such as those of Michael Coleman in New York, were marketed with the widest possible audience in mind, both in the United States and in Europe; The Chieftains and Alan Stivell continued a marketing tradition of casting Celtic identities in the widest and most cosmopolitan light in the 1960s; Altan and Capercaillie do the same today. The workings of this market is no simple matter and is far from being the imposition on "peripheries" of a fanciful and homogenizing metropolitan imagination, as is sometimes imagined when the "World Music" fashions of various periods are discussed. In the case of Celtic musics, recordings and recording company strategies have drawn on quite varied and multiple circuits of exchange and interaction,[25] in which one would have to include local scenes animated by socializing musicians of various ages and backgrounds, patterns of migration, internal and international tourism, and that complex of entrepreneurial and administrative activity revolving around arts councils, university departments, and festival organizations.

The ramifications of these criss-crossing circuits, in terms of musicians' changing horizons and the changing configurations of what, from a metropolitan perspective, counts as appropriately "Celtic" (or, indeed, "Irish," "Scottish," "Welsh," etc.) cannot be easily determined. The criss-crossing circuits have certainly produced, as all of the contributions to this particular volume demonstrate, no singular or unitary musical vision of the Celtic world, but rather a bewildering diversity. To note the commoditized aspect of Celtic musical identities is not, then, to suggest the inevitability of, as Lomax put it, "cultural grey-out" (Lomax 1968), but to ask questions about how, in the context of its actual social ramifications (as opposed to supposed ill-effects), the commodity form and commoditized attitudes toward music making produce such diverse sociomusical realities on the Celtic fringe.

Much music-collecting activity, habitually understood in terms of heroic nation building, needs to be considered in the broad context of Celtic commerce for domestic consumption. O'Neill's *Music of Ireland*, published originally in Chicago in 1903 and dedicated to "the multitude of nonprofessional musicians of the Gaelic- and English-speaking races all over the world who enjoy and cherish the music of Ireland" is a case in point. It was, and remains, a mass publishing phenomenon. Like the Celtic design "how-to" manuals, from the mid-nineteenth century (see Jones's 1856 discussed in Sheehy 1980, 64) to the mid-twentieth century (see Bain's *Celtic Art* of 1951, still very much in print), it constitutes a first port of call for anyone seeking a basic vocabulary, the elements of a broader composition. Just as many Celtic jewelers turn first to Bain's book to master fundamental ornamentational techniques, most musicians who want to learn a handful of jigs and reels in order to participate in a session continue to turn first to O'Neill's. O'Neill's canny recognition of the "musicians all over the world" who enjoy Irish music links it unambiguously to the transnational currency of the Celtic commodity form at that particular moment.

The point cuts across, without necessarily excluding, other interpretations of O'Neill as an exemplary Irish collector.[26] Ireland came to O'Neill, it is often argued, in relatively undisturbed social totality in the shape of a large and representative migrant community in Chicago, allowing for a view of the island that would have been more or less impossible back at home at this particular time. For Breathnach (1971) and, more explicitly, Carolan (1997) the energy, scholarly discipline, and personal integrity of O'Neill totally transformed the messy, opaque, and crypto-colonial efforts of the Victorian collectors. Here, at last, was the music of a hitherto "hidden" Ireland revealed, and here, at last, was the model for all future collecting: rational, abstract, zoned, monumental, and scientific. But it is difficult to avoid the conclusion that another set of deeply ideological schemes, just as intrusive as those of the Victorians, was at work in O'Neill's 1903 *Music of Ireland*: that of the New World's rationalism, zoning, monumentalism, and modernist appeal to scientific disinterest, starkly embodied in the urban design of O'Neill's adopted city, Chicago. This is, once again, to stress the necessity of thinking about Celtic musics as part and parcel of the modern world, the industrial city, the commodity form, and the patterns of rationality and intellectual order that emanate from it, and not as something eternally opposed.

To approach such artifacts and commodities as O'Neill's *Music of Ireland* in the vein of commodity critique is, of course, to engage in an act of criticism, but not an act of aesthetic or political dismissal. On the contrary: we and the other contributors to the volume attempt to root this criticism in the context of, in most of our cases, passionate and lifelong engagement with and dedication to the music we talk about. We recognize the struggle involved in extricating ourselves from or finding some productive vantage point within tired and often sterile debates about the relationship between tradition and modernity, radicalism and revisionism, and so forth.[27] We are committed to the view that we are helped rather than hindered in this by the fact that we reflect on *music*: music in the everyday and experiential lives of musicians, music in performance for diverse audiences, music in acts of public or domestic consumption, music in acts of self-assertion or disguise, music as pleasure and torment, as incorporation and exclusion, as location and dislocation, as recognition and misrecognition. If we think aloud, in a vein of somewhat uncomfortable self-reflection, as people who occupy somewhat ambiguous positions in relation to the circuitry of academia or professional musicianship, and as people positioned in complex ways between Celtic and non-Celtic worlds, we hope the process will do something to illuminate, to ourselves and, we hope, others, the compelling and consequential nature of the music we talk about and its grip on a global imagination.

NOTES

1. See Vallely on the Gaelic League in Ireland and Symon on the Scottish Feisan movement, both in this volume.

2. Chapman credits Trinity College Dublin Celticist Whitley Stokes with this insight (Chapman 1992, 30).

3. A number of Edwin Ardener's students at Oxford in the 1970s followed his pioneering work (for which see, among others, Ardener 1989) on the European peripheries, notably Malcolm Chapman, Maryon McDonald, Sharon McDonald, and Ed Condry, research framed specifically by the problematic of ethnicity and identity, and generally by anthropological structuralism. See, in particular, Chapman 1978, 1992, and 1994; MacDonald 1993; McDonald 1989.

4. Consider, for instance Emyr Humphrey's *Taliesin Tradition* (1983) and Cheryl Herr's Irish "erotics" (1995).

5. This should not be confused at all with the cultivation of the spoken Celtic languages, particularly in Wales, which Arnold quite explicitly saw as a hindrance to government and industrial progress.

6. For a valuable analysis see Trumpener 1997.

7. No doubt evoking Yeats's well-known fascination with Japanese Noh drama. See Fenellosa 1916.

8. Celtic revivalists had the more nuanced sense of the role of the imagination in political process, but were not themselves averse to appropriating

a contemporary language of hard science. Synge's 'ethnography' of the Aran Islands is a case in point (Synge 1992).

9. Bunting believed, for example, that "truly" ancient music could be identified by the ease with which a harmonic scheme could be discerned in them, and doctored his transcriptions from the Belfast Harping Festival with diatonic key signatures and piano accompaniments accordingly. According to Petrie, only vocalists could be relied on to preserve a melody, because they were constrained by texts; he largely ignored a huge corpus of instrumental dance music as a consequence. On the collecting tradition and its historiography, see, for instance, Bunting 1969; Breathnach 1971; Carolan 1997; Feldman and O'Doherty 1979; McCann 1995; Shields 1998. On Petrie specifically see Calder 1968. For an excellent review and polemical critique of what we are characterizing as the "realist" tradition see White 1998.

10. Corkery's *Hidden Ireland* was published in 1925.

11. We borrow Dave Harker's somewhat polemic and subsequently much discussed notion. See Harker 1985.

12. Our basic orientations on this issue come from Nairn 1977 and Hechter 1975.

13. See Lipsitz 1994 for an influential formulation of the issues.

14. See Stokes 1994 for a discussion of a Middle Eastern/Irish musical exchange. Since that article was written, the amount of Celtic/"World music" crossovers that one can find in record stores and hear on radio programs, such as Fiona Ritchie's *Thistle and Shamrock* ®, has increased exponentially. The point made in the article arguably remains: that "exchange" and "crossover" might be stressed at a discursive level, while, at the level of musical practice, the terms of exchange and crossover are usually being dictated by only one of the parties to it, with the consequence that important aspects of the process are actively misrecognized by the participants involved.

15. See Carson 1986. Carson's pocket-sized handbook contains an only slightly tongue-in-cheek section on session etiquette. This speaks volumes about the internationalization of the Irish traditional music scene.

16. Humphreys 1983, 133. We draw heavily on his account of the nineteenth-century *eisteddfod* in this section.

17. Hear, for example, the Davie Stewart and Jimmy McBeath recordings on *Songs of the Travelling People* 1994. There are various pilgrimage sites in western France and northwestern Spain where Roma are present as professional musicians.

18. For a historical view of the black/Irish connection, and a detailed reading of *The Commitments* (which complements ours to a large degree), see Taylor 1998.

19. See Hebdige 1979 for a classic statement.

20. Feld 2000 deals with the specifically central African dimensions of this discussion in a complex study of the circulation of "pygmy" musical

styles. For a useful account of the more general parameters of representation of others in "world music," see Taylor 1997.

21. We consider American country music's "whiteness" more as a matter of current popular perception and not as historical fact. Its links with the blues traditions of the Mississippi Delta are, of course, well established.

22. The theoretical issues have been thoroughly explored in the various contributions to Bellman 1998 and Born and Hesmondhalgh 2000.

23. The first theme of Bax's *Harp Trio*, of a vaguely pentatonic nature, and, of course, on a paradigmatically "Celtic" instrument, is a possible exception, but it is worth noting that this was an early work.

24. For a fuller account of this issue see the various chapters of Edelstein 1992, on which this paragraph draws.

25. See Gibbons 1988, Wallis and Malm 1983, and Taylor 1997 for useful discussions of the recording industry in Ireland, Wales, and "the Celtic World" more generally.

26. We draw on Breathnach's (1971) influential account and Carolan's recent detailed study (1997).

27. Our own questions about "internal colonialism," revisionism, nationalism—to a major degree shared by all of the contributors to this volume—have been shaped by the following: Bartlett 1988; Bew 1996; Boyce 1996; Cairns and Richards 1988; Chapman 1978 and 1992; Connolly 1996; Curtin, O'Dwyer, and Tuathaigh 1988; Davies 1989; Eagleton 1995; English 1996; Gramich and Hiscock 1998; Hechter 1975; Hutchinson 1996; Jackson 1996; Kearney 1997; O'Day 1996; Peillon 1984; Torode 1984; and Williams 1989. These issues have a sharp focus in the literature on Northern Ireland/The North of Ireland. For politically sensitive discussions of expressive culture in this context, see Buckley and Kelley 1995, Crawford 1998, Hughes 1991, Jarman 1997, McAuley 1998, and McNamee 1991.

BIBLIOGRAPHY

Anúna. *Omnis.* Celtic Heartbeat UD-53098, 1997.

Ardener, Edwin. "'Remote Areas': Some Theoretical Considerations." In *The Voice of Prophecy and Other Essays*, edited by Malcolm Chapman, 211–28. Oxford: Blackwell, 1989.

Bain, George. *Celtic Art: The Method of Construction.* London: Constable, 1951.

Bartlett, Thomas. "'What Ish Is My Nation?': Themes in Irish History 1550–1850." In *Irish Studies: A General Introduction*, edited by T. Bartlett, Chris Curtin, Riana O'Dwyer, and Gearoid O Tuathaigh, 44–59. Totowa, N.J.: Barnes & Noble, 1988.

Bellman, Jonathan, ed. *The Exotic in Western Music*. Boston: Northeastern University Press, 1998.

Bew, Paul. "The National Question, Land, and 'Revisionism'." In *The Making of Modern Irish History: Revisionism and the Revisionist Controversy*, edited by D. George Boyce and Alan O'Day, 90–99. London: Routledge, 1996.

Bohlman, Philip V. "Auf dem Weg zur Wallfahrt—musikalische Kolportage an den Grenzen zur Volksfrömmigkeit." In *Volksmusik—Wandel und Deutung*, edited by Gerlinde Haid, Ursula Hemetek, and Rudolf Pietsch, 505–22. Vienna: Böhlau Verlag, 2000.

Born, Georgina, and David Hesmondhalgh, eds. *Western Music and Its Others: Difference, Representation, and Appropriation in Music*. Berkeley: University of California Press, 2000.

Boyce, D. George. "Past and Present: Revisionism and the Northern Ireland Troubles." In *The Making of Modern Irish History: Revisionism and the Revisionist Controversy*, edited by D. George Boyce and Alan O'Day, 216–38. London: Routledge, 1996.

Breathnach, Breandan. *Folk Music and Dances of Ireland*. Cork: Mercier Press, 1971.

Buckley, Anthony, and Mary Kelley. *Negotiating Identity: Rhetoric, Metaphor and Social Drama in Northern Ireland*. Washington, D.C.: Smithsonian Institution Press, 1995.

Bunting, Edward. *The Ancient Music of Ireland: An Edition Comprising the Three Collections by Edward Bunting Originally Published in 1796, 1809, 1846*. Dublin: Walton's Piano and Musical Instrument Galleries, 1969.

Cairns, David, and Shaun Richards. *Writing Ireland*. Manchester: Manchester University Press, 1988.

Calder, Joanne. *George Petrie and the Ancient Music of Ireland*. Dublin: Dolmen Press, 1968.

Carolan, Nicholas. *A Harvest Saved: Francis O'Neill and Irish Music in Chicago*. Cork: Ossian Publications, 1997.

Carson, Ciaran. *The Pocket Guide to Traditional Irish Music*. Belfast: Appletree Press, 1986.

Carson, Ciaran. *Last Night's Fun*. New York: North Point Press, 1996.

Casanova, Jose. "Private and Public Religion." In *Public Religions in the Modern World,* edited by Jose Casanova, 40–66. Chicago: University of Chicago Press, 1994.

Casey, Conor. "The Use of the Didjeridu in Irish Traditional Music." Master's thesis, Department of Social Anthropology, The Queen's University of Belfast, 1994.

Chapman, Malcolm. *The Gaelic Vision in Highland Culture*. Montreal: McGill-Queen's University Press, 1978.

Chapman, Malcolm. *The Celts: The Construction of a Myth.* New York: St. Martin's Press, 1992.

Chapman, Malcolm. "Thoughts on Celtic Music." In *Ethnicity, Identity and Music: The Musical Construction of Place,* edited by Martin Stokes, 29–44. Oxford: Berg, 1994.

Chieftains, The. *Santiago.* RCA/BMG 09026-68602-2, 1996.

Connolly, Sean J. "Eighteenth Century Ireland." In *The Making of Modern Irish History: Revisionism and the Revisionist Controversy,* edited by D. George Boyce and Alan O'Day, 15–33. London: Routledge, 1996.

Cooke, Peter. *The Fiddle Tradition of the Shetland Isles.* Cambridge: Cambridge University Press, 1986.

Corkery, Daniel. *Hidden Ireland: A Study of Gaelic Munster in the Eighteenth Century.* Dublin: Gill, 1925.

Crawford, Mairtin, ed. *States of Sound: Musical Culture in Ireland.* Belfast: Fortnight Educational Trust, 1998.

Crichton Smith, Iain (Iain Mac a'Gobhainn). *Collected Poems.* Manchester: Carcanet, 1992.

Curtin, Chris, Riana O'Dwyer, and Gearoid O Tuathaigh. "Emigration and Exile." In *Irish Studies: A General Introduction,* edited by T. Bartlett, Chris Curtin, Riana O'Dwyer, and Gearoid O Tuathaigh, 60–86. Totowa, N.J.: Barnes & Noble, 1988.

Davies, Charlotte Aull. *Welsh Nationalism in the Twentieth Century: The Ethnic Option and the Modern State.* New York: Praeger, 1989.

Doyle, Roddy. *The Commitments.* New York: Vintage, 1987.

Eagleton, Terry. *Heathcliffe and the Great Hunger.* London: Verso, 1995.

Edelstein, Teri J., ed. *Imagining an Irish Past: The Celtic Revival 1840–1940.* Chicago: Smart Museum, University of Chicago, 1992.

English, Richard. "'The Inborn Hate of All Things English': Ernie O Malley and the Irish Revolution 1916–1923." *Past and Present* 151 (1996): 174–99.

Feld, Steven. "The Poetics and Politics of Pygmy Pop." In *Western Music and Its Others: Difference, Representation, and Appropriation in Music,* edited by Georgina Born and David Hesmondhalgh, 254–79. Berkeley: University of California Press, 2000.

Feldman, Allen, and Eamonn O'Doherty. *The Northern Fiddler: Music and Musicians of Donegal and Tyrone.* Belfast: Blackstaff Press, 1979.

Fenellosa, E. F. *Certain Noble Plays of Japan.* With an introduction by W. B. Yeats. Churchtown: Cuala, 1916.

Gibbons, Luke. "Synge, Country and Western: The Myth of the West in Irish and American Culture." In *Culture and Ideology in Ireland,* edited by Chris Curtin, Mary Kelly, and Liam O Dowd, 1–19. Galway: Galway University Press, 1984.

Gibbons, Luke. "From Megalith to Megastore: Broadcasting and Irish Culture." In *Irish Studies: A General Introduction,* edited by T. Bartlett, Chris

Curtin, Riana O'Dwyer, and Gearoid O Tuathaigh, 221–34. Totowa, N.J.: Barnes & Noble, 1988.

Gramich, Katie, and Andrew Hiscock, eds. *Dangerous Diversity: The Changing Face of Wales.* Bangor: University of Wales Press, 1988.

Harker, Dave. *Fakelore: The Manufacture of British 'Folksong', 1700 to the Present Day.* Manchester: Manchester University Press, 1985.

Hebdige, Dick. *Subculture: The Meaning of Style.* London: Methuen, 1979.

Hechter, Michael. *Internal Colonialism: The Celtic Fringe in British National Development, 1536–1966.* Berkeley: University of California Press, 1975.

Herr, Cheryl. "The Erotics of Irishness." In *Identities,* edited by Henry Louis Gates Jr., and Anthony Appiah, 271–304. Chicago: University of Chicago Press, 1995.

Hughes, Eamonn. "Border Country." In *Culture and Politics in Northern Ireland,* edited by E. Hughes, 1–12. Buckingham: Open University Press, 1991.

Humphreys, Emyr. *The Taliesin Tradition: A Quest for the Welsh Identity.* London: Black Raven Press, 1983.

Hutchinson, John. "Irish Nationalism." In *The Making of Modern Irish History: Revisionism and the Revisionist Controversy,* edited by D. George Boyce and Alan O'Day, 100–19. London: Routledge, 1996.

Jackson, Alvin. "Irish Unionism." In *The Making of Modern Irish History: Revisionism and the Revisionist Controversy,* edited by D. George Boyce and Alan O'Day, 120–40. London: Routledge, 1996.

Jarman, Neil. *Material Conflicts: Parades and Visual Displays in Northern Ireland.* Oxford: Berg, 1997.

Kearney, Richard. *Postnationalist Ireland: Politics, Culture, Philosophy.* London: Routledge, 1997.

King, Chris. *Our Celtic Heritage: Looking at Our Own Faith in the Light of Celtic Christianity.* Edinburgh: St. Andrew Press, 1997.

Lipsitz, George. *Dangerous Crossroads: Popular Music, Postmodernism, and the Poetics of Place.* London: Verso, 1994.

Lomax, Alan. *Folksong Style and Culture.* Washington, D.C.: American Association for the Advancement of Science, 1968.

MacDonald, Sharon, ed. *Inside European Identities.* Oxford: Berg, 1993.

Magowan, Fiona. "Out of Time, Out of Place." In *The Didjeridu from Arnhem Land to the Internet,* edited by Karl Neuenfeldt, 123–82. Sydney: Perfect Beat Publications, 1997.

McAuley, Tony. "Showing Off: The Irish Showband Scene." In *States of Sound: Musical Culture in Ireland,* edited by Mairtin Crawford, 12–15. Belfast: Fortnight Educational Trust, 1998.

McCann, May. "Music and Politics in Ireland: The Specificity of the Folk Revival in Belfast." *British Journal of Ethnomusicology* 4 (1995): 51–75.

McDonald, Maryon. *"We Are Not French": Language, Culture and Identity in Brittany.* London: Routledge, 1989.

McKennitt, Loreena. *The Mask and the Mirror.* Warner Brothers, 9 45420–2, 1994.

McNamee, Peter. *Traditional Music: Whose Music?* Belfast: Institute of Irish Studies, The Queen's University of Belfast, 1991.

Meek, Donald E. *The Quest for Celtic Christianity.* Edinburgh: The Hansell Press, 2000.

Mitchell, Timothy. *Colonising Egypt.* Cambridge: Cambridge University Press, 1988.

Moloney, Paddy. Liner notes for *Santiago* (The Chieftains). RCA/BMG 09026-68602-2, 1996.

Nairn, Tom. *The Breakup of Britain: Crisis and Neonationalism.* London: New Left Books, 1977.

Negus, Keith. "Sinead O Connor: Music Mother." In *Sexing the Groove: Popular Music and Gender,* edited by Sheila Whiteley, 178–90. London: Routledge, 1997.

Nolan, Mary Lee, and Sidney Nolan. "Location and Environment: Shrines as Holy Places." In *Christian Pilgrimage in Modern Western Europe,* edited by M. L. Nolan and S. Nolan, 291–338. Chapel Hill: University of North Carolina Press, 1989.

O'Day, Alan. "Revising the Diaspora." In *The Making of Modern Irish History: Revisionism and the Revisionist Controversy,* edited by D. George Boyce and Alan O'Day, 288–315. London: Routledge, 1996.

O'Driscoll, Robert. *The Celtic Consciousness.* New York: George Braziller, 1981.

O'Neill, Francis. *O'Neill's Music of Ireland: Eighteen Hundred and Fifty Melodies, Airs, Jigs, Reels, Long Dances, Marches, Etc.* Chicago: Lyon and Healy, 1903.

Pennick, Nigel. *Celtic Sacred Landscapes.* London: Thames and Hudson, 1996.

Peillon, Michel. "The Structure of Irish Ideology Revisited." In *Culture and Ideology in Ireland,* edited by Chris Curtin, Mary Kelly, and Liam O Dowd, 46–58. Galway: Galway University Press, 1984.

Selby, Bettina. *Pilgrim's Road: A Journey to Santiago de Compostela.* London: Abacus, 1994.

Sheehy, Jeanne. *The Rediscovery of Ireland's Past: The Celtic Revival, 1830–1930.* London: Thames and Hudson, 1980.

Shields, Hugh, ed. *Tunes of The Munster Pipers: Irish Traditional Music from the James Goodman Manuscripts.* Dublin: Irish Traditional Music Archive, 1998.

Songs of the Travelling People: Music of the Tinkers, Gipsies and Other Travelling People of England, Scotland and Ireland. Saydisc CD-SDL 407, 1994.

Spivak, Gayatri Chakravorty. "Acting Bits/Identity Talk." In *Identities,* edited by Kwame Anthony Appiah and Henry Louis Gates Jr., 147–80. Chicago: Chicago University Press, 1995.

Stokes, Margaret. *Early Christian Art in Ireland.* London: Chapel and Hall, n.d.

Stokes, Martin. "Place, Exchange and Meaning: Black Sea Turks in the West of Ireland." In *Ethnicity, Identity and Music: The Musical Construction of Place,* edited by Martin Stokes, 97–115. Oxford: Berg, 1994.

Synge, John Millington. *The Aran Isles.* London: Penguin, 1992.

Taylor, Timothy D. *Global Pop: World Music, World Markets.* New York: Routledge, 1997.

Taylor, Timothy D. "Living in a Postcolonial World: Class and Soul in The Commitments." *Irish Studies Review* 6, no. 3 (1998): 291–302.

Torode, Brian. "Ireland the Terrible." In *Culture and Ideology in Ireland,* edited by Chris Curtin, Mary Kelly, and Liam O Dowd, 20–29. Galway: Galway University Press, 1984.

Trosset, Carol. *Welshness Performed: Welsh Concepts of Person and Society.* Tucson: University of Arizona Press, 1993.

Trumpener, Katie. *Bardic Nationalism: The Romantic Novel and the British Empire.* Princeton: Princeton University Press, 1997.

Turner, Victor, and Edith Turner. "St. Patrick's Purgatory: Religion and Nationalism in an Archaic Pilgrimage." In *Image and Pilgrimage in Christian Culture: Anthropological Perspectives,* edited by V. Turner and E. Turner, 104–39. New York: Columbia University Press, 1978.

Wallace, Martin. *The Celtic Resource Book.* London: National Society/Church House Publishing, 1998.

Wallis, Roger, and Krister Malm. "Sain Cymru: The Role of the Welsh Record Industry in the Development of a Welsh Language Pop/Rock/Folk Scene." *Popular Music* 3 (1983): 77–106.

Williams, Raymond. "Welsh Culture." In *Resources of Hope,* 99–119. London: Verso, 1989.

White, Harry. *The Keeper's Recital: Music and Cultural History in Ireland 1770–1970.* Notre Dame, Ind.: University of Notre Dame Press, 1998.

1

Shared Imaginations: Celtic and Corsican Encounters in the Soundscape of the Soul

Caroline Bithell

Until relatively recently, the assumption of an early Celtic presence in Corsica remained unquestioned, clear evidence appearing to be offered in the separate realms of material remains, character and behavior, and belief systems. At the most tangible level, irrefutable proof seemed to be provided by the presence of the granite dolmens, warriorlike menhirs and other megalithic structures that litter the Corsican landscape at a time when such monuments were universally believed to be the work of the Celts.[1] Resonances were also found in the associated cult of the dead, which was similarly identified as "Celtic." With respect to character and lifestyle, the remarkable similarities between descriptions of Celts and Corsicans found in the writings of Greek and Roman chroniclers have already been remarked upon by McKechnie (1993, 121).

In our own time, the Corsican author of the recent *Histoire Secrète de la Corse* offers a list of traits attributed to the Celts, or Gauls, by the writer A. Thierry—"personal bravery, of candid spirit, impetuous, open to all impressions, eminently intelligent; besides that an extreme mobility, a marked repugnance towards notions of discipline, a great deal of ostentation, and finally a perpetual disunity, the fruit of excessive vanity."[2] In this, he proposes, one can clearly recognize the Corsican, this fact offering indisputable evidence of the presence of the Celts among Corsica's invaders (Angelini 1977, 61). In a similar spirit, on the basis of his experience of living for a number of years in Glasgow, the Corsican writer Joseph Chiari identified numerous points of contact between the Scottish and Corsican character, which he attributed, apparently without hesitation, to shared Celtic roots (cited in McKechnie 1993, 122). An exploration of the substance behind such assumptions and associations inevitably involves engaging with recent developments in the Celtic debate. This, therefore, is where I begin.

CELTS, CORSICANS, AND HISTORIES

Accounts found in classical sources (including Diodorus, Strabo, Livy, and Tacitus) routinely present a picture of the Celts as passionate, high-spirited, erratic, boastful, and prone to drunkenness, violence, and general debauchery. That we are dealing here largely with stereotypes is now widely recognized, although it is only in recent decades that anthropologists have engaged in the extensive and often controversial deconstruction of such stereotypes that has allowed Maryon McDonald to refer to the Celts as "perhaps the best-known invention of the classical imagination" (McDonald 1993, 225).[3]

To both the Greeks and the Romans, the populations they referred to as Celts (or alternatively as Gauls, the two appellations being apparently undifferentiated) were in many respects simply part of the barbarian horde, together with the existing inhabitants of other lands that they saw fit to grace with their more civilized presence. At the most basic level, we can thus see those identified as Celts as conveniently and inevitably occupying the category of "other," their main function being—via the now familiar process of structural opposition or inversion across boundaries, together with the propensity for exaggeration to which this typically gives rise—to throw into sharper relief the more noble and civilized nature of all aspects of the classical lifestyle, from personal behavior to government. Chapman also makes the obvious point that those resisting invasion, conquest, or oppression will inevitably behave in a manner that allows their would-be vanquishers—with a certain irony—to portray them as violent, aggressive, belligerent, and uncontrollable (Chapman 1992, 177). In their encounters with the Romans, the Celts, irrespective of any expansionist ambitions of their own, were inescapably forced into a position where they fell prey to the unresolvable contradiction of fighting for peace.

In the light of these considerations, it should not appear surprising that in classical times a rather similar picture should have been painted of the indigenous peoples of Corsica. Indeed, in many cases, early characterizations of Corsicans and Celts are directly linked by their authors: In each case, Herodotus, Strabo, and Diodorus of Sicily feature prominently among the most commonly cited sources. At the most obvious level, the overlap can be attributed to the fact that Celts and Corsicans were sited on the same side in the opposition civilized versus barbarian.

It has to be said, for the record, that the picture given of these early Corsicans was by no means entirely negative. Diodorus expresses great admiration for the Corsicans' pronounced respect for justice. Among themselves, he reported, they lived "lives of honor and justice, to a degree surpassing practically all other barbarians" (cited in Carrington 1984, 80). The Corsicans were, however, given ample opportunity to live up to their more ferocious reputation in the fate accorded them by history. Like other islands in the Mediterranean, Corsica was for centuries plagued by onslaught and occupation by a succession of usually hostile forces keen to command such a strategic vantage point. Before the Romans, parts of the island had been settled by Greeks, Etruscans, and Carthaginians. Following several centuries of Roman rule, it was in turn occupied or overrun by Vandals, Ostrogoths, Byzantines, Lombards, and Saracens. Such a climate meant that its indigenous population was repeatedly forced into a position of defensiveness, often retreating to the relatively impenetrable mountainous regions of the interior. In view of the hostile or at the very least wary reception that they would have received, these occupying forces—whether they turned out ultimately to be a marauding or civilizing presence—could hardly have been expected to construe the island's existing inhabitants in a particularly positive light.

The characterization of Celts and Corsicans as wild and barbaric is by no means limited to classical writings. In medieval times and later we find many records belonging to an ecclesiastical context whose authors give vent to a sense of moral outrage at the propensity of their subjects for loose living. Gerald of Wales, despite his own Welsh blood, offers us the following characterization of the Welsh he encountered on his twelfth-century peregrinations: "involved in such an abyss of vices, perjury, theft, robbery, rapine, murders, fratricides, adultery, and incest, [they] become every day more entangled and ensnared in evil-doing" (cited in Chapman 1992, 199). In short, their behavior was no better than could be expected of the average heathen. In Corsica of the sixteenth and seventeenth centuries, successful evangelization was, according to the reports of a series of papal emissaries, apparently still being hindered by the resistance of the population not to Christian dogma itself but to the suggestion that they should relinquish the very types of unchristian behavior that had so impressed Gerald (see Casanova 1931–38).

As Chapman has been keen to point out, however, the early descriptions of the Celts, as of other populations occupying the category of "other," are likely to have been based on a mixture of empirical and conjectural ingredients. Having decided that these descriptions carry little reliable historical weight, we are not necessarily justified in going to the opposite extreme of declaring them to be entirely fictitious. While some aspects of the ideas people have about others have to be consigned to the realm of surmise and often extravagant elaboration, others result from misunderstandings and misinterpretations when confronted with an alien social reality as genuinely observed and experienced (Chapman 1992, 199)—a phenomenon that has been termed by Edwin Ardener "categorical mismatch" (see Ardener 1982). This perspective could well be applied to the vendetta that blighted Corsican society until the early decades of the present century, disputes between rival families often continuing for several generations with considerable loss of life on both sides (see, for instance, the figures from 1714 reported in Marcaggi 1926, 35).

For continentals, such behavior was seen as proof of outright lawlessness in which the most primitive instincts were allowed free rein. In the moral landscape of the Corsicans themselves, however, the bandits who inhabited the maquis in an attempt to evade arrest and imprisonment on the one hand and to avoid themselves falling victim to the demand for revenge on the other were "bandits of honor," often revered or at least respected, at the same time as being pitied for the heavy destiny that they had been obliged to embrace. As Carrington has pointed out, the vendetta itself was "a spectacular expression of the cult of the dead," the purpose of the bloody retribution that was unfailingly exacted being to appease the original victim who would otherwise allow his kinsmen no peace (Carrington 1995, 8). From a more modern perspective, the system of the vendetta served as a demonstration of the islanders' refusal to be bound by state-enforced law.

Certain elements in the outsider's observations of the Celtic or Corsican character can nevertheless be directly associated with aspects of lifestyle. As Laade has pointed out, a range of features of character commonly attributed to the Corsicans, such as contempt for manual labor, frankness and openmindedness, hospitality, a natural nobility, a propensity for their honor to be easily offended, a predisposition toward blood revenge, a fondness for weapons and male adventure, loyalty without submission, and an inclination toward reflection and poetic expression, can be understood to derive from specific sociocultural determining factors related to a pastoral lifestyle (Laade 1981, volume 1, 10). Like many of the "modern" Celtic populations, the Corsicans have equally been associated with the unpredictability of nomadic mountain dwellers, absorbing into themselves as if by osmosis the wildness of the landscapes they inhabit (see Chapman 1992, 187). It is interesting to note that, as early as the twelfth century, Gerald of Wales found the Irish "a rude people" essentially on the grounds that they had "not yet departed from the primitive habits of pastoral life": they were "not only barbarous in their dress, but suffering their hair and beards to grow enormously in an uncouth manner" (cited in Chapman 1992, 191). This brings to mind an occasion during my own time in Corsica when my companion (incidentally part Irish) was greeted at a mountain fair with almost certainly misplaced deference on account of his own thick beard and flowing locks. He apparently reminded my Corsican friends of "the real Corsicans, the ancients."

OF MEGALITHS, BRAINS, AND BLOOD

It was only in the 1940s that serious research began into the history and possible provenance of Corsica's distinctive megaliths, many of which had until then lain undiscovered in the maquis, and, with the growing acknowledgment that the case for Celtic origins so vehemently reinforced in the eighteenth century was untenable, the notion of Celtic builders was abandoned. The island's megalithic culture is now generally believed to have been introduced by settlers from Asia Minor and the Aegean in the fourth millennium, although the fact that the greatest concentration of stones is found close to the west coast of the island, together with the observation that they have no counterparts in Sardinia, the Balearics, or Italy, has led Angelini to suggest that their builders must have come from the west, that is, from the Atlantic, leaving similar traces in the Canary Isles and the Basque Country (Angelini 1977, 29). Although he acknowledges that the Celts were not actually responsible for erecting Corsica's megaliths, Angelini does nevertheless continue to argue for a Celtic presence on the island, proof of which he finds in the legends associated with the stones (60). This is related to an assumption that, on their later arrival in Corsica, the Celts settled around the stones and incorporated them into their religious rites (58). Hence an association between the stones and the Celts persists.

It is perhaps because of the former unquestioned equation of the Celts with the megaliths that early historians concerned with racial origins tended to identify the Corsican population as being of Celtic, as well as Ligurian and Iberian, descent. At the end of the nineteenth century, however, Jaubert had already proposed, on the basis of cranial measurements, that the idea of Celtic and Ligurians origins should be rejected, arguing instead for descent from the Berbers—to whom he also believed the megaliths should be attributed (see Hörstel 1908, 59; cited in Laade 1981 volume 1, 5). An equally close relationship has apparently been established with the Guanches of the Canaries, with Pierre Rocca's claims that the Corsicans are related to the Guanches on the basis of their cephalic index, their cranial capacity, and their facial angle (see Angelini 1977, 32). Angelini proposes links with both the Guanches and the Basques, supported in this case by evidence both linguistic (on the basis of similarities in surviving place names, especially those with certain prefixes) and biological (in the surprisingly high incidence among each of these populations of the blood group O). Few traces remain of the language spoken by the Corsicans in pre-Roman times. Meanwhile, the Guanche language, which became extinct in the sixteenth century, is believed to have been a Berber language.

To add to the conundrum, other studies have equally identified similarities between the Celts and the Berbers, not only in terms of physical appearance but also with respect to genetic and linguistic affinities. A correspondence between the ABO blood groups of Berber and modern "Celtic" populations has been remarked upon, while claims have also been made for a close structural affinity between the Celtic and Berber languages. In addition, it has even been suggested that the rhythms of Irish traditional music show links with the melodies of North Africa (see Laidler 1998). Regardless of the scientific status accorded to these theories and their ability to prove the case, the very fact that they have been proposed, that they appear attractive and plausible and are given widespread credence lends them an undeniable authority.

THE MEGALITHIC FAITH AND THE CULT OF THE DEAD

Even if any straightforward equation between Celts and Corsicans does not ultimately bear scrutiny, the notion of a certain shared ancestry in more remote times (not necessarily based on blood ties) nevertheless remains as more than a tantalizing possibility. Echoes of the ancient megalithic faith, now firmly recognized as pre-Celtic and whose diffusion is described by the onward march of the stones across Europe, can still be found in Corsica as well as in what we now refer to as the Celtic lands.[4] In particular, striking commonalities have been observed with respect to the shamani-clike rites and beliefs associated with the cult of the dead, vestiges of which are still to be found not far beneath the surface of present-day Corsica.

Christianity was introduced into Corsica from the third century A.D. onward, although in the sixth century Pope Gregory the Great condemned the Corsicans for their persistence in worshipping stones (Carrington 1995, 40). As in many other parts of Europe, Christian practices in many cases merely overlaid, rather than displaced, previous pagan customs, with the Mediterranean saints continuing to play the roles of the gods of the ancient world and the rhythms of the Catholic liturgical calendar often mirroring those of the old agrarian ritual cycles. Among many of the older generation in particular, Christian and pre-Christian practices still coexist without any apparent sense of paradox. A ritual involving the interpretation of oil droplets in water to determine the presence of the Evil Eye and drive out hostile forces is still enacted by the *signatore*–a practice that, despite the Christian prayers now associated with it, is thought to date back to the Chaldeans (Carrington 1984, 71). Divination using animal shoulder-blades is now rare but by no means forgotten.

The tenacity of the ancient cult of the dead is reflected in the remarkable degree of veneration accorded to the ancestors, especially at All Souls', when everyone visits the family graves and candles are left burning through the night in all the tombs and roadside shrines. In some parts of the island, doors are left unlocked and food set out for the dead who will return to their homes on that night. In the Casinca, members of the *confréries* and their fellow villagers involved in a nocturnal procession from one village to the next that forms part of an elaborate Good Friday ritual—itself an intriguing reflection of the continued preoccupation with death—stop en route at the graveyard to give thanks to the ancestors for the sacred songs that they customarily sing on that night. They are then refreshed with quantities of homemade wine and cakes before setting off again into the night, their glowing torches reflecting on their white robes and lighting the way as they thread their path around the hillside. This creates a somewhat uncanny spectacle that brings to mind the tales of phantom funeral processions attested in Corsica as well as in Wales, Scotland, and Brittany.

Outside the confines of religion, even more arcane aspects of the cult of the dead find expression in the shamanlike figure of the *mazzere*, who acts as a type of emissary for death, recognizing in the animal he or she is compelled to kill during nocturnal hunting expeditions in the maquis the likeness of a fellow villager who is doomed to die within a short space of time—hence Carrington's description of the *mazzeri* as "night-hunters of souls" (see Carrington 1984).[5] Writing as recently as the 1990s, Carrington reports that thirty *mazzeri* are still known to be in operation in the southern part of the island and that in recent years they have attracted interest from a number of young nationalists who view them as venerable representatives of the ancient indigenous culture so long neglected and devalued (Carrington 1995, 56). Roccu Multedo sees a particularly close relationship between the phenomenon of mazzerism and the cult of the dead in Corsica and the Welsh legends of death (Multedo 1994). Most recently, Carrington has proposed that mazzerism possibly derives from a period that considerably predates even the arrival of the megalithic faith in Corsica (Carrington 1995, 77).

To attempt a connection between the much-vaunted Celtic "cult of the severed head" and the Corsican flag with its Moor's Head—inherited from the kings of Aragon and declared the official emblem of an independent Corsica by Pasquale Paoli in the eighteenth century—is far-fetched but offers food for thought. Angelini does indeed go so far as to suggest a phonetic analogy between the French *tête de Maure* (Moor's head) and *tête de mort* (head of death), the latter, however, reminding him not of the Celtic head but of the pirate flag and leading to the proposition that the head on the Corsican flag is a symbolic reminder of the death of the goddess Isis and her rule (Angelini 1977, 13).[6] The Moor's Head continues to operate as a powerful symbol, in particular in nationalist contexts, and has been adopted as an emblem by many contemporary groups (i.e., musical ensembles).

CORSICA AND SCOTLAND IN THE ROMANTIC ERA

History, like everything else, has its fashions. That the facts are colored by the identity and allegiance of the author of the historical record and by the political context in which the texts were penned is now accepted. Chapman and others have shown how the "barbaric" Celts of classical and medieval times underwent a remarkable change of fortune during the Romantic era, being redefined in more noble, heroic, and exotic terms as the observers of the day directed their gaze through a different colored lens. Again, not surprisingly, a similar transformation took place with respect to Corsica.

Images of Corsica in French literature over the ages have oscillated between that of a wild, impenetrable land, its barbarous inhabitants completely given over to the excesses of blood revenge and terrorized by ruthless bandits and, on the other, a paradisical retreat, still unsullied by the more destructive forces of progress and one of the last bastions of the principles of democracy and honor—with a backlash to the former as travelers lured to the island by the more romantic images often discovered a far harsher reality (see Jeoffroy-Faggianelli 1979). Whatever the particular slant adopted, these portrayals served to reinforce a sense of otherness, constructing Corsica as the antithesis to life on the more—or less—civilized mainland.

In the latter half of the eighteenth century, the more romantic and heroic images gained a clear upper hand. Rousseau was sufficiently impressed by what he knew of the island and its affairs to write in his *Contrat Social* (published in 1762): "There is still in Europe one country capable of legislation, and that is the island of Corsica. The valor and constancy with which this brave people has known how to recover and defend its liberty well merits that some wise man teaches them how to preserve it. I have some presentiment that one day this little island will astonish Europe" (cited in Carrington 1984, 265–66). These oft-quoted words have left a lasting legacy and many of today's generation of Corsicans—including musicians, who have been known to include the above pronouncement in their disc notes—still strive to fulfil the philosopher's predictions.

In the eighteenth and nineteenth centuries, the island also became a popular haunt of a host of British Romantic writers and artists and it was during this period that a series of connections were made between Corsica and Scotland. The most direct, however, was that forged by the young James Boswell, who, on the advice of Rousseau himself, visited Corsica in the autumn of 1765 in the course of his "grand tour" with the particular aim of making the acquaintance of Pasquale Paoli. In 1755, Paoli had been invited to return from exile in Italy to be elected General of the Nation and had then served the island in its fight for independence from Genoa for a period of ten years, instigating what Rousseau had identified as one of the most enlightened systems of government in the whole of Europe. Boswell—having suffered only brief trepidation following warnings, as he prepared to set sail from Livorno, that "I run the risque of my life in going among these barbarians" (Boswell 1923, 6)—was suitably in awe of what he saw and heard and benefited from Paoli's confidences over a number of days. Having already aligned himself with other national struggles for independence, Boswell now became a lifelong friend and supporter of Paoli and was singularly responsible for a dedicated campaign that led ultimately to the short-lived Anglo-Corsican Kingdom created when the British finally came to Corsica's defense (this time against the French) in the last decade of the eighteenth century.

In 1763, the British government had proclaimed the Corsicans to be "rebels" and had forbidden any British subject to lend support to their cause in any way. As soon as he set foot on Italian soil after his Corsican sojourn, however, Boswell immediately began to bombard the press with anonymous letters and articles speculating on the reasons for his own recent interviews with Paoli and calling for British intervention on the general's behalf. The slim volume that he published in 1768, not long after his return to Britain—*An Account of Corsica, the Journal of a Tour to that Island and Memoires of Pascal Paoli* (Boswell 1923)—ran to three editions each in England and Ireland as well as appearing in a number of translations, and earned its author a certain notoriety.

It was followed later in the same year by the collection *British Essays in Favor of the Brave Corsicans*, edited by Boswell, who was himself the author of several of the essays. He energetically set about raising funds for Paoli in Scotland and when the French invaded Corsica in 1768 he was able to assist with both money and guns. However, despite his attendance at the Shakespeare Jubilee in Stratford dressed in the costume of a Corsican chief, which he had had specially made for the purpose—after which several more anonymous notices found their way into London periodicals commenting on the stir his appearance had caused—Britain unfortunately failed to offer such timely intervention as Boswell had hoped for and Paoli's patriots were defeated by French forces at the Battle of Ponte Novu in May 1769. The anniversary of this date is still an important event in the Corsican calendar, when those of a nationalist bent broadly interpreted—including many of the island's intellectuals as well as young activists—gather at the bridge where the Corsicans made their final stand to celebrate a mass, throw flowers into the water in homage to the slain, and sing rousing traditional songs, including some that tell the story of the battle itself.[7]

One might reasonably imagine that the way had already been paved for Scottish sympathy for, and active interest in, Corsica as a consequence of the mid-eighteenth-century fervor for Scottish Highland culture. The *Ossian* poems, which had caused such a sensation when they were "discovered" by MacPherson in 1760, fueled enthusiasm both for the mystic Celtic past and for the continuing tenacity of aspects of the ancient way of life in the free-spirited Scottish Highlands and Islands, whose more "barbaric" aspects could now, following the dismantling of clan society after the 1745 Rising and the Battle of Culloden in 1746, be viewed with greater dispassion from the relative safety of the more progressive urban Lowlands (James 1999, 128). The poems had equally inspired the young Boswell, despite the early suspicions of his mentor, Samuel Johnson, concerning their authenticity. The Corsicans—with their reputation for being courageous and resilient, if somewhat hot-headed, and retaining the naturalness and innocence of a people as yet untarnished by civilization—offered a living example of just such a society without the complications of being too close for comfort. Interestingly, Corsica's most famous son, Napoleon Bonaparte (born in 1769 and enthusiastically patriotic in his youth before the turn in the family's political fortunes that forced them to flee for their lives at dead of night), also apparently became a dedicated admirer of MacPherson to the extent that he later commissioned a series of Ossian-style paintings to adorn his chambers.

During his time in Corsica, Boswell had entertained his new friends by playing "some of our beautiful old Scots tunes" on his flute, commenting on their reception: "The pathetick simplicity and pastoral gaiety of the Scots musick will always please those who have the genuine feelings of nature. The Corsicans were charmed with the specimens I gave them" (Boswell 1923, 53). The Scottish travelers who continued to be attracted to the island in the nineteenth century inevitably recognized a certain resemblance in terms of landscape, which added to the sense of affinity. In particular the southern town of Ajaccio (now the administrative capital) became popular with the British in general in the second half of the century, largely due to the efforts of a Miss Thomasina Campbell, who described her peregrinations around Corsica in her book *Southward Ho!* (1868). Edward Lear's engravings in his *Journal of a Landscape Painter in Corsica,* which appeared two years later, added a more vivid and dedicatedly romantic edge. The perceived affinity with Scotland endures. A recent article in *The Sunday Times* (13 June 1999) concerning Caroline Cameron's attempts to buy the former Foreign Legion barracks in the southern port of Bonifacio and develop it as a center for Mediterranean culture reports that her husband initially fell in love with the island in part because "it reminded [him] of Scotland without the midges."

SHARED HISTORIES AND COMMON CAUSES

In the context of his writings on flamenco, Mitchell invokes the conclusions reached by Roosens in *Creating Ethnicity* (1989) to the effect that "beliefs and feelings are of much greater importance in self-definition than any objective cultural continuity" (Mitchell 1994, 62–63), a perspective that can usefully be applied not only to the modern Celts' conviction of their direct descent from the ancient Celts and the fundamental role that this plays in their mode of engagement with the world of today, but also to the abiding Corsican sense of kinship with the Celts, both ancient and modern. This "quasi-kinship" (Geertz 1973, also cited in Mitchell 1994, 63) between Corsicans and Celts has been further reinforced in the present in the context of a certain degree of shared experience on the sociopolitical plane.

One of the most conspicuous features that Corsica shares today with many of the peoples of the so-called Celtic fringe is a fervent nationalist movement. The fact that today's Celts tend to occupy a minority position in political terms accounts in large part for the ideological links that have developed between, for example, Northern Ireland, the Pays Basque, and Corsica as brothers in suffering at the hands of more or less oppressive regimes.

Corsican identity has long been written between the lines, occupying a space beyond the confines of official reality. After spending several centuries in the hands of the rival republics of Pisa and Genoa, and following its brief spell as the Anglo-Corsican Kingdom between 1794 and 1796 (the securing of which cost Nelson his eye), Corsica suddenly found herself to be "French."[8] Although a reluctant subject who continued to put up a dedicated fight against her new overlords into the early years of the nineteenth century, the island did then settle into a period of relative calm.

In the present century, however, increasing dissatisfaction with life under French rule—which, in parallel with the situation in Scotland and Wales, intensified with the experience of the postwar generation and in particular with the loss of the colonies that had previously offered stable employment for large numbers of Corsicans—naturally led to a situation where questions of identity occupied a central place in the island's concerns. Since the 1970s, nationalist organizations demanding varying degrees of autonomy and supported in many of their concerns by a significant proportion of the population have been a prominent presence. In the face of the refusal of the French government to cede to their demands to an extent that they find acceptable, the political climate remains volatile. Corsica's position as part of the French state has, of course, brought her into particularly close contact with France's other most notoriously disgruntled minority, the Bretons, with whom Corsican militants have shared both platforms and prisons.

As McDonald has pointed out, "the apprehension of mismatch . . . will usually have a dominant discourse . . . in which to find ready expression" (McDonald 1993, 228). Others will recognize the discourse, even if they are unfamiliar with the new situation to which it is being applied. They can then attribute to this situation the appropriate set of conditions, which might, for want of better information and a deeper understanding, really be little more than assumptions. A related trend sees a transference of aspects of this discourse from one situation to another. Not surprisingly, therefore, the discourse of French domination in Corsica has much in common, at surface level, with the discourses of English domination in Wales and Ireland, Spanish domination in the Basque lands, and French domination in Brittany, even if both the historical determinants and the conditions that form the backdrop to the present manifestation of the conflict are in each case quite different. The details of the situation are, however, less important to those united in occupying the victim position than the overriding experience of oppression and injustice that brings with it a moral as well as an emotional obligation to enter into a relationship of solidarity and mutual support, both ideological and, in some cases, practical. Hence the assertion common among Corsica's political activists and sympathizers, singers included, that "we are the friends (or brothers) of all minorities."[9] Most recently, the singer Petru Guelfucci and his group Voce di Corsica, who have performed to huge acclaim in Quebec, have found themselves in the curious position—whose irony is by no means lost on them—of sharing a common ground with the French-speaking Canadian population in their fight for equal recognition in a predominantly English-speaking territory.

Like today's Celts, the Corsicans are also clearly distinguished from the rest of the "nation" to which, by an accident of history, they now belong by their use of an entirely separate language that cannot be understood by those speaking the majority language (even if the difference is not quite as profound as in the case of the Celtic languages). A Romance language that developed from Latin during the period of Roman occupation, the Corsican language as it is spoken today is closely related to Sardinian, Sicilian, and the dialects that have become modern-day Italian and, to a lesser extent, Spanish and Portuguese. It has always operated as an essentially oral language and different areas of the island have their own linguistic variants, with the main divide being between north and south. It is only in latter years that attempts have been made to establish a unified orthography. In the context of the French state, however, the Corsican language has until recently been consigned to the status of a dialect of Italian, which as a foreign language could be accorded no formal recognition on French soil.[10] Needless to say, this has hardly helped smooth relations between the long-suffering Corsicans and their latest governors and the language question continues to play an important role in the island's demands for greater autonomy.

An examination of the language issue as a political preoccupation in Corsica and, for example, Wales does, however, reveal some interesting differences. Ethnicity in Wales today is defined almost exclusively in terms of language. As Trosset has noted, though by no means everyone accepts the equation "language = identity," this idea has nevertheless firmly set the terms for debate to the extent that all debates about Welshness inevitably center on the language issue (Trosset 1993, 40). The true Welsh are the "Welsh Welsh" who live in "Welsh Wales" (*Cymru-Cymraeg*), which, geographically speaking, is for the most part situated in the western reaches of the principality where a more rural lifestyle continues to hold sway and where one is furthest away from possible contamination from across the border. The English-speaking Welsh (such as myself) are not thought of by the Welsh-speaking Welsh as—and are alive to the considerable complexities involved in thinking of themselves as— "really" Welsh. Indeed, as Trosset notes, "among Welsh-speakers . . . everyone who does not speak Welsh is considered to be a *Sais*, literally 'a Saxon'" (Trosset 1993, 32). There is certainly no concern here with blood groups, skull measurements, or any other biological definition of ethnicity. Everyday definitions of Corsican-ness are less problematic for the majority of Corsicans insofar as it is obvious to everyone where the boundaries are and there is no disputing the fact, even by those who are happy to see Corsica as a part of France, that the whole island is Corsica.[11] Those not fluent in the Corsican language are not simply redefined as French: Those identified as French have literally "come from Lyon," or wherever. Language issues have nonetheless played a vital part in "the struggle," and the "minority language" status of Corsican has certainly served to reinforce a sense of identification with the Celtic nations of the British archipelago.[12]

The "fringe" status enjoyed by both Celts and Corsicans in a geographical sense also accounts for certain cultural parallels that might in their turn be suggestive of a more profound kinship. Typically occupying a place apart in time as well as in space, these cultures have often preserved, independently, fashions and traits that in earlier times were widespread in continental Europe as a whole but that have later come to be seen as a central identifying feature of the "traditional" heritage of the areas in which they have survived. This trend has often been observed with respect to what comes to be seen as "national costume," while Chapman (1994) has also addressed the question of traditional "Celtic" musical instruments within the framework of this debate. Dance music represents another case in point that has relevance to the present discussion. What passes today for Irish dance music is a case of a musical style and repertoire, together with its associated dances, having been preserved in Ireland (at the periphery of its catchment area) long after it had been superseded at the center by newer fashions. A similar style of music is currently being resurrected in Corsica in association with the revival of the quadrille, a lost part of the "traditional heritage" now being reclaimed and promoted by an enthusiastic network under the auspices of the association *Tutti in Piazza* ("Everyone in the Square"). The delicious whimsicality of this circumstance was neatly captured by an Irish resident on the island who commented: "To me, what they're playing is Irish music. But it's not, it's Corsican." And indeed, the tradition they are continuing is that of the old Corsican violinists from villages such as Sermanu, whose tunes fill many a reel in the field recording collections of Quilici and Laade (which together cover a period from the late 1940s to the early 1970s). Meanwhile, the delightful and popular "Panica Nera" on Canta u Populu Corsu's disc *Ci Hè Dinù* (Ricordu 1982), an original instrumental composition by group member Christophe Mac Daniel, sounds just about as "Celtic" as you can get.

Finally, as we have seen, history has endowed both Celts and Corsicans with a reputation for being troublesome and prone to all manner of uncivilized behavior.[13] Stereotypes of this nature can become self-fulfilling prophecies as struggling minorities either unconsciously live up to their reputations or make a more conscious choice to behave in a certain (oppositional) manner in order to emphasize their lack of identity with the "colonizer." Angelini, following his quotation of Thierry's description of the Celts and his recognition of the Corsican in this description (see earlier), concludes: "We delight in the qualities set forth. We are bad at accepting failings and yet haven't we seen in Corsica at times of domination . . . indiscipline and disunity triumph?" (Angelini 1977, 61). Similar processes can, of course, be seen to be at work in the more discrete realm of musical activity, as I now aim to demonstrate.

MUSIC AND ITS ROLE IN THE ARTICULATION
OF IDENTITY IN PRESENT-DAY CORSICA

My intention in the second half of this chapter, in which I focus directly on music in Corsica, is not to propose any primary kinship between Corsican and Celtic musics at the intrinsic level of musical language but rather to explore points of contact in the role played by indigenous music in these cultures today and in the recent past and, with specific reference to the Corsican case, to highlight issues of musical meaning and representation that relate to themes in the preceding discussion. I also consider the ways in which the evolution of a wider cultural and political consciousness in recent years has informed musical practice at a multitude of levels.

My examination of developments in Corsican music from this broader sociopolitical perspective will, I trust, suggest further resonances with aspects of the dialogue between music and politics in today's Celtic nations and inspire comparisons with other studies devoted to one or other area of the so-called Celtic fringe. Rather than belaboring every such resonance, however, I for the most part allow them to speak for themselves, being confident that the reader will readily make his or her own connections, in the course of which I hope that further new perspectives on developments in Celtic areas might emerge.

The prime focus of musical expression in Corsica is the voice. Historical evidence relating to instrumental music or older indigenous dances is comparatively thin. The oldest stratum of traditional song features a range of mostly familiar monodic song types, including laments, lullabies, songs of departure, threshing songs, and the *chjam'è rispondi*, a form of sung improvised debate. More recent genres include serenades, satires, election songs and soldiers' songs. The notion of a song as consisting of text and melody forming a single immutable unit is, however, a relatively recent one. The collections of field recordings made in the middle decades of the twentieth century offer plentiful examples of the lengthy improvisations sung to a comparatively restricted range of melodic prototypes that are more characteristic of the tradition. A number of polyphonic song types have also been preserved, including the *paghjella*, typically sung at fairs, patron saints' day celebrations, gatherings of shepherds (e.g., for sheep-shearing), and informal gatherings of friends, and settings of the Latin mass and other liturgical and paraliturgical texts that operate as part of local oral traditions and that vary from one village to the next.[14]

Most of the older songs are based on a modal tetracord or pentacord, with more elaborate melodies employing two conjunct tetracords. Within this framework, pitch relations are relatively labile, with certain intervals often being subject to slight expansion or contraction. The third degree of the scale tends to be particularly flexible, with an apparently wide margin of both individual and regional variation. In the case of the melismatic figurations (known in Corsican as *rivucate*, sing. *rivucata*), which are characteristic of many of the older monodic songs and also of the two upper voices in polyphonic songs, a range of quarter tones and other divisions are used, although it is rarely possible to distinguish the precise placement of a note. (It should be noted that, while they have often been described as ornamentation, the *rivucate* are not considered by the singers themselves as secondary features but as an integral and indispensable part of a satisfactory performance.) In addition, a single note can be kept in motion by means of a rapid microtonal variation with the result that the tuning of that note might be perceived to change during its execution. In the case of polyphonic singing, this technique allows the singers to adapt constantly to one another so as to remain "in tune."

Melisma plays a crucial part in maintaining a constant balance between tradition and personalization. The art of mastering the technique of using *rivucate* lies in finding a balance between, on the one hand, intimate knowledge of the tradition and the ability to reproduce it and, on the other, one's own creativity. A singer has to learn, by repeated listening and imitation, where the *rivucate* should or should not be placed and understand the parameters that dictate the forms they might take; but the singer must then be able to liberate himself or herself from the constraints of mere reproduction and be able to arrive at his or her own personalized and spontaneous interpretation. Thus while the *rivucate* might come at predictable points within the line, their actual structure will differ from one performer or performance to another. The ultimate aim is for each *rivucate* to be unique yet at the same time recognizably traditional.

Corsican songs rarely conform to a strict meter. Even where a melody is clearly conceived according to an underlying rhythmic or metric unity, it is rarely executed in a regular or symmetrical manner. Some notes are drawn out, with a special emphasis being placed on long sustained final notes, while others are extended by means of melismatic elaboration. Despite the overall impression of rhythmic flexibility and metrical freedom, however, the notion of timing—sometimes referred to by the singers themselves as "rhythm"—remains a crucial component of the singer's art, the ideal delivery of the vocal line involving a judicious interplay of suspense and propulsion.

The songs of the oldest extant layer are characterized by a vibrant timbre (sometimes described in the literature as "forced") with varying degrees of "gutterality" and, more often, nasality as often found in rural voices accustomed to singing in the outdoors. This choice of timbre in turn allows for the use of related vocal techniques. Other features of the older Corsican style of singing (often strikingly reminiscent of those found in flamenco) include: specific uses of breath control to add impulse to the melodic line; the associated practice of inserting aspirants at the beginnings of phrases in order to emphasize the vocal attack, resulting in a soblike quality; an alternation between an open and closed mouth, which is associated with nasalization techniques; and the markedly extended nasalization of final syllables, which approaches the phenomenon of overtoning. Each of these makes a particularly significant contribution to the texture of polyphonic singing.

All of these elements combine to form a style of singing that is, to the majority of outside listeners, obviously, distinctively, and profoundly "other." The reader will already have begun to appreciate the scope for its practitioners to be perceived, from a supposedly more "civilized" perspective, to fall far short of the skills required of a "proper" musician, namely the ability to sing in tune, maintain a certain "purity" of tone, keep time, and reproduce faithfully what is written in the score. Furthermore, this way of singing does not operate at a level that can easily be cultivated, as witnessed by rare attempts by non-Corsicans to emulate it. The main area of difficulty for those trained in Western or classical music is that of modality—whereby modality is understood to signify not simply the use of pentatonic scales or old Church modes, but the density of vocal modulation and melisma with its use of microtones and flexible pitches. The situation is completely different from that of learning an average "folk song" where the main points of reference might be the "melody" and the text. Here, where vocal inflection often constitutes the very fulcrum of the song, matters are rather different, these inflections or modulations constituting an intrinsic part of the melody, rather than an optional, ornamental extra.

The fact that the youngest generation of singers continue, at the dawn of the twenty-first century, to sing in much the same way, even when performing their own compositions on stage, demonstrates the extent to which aspects of musical style and performance practice, such as those referred to earlier, appear to be culturally ingrained. This assessment is supported by one musician's reference to the difficulties he encountered when first working on his own newly composed *chansons* with fellow members of the group of which he was a part due to their inability to "keep time," which in turn was largely a result of their inability to sing without melisma. Their ears at that time were not tuned to a "regular" style, in terms of meter and singing on the note: They automatically reproduced the material in what we might call a "long" style (typical of many rural idioms in the Mediterranean region), drawing out the individual notes and punctuating the line as a whole with relatively flexible melismatic elaborations.[15]

From my first encounter with the distinctive Corsican style of polyphonic singing in particular, I was struck by the way in which the sheer power and intensity of the music seemed to cut a path straight to the soul. These were not songs in the usual sense of the word, but incantations. I can think of no more eloquent and evocative description than that offered by Dorothy Carrington of her first encounter with a group of *paghjella* singers at the Fair of the Santa di u Niolu more than half a century ago:

> The sound was like none I had ever heard before; yet I recognized it as one I had always longed to hear. The three strong voices . . . rose and fell in a series of deliberate discords; this rich harsh clashing music was more poignant, far, than any of the wailing solos I had heard, even the *voceru*, so remote and rending that it seemed to issue from the birth-pangs of the world. . . . The cries of loneliness and thwarted love, however moving, seem insufficient for this music, which by its violence and mystery exceeds the range of even the more extreme personal emotions. (Carrington 1984, 239–40)

CORSICAN MUSIC IN THE TWENTIETH CENTURY: CHANGING FORTUNES AND PERCEPTIONS

The twentieth century brought rapid change to Corsica, accompanied by an inexorable process of social, economic, and cultural decline, in which both the practice and the status of traditional music were severely compromised. The decimation of the male population and the economic devastation caused by the two world wars, together with the rampant emigration, depopulation of the interior, increasing urbanization, and linguistic decline that followed in their wake, all took their toll on the musical life of the island. Many of the old songs were deprived of their functions as the activities with which they had once been associated were abandoned. The interwar years saw a move away from indigenous *chant* to the continentally derived *chansonette* as Corsican music entered a period of decline from which it was not to emerge until the 1970s (de Zerbi 1993, 15). The traditional modal melodies with their characteristic melismatic interpretation were displaced—in terms of public presentation and endorsement, at least—by jolly, even-tempered melodies with guitar or mandolin accompaniment and standard tonal harmonization, which could hold their own in continental circles as "proper" music.

In the eyes of many of those who were to be swept up by the cultural revival of the 1970s, the *chanson* singers—exemplified by the enormously successful Tino Rossi, who recorded his first "hit" (the lullaby "Ciuciarella") in 1932 and whose name could at the time scarcely be evoked without the adage *il chante la Corse* ("he sings Corsica")—were to come to represent a betrayal of the true Corsican tradition, whose integrity they had traded for a comparatively facile, commercially attractive style of song, even abandoning the mother tongue that was central to insular identity in favor of the language of the dominant culture, French. In their own era, however, the *chanteurs de charme* belonged in the context of an attempt to counter the enduring popular continental image of Corsica as wild and backward, bristling with bandits and assassins. The Corsica of the *chansonette*, by contrast, was *l'isula bella* ("the beautiful island"), peopled with beautiful girls living out a rural idyll of innocence and tranquillity against a backdrop of glowing sunsets. The siting of the songs in a Parisian frame of reference and their attraction in particular for the Corsicans of the diaspora also needs to be stressed. They appealed to a gaze that was colored by the romanticism and idealization that distance inspires. Salini draws attention to the fact that the numerous Amicales des Corses (Corsican friendship societies), established by populations of Corsicans living in self-imposed exile from their island of birth, provided the *chanteurs de charme* both with a receptive audience and with an eminently suitable context for the

evocative style and emotional symbolism of their performances
(Salini 1996, 194). The appearance of an increasing number of texts
in the French language was perhaps inevitable, occasioned in part
by the desire of the record companies to appeal to a wider audience.
Songs in French eulogizing the island for its environmental attrac-
tions and the tranquil existence enjoyed by its inhabitants can also
be understood in the context of tourist appeal where Corsica is presented as *la plus prôche des îles lointaines* ("the closest of the far-away
islands").

Despite the fact that the *chanteurs de charme* were essentially an
export item, the immortalization of their performances in the form
of records meant that they had a direct affect on musical life within
the island as amateur singers were inevitably to appropriate both
the repertoire and the style of singing. With the advent of the recording industry, therefore, a shift had already begun away from locally
specific repertoires to one that was more general, "the repertoire that
everyone knew," accompanied by radical changes in vocal style as
many singers—especially women—abandoned the comparatively
raw insular sound in favor of the more lyrical and operatic voices of
their favorite artistes.

As the style's wide dissemination via the media rapidly established it as the norm, this was the sound that listeners came to identify as Corsican. The extent to which such identification had taken
root by the late 1940s is revealed in the indignant horror that greeted
examples taken from the field recordings of traditional Corsican music collected during Félix Quilici's 1949 mission, made under the
auspices of Radiodiffusion Française, when they were broadcast that
same year in a series of programs by Radio Monte-Carlo; heated debates followed in the press. "It's a disgrace! They're making fun of
us!" was, according to one correspondent, the general reaction. "We
were expecting 'Nina-Nana' [a lullaby]," he continues, "and what
we got, instead of these nostalgic airs, were *chjam'è rispondi* fit to
chill the spine! Heavens above! complained a refined Ajaccian,
whatever will the continentals think of us?" (Nice Matin Corse 21
Sept. 1949, cited in Pizzorni-Itié 1997, 68). "Or perhaps it is the case,
proposed another, that, when the recordings came out, someone
mixed up the records, because what we heard—oh! our poor ears!—
was more reminiscent of the confines of the Sahara than 'The mountain of the Cuscione' [again, the title of a popular Corsican lullaby]"
(Journal dela Corse 17 Sept., cited in Plizzorni-Itié 1997, 68).[16]

To the ears of Corsican town dwellers, everything about the rural styles of singing sounded alien and, by implication, barbaric. This was the age in which traditional singers were perceived as being perpetually drunk and singing horribly out of tune. Their singing was, in keeping with their lifestyle as a whole, a display of their inability to embrace any sort of discipline or order.[17] The Corsican language was similarly stigmatized. One acquaintance described to me how its use was strictly forbidden at the girl's *collège* she attended in Bastia. If she did speak Corsican, even outside the classroom, she was called a shepherdess.[18]

In the latter decades of the twentieth century, a conscious reversal of this value system was set in motion with a positive reframing, from an emic perspective, of those features that had so horrified urbanized postwar audiences. On several occasions during my original fieldwork (1993–95), I found myself party to what I came to recognize as an evolving popular discourse on the merits and values of traditional indigenous music, based largely on a system whereby it was directly, and in this case favorably, juxtaposed to "other" music, variously identified as French, continental, Anglo-American, or Western. Inevitably, perhaps, there is an overlap between this discourse of musical difference and the broader discourse of colonization.

It is common for singers in Corsica today, for instance, to talk of a "colonization of the ear," alluding to the domination of the equal-tempered scale and the duality of major and minor to which most European ears have now become accustomed, depriving them of the ability to clearly distinguish and reproduce other intervals. Comment has already been made on the characteristic flexibility of pitch in traditional Corsican singing. The middle or neutral third, known in Corsican as the *terza mezzana*, has in latter years come to be identified by Corsicans themselves as one of the most characteristic hallmarks of the Corsican singing style that now needs all the help it can muster to hold its ground against the encroaching tide of major and minor thirds. Retaining or reclaiming this aspect of the indigenous musical heritage can, for some, become part of a conscious resistance to colonization.

The apparent rhythmic liberty of traditional singing styles can similarly assume a political dimension. Within a particular melodic figure, part of the function of the *rivucate* (melismas) is to militate against an impression of rhythmic regularity or predictability. Regularity can, in the terms of the colonization debate, be seen as something imposed from outside, and slavish adherence to a regular beat is, in this context, clearly both undesirable and distasteful. The older indigenous singing, by contrast, unfolds naturally in its own time. Maintaining rhythmic freedom can thus take on the aura of a revolutionary campaign with the slogan *Il faut casser la logique!* ("You have to break the logic!")

The favorable comparison between Corsican music and its supposedly more derivative French or continental counterparts was further reinforced by the analogies that were suggested on a number of occasions with wine, cheese, and milk, the mass-produced, pasteurized, and processed varieties being associated with the continental mainland and the increasing blandness of its products resulting from its dedication to the mass-market ethos (now encroaching on insular territory in the form of hypermarkets in the larger towns), while the less refined and to some extent less predictable Corsican equivalents stood for spontaneity, lack of artifice or stylization, and a natural organic wholesomeness.

Such missionary fervor does not mean that the types of musical distinctions referred to are in any way imagined or fabricated, even if they are on occasion prone to exaggeration. Nor does it in any sense detract from the validity of attempting to reestablish the Corsican musical language in a Mediterranean as opposed to a Continental (and predominantly urban) frame of reference. In Michel Raffaelli's assessment, "The song of the Mediterranean is Arabo-Andalusian, Iranian and Lebanese song. We, too, have this Oriental song, but colonization killed it for us. People became ashamed of it" (in de Zerbi and Diani 1992, 35). In this context, the distaste that informed the rejection of *paghjella* singing through the postwar years and into the early years of the revival with the accusation "they sound like Arabs" is reframed as a positive concept of the "Oriental" with its suggestion of a higher form of artistic culture. While any identification of Corsican music with Oriental music inspired by the opposition established to Western music as a whole is certainly not as straightforward as it is sometimes made to sound, there is, nevertheless, a kinship that cannot be denied with respect to some aspects of some types of musical expression.

The current interest in Oriental musics is part of the process of rediscovering the deep roots of the Corsican vocal tradition. Part of the reason for making the connection in Raffaelli's case is to draw attention to similarities in vocal technique and in the conception of the voice and the vocal line, in particular with respect to its modal flex-

ibility, its melismatic nature, and its rhythmic liberty, and by so doing, perhaps, to add a greater sense of legitimacy to this style of music by relating it to non-Western traditions that might be seen as
"classical" in their own right.[19] The results of such reflection can
then be applied equally to new compositions and to the interpretation of traditional material, where they serve in part to counteract
the tendency to subconsciously "westernize" or modernize the
singing style.[20]

THE RIACQUISTU AND
THE SOLDATS-CHANTEURS

A growing sense of economic abandonment by the French state, coupled with a climate of increasing sociopolitical oppression, lay behind
the cultural and political movements that began to flourish anew in
Corsica in the late 1960s and early 1970s. In a broader context, Corsica
was not immune from the reactionary, anti-authoritarian spirit that
swept across most of the western world in the 1960s in response to the
increasing imposition of a global, capitalist ethic at the expense of local systems and networks. In Corsica, this sense of political awaken-
ing took the form of a return to the question of cultural identity that
had lain dormant since its airing by the *félibres* and their journals in
the late nineteenth and early twentieth centuries. The new regionalist
and autonomist groups that now began to blossom subscribed to the
principles of cultural as well as political reacquisition.

The ensuing decade saw a vastly increased output across several
disciplinary areas—historical, political, archeological, scientific, literary, and artistic. Corsican was reinstated as a language in its own
right, as opposed to a mere dialect, and classes were established at
community level where the language could be learnt and practiced.[21] Many of those active in cultural contexts were also
prompted to reclaim the Corsican versions of their Christian names,
which they now used for their professional or semiprofessional
work, as a further statement of their Corsican identity.[22] *A gener-
azione di u settanta*, literally "the generation of the seventies," is the
name by which this era in Corsican history has come to be known.
It is also referred to as *u miraculu di u settanta* ("the miracle of the
seventies"). The process of cultural revival which it fueled is referred to in Corsican as the *riacquistu*, literally, "reacquisition."

Music, too, had its place within this ferment of activity. Alongside the fighters for political autonomy, there developed the notion of *militants culturels* ("cultural militants"), an epithet applied predominantly to those who sang in the newly formed "groups."[23] The act of singing in the Corsican language was in itself a powerful political statement and the old songs—which offered such blatant proof of Corsica's non-Frenchness—now came to play a vital role in the demands for political recognition.[24] This new alliance between music and politics saw a transference of the fervor that had built up in connection with political action to the realm of musical activity. The groups that came together in the 1970s and identified themselves as *groupes engagés*, epitomized in the example of the now legendary Canta u Populu Corsu, typically engaged in a variety of activities that included visiting old singers in the villages to learn their songs and their manner of singing and then disseminating the material via their own recordings and through *veghje culturale* ("cultural evenings"), where they performed the songs, and later *scole di cantu* ("schools of singing"), where they taught them to others. In addition, they began to seek out old field recordings from which they could add to their repertoire, thereby bringing songs that had been little known or forgotten back into circulation.

Initially, Canta was concerned primarily with the restitution and transmission of the repertoire: their overriding concern was that the songs should be sung again. Soon, however, encounters with musicians from other cultures who were already using their art as a more direct vehicle for political assertion (in particular in parts of South America) awakened individual members of Canta to the fact that "the *chanson* could also carry a message" (interview 1994). Coupled with the rapid deterioration of the political situation, this realization led increasingly to new *chansons* composed by the groups themselves, expressing their reactions to contemporary concerns and incidents. A retrospective report in *Kyrn* magazine (May 1981) highlights the dramatic nature of the change in the group's orientation: "Gone the laments and the lullabies, 'Canta' seeks and finds its inspiration in the noise of the light armoured-cars, the acrid smoke of the tear-gas grenades, the grey walls of the Parisian prisons and the maquis where the 'clandestine' wages the battle of national liberation" (32).

New songs now began to appear with such titles as *A Rivolta* ("The Revolt"), *Clandestinu* ("Clandestine"), *Compañero, Corsica*

Nazione ("The Corsican Nation"), *Corsica Nostra* ("Our Corsica"), *Let-
tera di u Prigiuneru* ("Letter of the Prisoner"), *Suldatu di u Populu Và*
("Soldier of the People Advance"), and *Un Soffiu di Libertà* ("A
Breath of Freedom"). For many of these songs, invocations of *unità*
("unity"), *libertà* ("liberty"), *verità* ("truth"), and *sulidarità* ("solidarity") offered a ready rhyme. Some songs were dedicated to "events"
in the struggle, such as the incident at Aleria[2]; others were composed
in honor of Corsica's own contemporary martyrs, both those who
had lost their lives and those who had been imprisoned for their nationalist activities or allegiances (themselves often active as singers
with one or other of the groups). Others again—such as *A Pasquale
Paoli* and the *Paghjella di Ponte Novu*—celebrated moments of glory
in the island's past. The overridingly political content of many of
these songs was further reinforced by the commentaries that accompanied them in performance and the groups who sang them were
increasingly referred to in the press as *soldats-chanteurs* ("soldier-
singers").

To many of the older generation of islanders, this political rhetoric
sometimes smacked alarmingly of terrorism. If a Canta song was
played on the radio at this time, the radio base would be bombarded
by people ringing up to complain, typically reiterating the by now familiar objection that they were "singing like Arabs." Petru Guelfucci
(now one of the island's most successful singers and one of the original members of Canta) observes that what people were responding to
was more the "political coloration" of the group's activities, but since
they were not able to attack them directly for their politics, their rejection was transferred to an attack on their style of singing (interview
1995). Meanwhile, the mayors of a number of communes prohibited
concerts or *manifestazione culturale* from being held in their villages,
accusing the groups of attempting to impose a political ideology on
their audiences. The manner in which the authorities sometimes
sought to reinforce these bans, however, only served to increase the
revolutionary fervor of those affected and to implicate traditional music, together with the new *chanson engagée* or *cantu indiatu*, ever more
deeply in the nationalist cause. By the early 1980s, Canta had become
more or less synonymous with the nationalist struggle, functioning as
"a sort of legal expression of the clandestine struggle which was developing at the time" (de Zerbi and Diani 1992, 67).[26]

The nationalist movement in Corsica inevitably drew inspiration
in general from what was going on in other parts of the world, in

particular in the Pays Basque, Northern Ireland, and Chile, which at that time were very much in the news. Fusina comments on how reports in the press of outbreaks of violence in Northern Ireland attracted the attention of young Corsicans, especially when the emphasis was on "the exemplary destiny of romantic heroes in an eternal struggle against outside domination" (Fusina 1993, 143). A number of new compositions were inspired by these other struggles and conceived as an expression of solidarity. Jean-Paul Poletti's *Surella d'Irlanda* ("Sister of Ireland," featured on Canta's 1978 disc *A Strada di l'Avvene*, Ricordu 1978), for example, evokes the troubles in Northern Ireland and its perennial resistance to English colonization. The text opens with a reference to reading of Ireland's tribulations in the newspaper and expresses the sense of brotherhood (or in this case sisterhood) that the writer derives from the knowledge that both islands are oppressed by the same hand of iron, imprisoned and condemned to death by the colonial order. Another later song inspired by events in Northern Ireland was A Filetta's *Sintenza per tè* ("A Sentence / Judgement for You," from *In L'Abbriu di e Stagioni*, Kalliste 1987), which was dedicated to Bobby Sands.

Canta now became increasingly active on the circuit of festivals and concert tours outside the island, presenting programs that consisted of a combination of traditional songs, including local polyphonic settings of the Latin mass, and their own political *chansons* as part of a semiformalized "internationalization of the Corsican problem." They also took to the stage specifically as a gesture of solidarity with other minority struggles, for example in Brittany and the Pays Basque, appearing in particular in support of political prisoners. Boswell's earlier efforts were equaled as regular reports appeared in the press detailing Canta's latest success in spreading the message of Corsica's oppression across the continent while also "bringing Corsica's support to those fighting against fascism and repression" (report in *Le Provençal* 12 June 1980, reproduced in de Zerbi et al. 1993, 216). Meetings with other "soldier-singers" in the context of these gatherings inevitably led to direct exchanges of both songs and discourses, as well as to more general musical influences, and Canta now began to include occasional "foreign" songs in its own repertory, the texts sometimes remaining in their original language and sometimes being adapted into Corsican.

The move toward newly composed *chansons* brought with it a change in musical language. As the style matured, the melodic basis moved further away from the traditional model and, aided by the addition of instrumental accompaniment, the songs became increasingly rhythmic and at the same time began to lose touch with the strongly modal character that distinguishes the island's traditional unaccompanied singing. Turchini characterizes the new style as a meeting between the traditional polyphonic *paghjella* style and a more contemporary harmonic style centered on the arpeggio (Turchini 1993, 199). The way in which the vocal harmonies were added was, however, far removed from the manner of constructing the traditional polyphonic sound. The pattern increasingly adopted was that of a solo voice singing a verse with the other voices joining in a refrain with choruslike harmonies dictated by the triadic chordal progressions of the guitar, which now featured prominently as accompanying instrument. This new style was further enriched by the conscious assimilation of elements from other musical cultures, specifically justified by some on aesthetic grounds. One member of the group I Chjami Aghjalesi, for example, explained to me in 1995 that while the group's own creations are, in their own eyes, firmly rooted in the tradition, what they have added is "the rhythm." This move to a more upbeat presentation was inspired by a search for "something a bit happier," but since there was no rhythmic tradition in Corsica, he explained, they had to look for inspiration elsewhere. Portuguese *fado* offered one such inspiration.

The stylistic choices that were made can also be seen to be related in some instances to the songs' function as vehicles of a political ideology. While the overt message is carried by the lyrics, a number of features incorporated into the musical setting (presumably often subconsciously) serve to stimulate an emotional response in the listener. Such features include melodies that have a comparatively wide range and feature a high proportion of ascending patterns, the choral style of triadic harmonization and in particular the use of dominant seventh chords with their feeling of suspense, and the manner in which the voice is projected, the combination of these factors in some indefinable way seeming to evoke an image of heroic resistance, determined self-assertion, and the claim to a more just and hopeful future. It could also be observed that, as the musical interest increased in the sense of becoming more varied and the idiom became more widely recognizable, so the appeal of the material was no longer dependent on an understanding of the text and so became more accessible to foreign as well as local audiences. Meanwhile, within Corsica, this style has now come to be seen as traditional in its own right, especially by the younger generation who have, after all, grown up with it, many becoming ardent practitioners in their own right.[27]

POLYPHONIC RENAISSANCE AND
THE SALVAGE OF THE CORSICAN SOUL

This is not to say that the older styles and repertories have again been abandoned. While the number of groups operating in the Canta mold continues to multiply, so too does the number committed to a cappella polyphonic singing. Indeed, many groups cultivate both, moving with apparent ease between rousing revolutionary-sounding choruses and heart-stopping renditions of extracts from their local village mass in the same concert performance. In the early days of the *riacquistu*, particular attention had been paid to the polyphonic heritage. The *paghjella*, which had survived as a living tradition only in the villages of the island's isolated interior, mainly among those still practicing a pastoral way of life, now came to function as "the symbol of the profound Corsican being, the major expression of its musical discourse" (Berlinghi 1993, 230). According to Petru Guelfucci, the original motivation of Canta u Populu Corsu was intimately connected with the salvage and safeguard of the polyphonic tradition: It was indeed as a result of a visit on the part of other future members of the group to the saint's day celebrations near Guelfucci's own village of Sermanu, an occasion characterized by extensive polyphonic singing, that Canta was first formed. Iviu Pasquali similarly talks of an act of salvage by people who realized that "in losing these songs which had come down to us from the beginning of time we were soon going to lose a part of our soul" (Pasquali 1993, 7).

The unprecedented scale on which the *paghjella* has been taken up by young people during the past decade even in those parts of the island that do not have a history of *paghjella* singing—albeit largely as a direct result of the influence of the groups and their recordings and of the *scole di cantu*—suggests nevertheless that there are certain qualities embodied in the singing of polyphony that continue to appeal strongly to the Corsican male psyche. The psychosocial function of the *paghjella*—the act of men singing together—has always taken precedence over the function implied by the text, whether it be a lullaby, a lament, or a serenade, such singing owing its perennity in considerable part to the immediate metaphysical benefits derived from the collective acoustic experience for which the text serves largely as a pretext. For today's youth, the *paghjella* is the perfect embodiment of the notion of *patrimoine*. On the one hand, it has become emblematic of the old indigenous way of life whose values remain enshrined in the songs. By singing them, young culturally disinherited singers hope that they will somehow find their way back to the Corsica of their ancestors, in spirit if not in practice. In this sense, the act of singing *paghjelle* represents a literal return to the old ancestral rhythms.

On the other hand, in the context of the nationalist discourse of identity, the *paghjella* operates as a symbol of unity and solidarity. *Paghjella* singing in particular has always been experienced, by both singers and audience, as something liberated and primal, unrestrained by any externally imposed discipline. Together with the fact that the development of the song is controlled by the singers themselves in an essentially democratic manner—with reference to the independence of each voice within the wider collective framework—this would seem to marry well with the desire for self-determination on a social and political level.[28] The attractiveness of the Corsican style of polyphonic singing to contemporary "world music" audiences has also been an important factor that, together with the new state of grace in which polyphony has come to find itself in the island itself, has led to a wealth of new polyphonic "creations."

FORGING NEW FUTURES

Whether they relate to the polyphonic or *chanson* framework, today's groups are consciously striving in their new compositions to find an appropriate marriage of tradition and modernity that will allow them to explore their own creativity and give expression to contemporary concerns and values while remaining faithful to their roots. In a discussion regarding the style of new polyphonic compositions devised by the group Voce di Corsica, Benoit Sarocchi agrees that certain elements of the traditional musical language are consciously retained. They want fellow Corsicans who hear their songs to be able to say, "I don't know it, but it is from here" (interview

1995). Some of the new songs incorporate traditional motives but combine them with more original elements while others owe their "Corsican" sound to more general stylistic or procedural features such as the arrangement and interaction of the voices, the behavior of the individual voices, the melismatic style, the timbral qualities, the nature of the cadences, and, in particular, the *tierce de Picardie* type ending. At a broader level, the readoption of traditional Corsican instruments, the fact of singing in polyphony, and the inclusion of improvisatory elements are all seen to provide a strong sense of continuity between contemporary developments and "the tradition," while the utilization of the Corsican language is for many enough in itself to allow a song to qualify as traditional. While any more detailed analysis of these developments lies beyond the scope of the present article, it should be noted that some of the features mentioned above are interpreted at a relatively liberal level.[29]

Corsican groups continue to take opportunities to perform outside the island, both through individual concert tours organized by continental agents and through the festival circuit. Many invoke the need to actively look beyond the confines of the island and its sometimes stifling concerns and value meetings with musicians from other cultures as a means of maintaining a sense of proportion, at a sociopolitical as well as a musical level. As Iviu Pasquali (of the group Madricale) expresses it, "it also demonstrates to us that we are not the centre of the world" (Pasquali 1993, 40). At the same time, part of the motivation is to make Corsican music known to a wider audience; in the words of Patrizia Poli (of the ensemble Les Nouvelles Polyphonies Corses/Soledonna), "to show the whole world the strongest things we have, the most beautiful things we have" (interview 1995), thus helping to counteract the often negative image of Corsica abroad. This desire to export the best of what Corsican culture has to offer as a means of drawing attention to the island in a positive way is their manner of demonstrating their "engagement" to the cause, while their commitment to portraying Corsica in as advantageous a light as possible necessarily entails working on producing a quality product.

Patrizia Gattaceca (Les Nouvelles Polyphonies Corses/Soledonna) also draws attention to the part played by musical exports in creating a presence at an international level for the Corsican language: "[song] is a vector of our language. It permits us to convey it everywhere" (cited in de Zerbi and Diani 1992, 75). This connection with the language issue was again emphasized in a media interview with the group Voce de Corsica following their appearance at the award ceremony of the 1995 *Victoires de la Musique* in which they had been awarded first prize in the category of traditional music, when they expressed the conviction that, having accorded this degree of recognition to Corsican culture, the French government would no longer be able to maintain its entrenched position vis-à-vis the language itself. In the words of Petru Guelfucci: "It will no longer be possible, at a political level, to continue to maintain a double parlance. Since we win prizes, our language must be given recognition, it must be given a statute, and the means to develop" (*La Corse* 15 February 1995).

At the same time as acting as ambassadors for Corsican culture, today's groups continue to forge links with other musical cultures, in some cases working on recordings together with established musicians from outside the island. Les Nouvelles Polyphonies Corses' first disc (*Les Nouvelles Polyphonies Corses*, Philips 1991) famously included instrumental contributions from Manu Dibango, Ryuichi Sakamoto, Shaymal Maltra, Ivo Papasov, John Cale, and Jon Hassel, while Cinqui Sò's *Tarraniu* (Albiana 1996) features the Sardinian singer Elena Leda, the Occitan singer Miquèla Bramerie, and the Catalan musician Pedro Aledo. A number of semicomposed, semi-improvised performances have also taken place in the context of festivals as a literal enactment of the notion of a *rencontre* ("meeting").

This impulse to reach out and embrace the other would appear to belong to a new climate of global dialogue and the recognition of a shared humanity. Indeed, the language of universal love and fraternity permeates many of the edicts of today's groups, as exemplified by the statements of Jean-François Bernardini of the group I Muvrini, who says: "We want to make our concerts into places of meeting and dialogue. To show, certainly, our face, our identity, our differences. . . . But what we want to say most of all through our songs is that we are all citizens of an identical love!" (*Corse-Matin* 30 May 1994). Canta u Populu Corsu's 1995 disc *Sintineddi* (Albiana 1995) was described on its release by a spokesman for the group as "a veritable gift of fraternity" (*Corse Matin* 2 July 1995), while a song on the disc entitled *Beal Feirste* ("Belfast") says, in the words of the disc notes, "that the time has come for the people of Ireland to strike out the chords of fraternity." This new perspective can perhaps be seen as the other face of nationalism—a perspective that has both been inspired by, and in its turn lent further endorsement to, the increasingly ecumenical approach to the musical product itself.

THE PERFORMANCE OF IDENTITY IN
CONTEMPORARY CORSICA AND THE CELTIC FRINGE

Chapman (1994) has drawn attention to the "two rather distinct spheres" that might be seen to exist with respect to the performance of identity in Celtic areas today: On the one hand "the area of self-conscious 'Celtic' activity" typically entered into by "intellectual incomers with folkloric tastes" and "some small part of the university-educated local youth," and, on the other, "genuinely popular activity in the 'Celtic' areas" (30). This latter often has little to do with the cultivated style of the former group, which has, nonetheless, been disseminated and marketed to the rest of the world as distinctively "Celtic," often fueling a quite unrealistic expectation that this is the sort of thing that people in Brittany or Wales or wherever commonly do of an evening, whereas in truth a fair proportion of them are settling down for a fix of their favorite soap, whether it be London's "Eastenders" or (its Welsh equivalent) *Pobol y Cwm*.

This model does not lend itself so readily to the Corsican example. Despite the fact that there has been a very definite "return" to traditional music in Corsica in recent decades which, in itself, has in many cases been deliberate and self-conscious, the current state of traditional musical practice cannot fairly be described in revivalist terms. The situation is also very different from that pertaining in Wales, for example, where there is an indisputable element of "invention" or at least repackaging in what now passes for traditional Welsh culture, at least as far as its roots in "ancient times" is concerned, together with what is often a rather formalized compartmentalization of "traditional" activity, with the annual cycle of *eisteddfodau* serving as the prime arena in which people act out their Welshness—even if, as Trosset (1993, 42) has pointed out, this enactment takes place for the Welsh themselves and not for any outside observer. There is not, in Corsica, such an obvious break in continuity, either between past and present or between the stage and grassroots manifestations of present-day culture.[30]

While it was true in the postwar years that the inhabitants of Corsican *towns* "[knew] little or nothing about this music, and [had] no interest in it" (Chapman 1994, 30), having acquired more cosmopolitan musical tastes en route to their membership of a more modern age, the situation in the *villages* was often quite different. Here, many of the musical genres now included in the repertories of the more traditional groups remained part of a way of life that, while being under threat, was still practiced in direct continuity with the past. It is true that many of those who were at the forefront of the *riacquistu* in its early days and became the most fervent promoters of traditional music had benefited from an outside perspective through having lived and studied, as young adults, in France or Italy (in particular at the universities of Nice and Aix-en-Provence) where their education had often undergone both a political and a musical fine tuning.

They did not, however, simply reinvent some rather spurious and fragmentary notion of an authentic past. Rather, they either sought out those rural traditions, still being practiced by a minority, to which they had lately been alerted, or came to see in a new and more appreciative light (inspired partly by the simple fact of distance as well as by a heightened consciousness) the village traditions with which they had grown up. In the context of cultural renewal and the salvage of nationhood, these now became treasures to be preserved and nurtured—a responsibility as well as an opportunity. Moreover, it tends to be items of repertoire—such as rarely sung musical variants or texts, collected either from an isolated singer or relearned from old field recordings—which have been revived, rather than the style of singing, which—as noted earlier—has to be seen as something distinct and that is a more enduring, "natural," and apparently in-bred inclination.

The fairs and festivals that take place out of doors in the summer months are still community events and while they now attract all manner of fairground paraphernalia quite foreign to their true nature and are, to the regret of many, "no longer what they used to be," the songs that are sung there are still much the same songs as in the past, with improvised poetic debates and spontaneous *paghjella*-singing taking pride of place. Although they might now be in the minority, shepherds do still sing when they take their flocks up the mountain or gather their friends together for the shearing. In a few villages, groups of friends still go out serenading. Religious ritual remains for many an integral part of community life. Comparatively "ancient" polyphonic masses continue to be sung in isolated chapels on mountaintops or in olive groves in honor of particular saints.

Thus while the profusion of recordings that have come out of Corsica in recent years are a fair reflection of the high density of musical activity at "group" level, what is not immediately evident from this is that there is a parallel population of those who are still to be found in respectable if diminished numbers singing their hearts and lungs out at fairs and similar gatherings and for whom such an activity remains in the realm of "being" as opposed to "performing." Nor is there a clear dividing line between the groups and the village singers. Notwithstanding what I have written elsewhere about differences in musical perception and interpretation between older and younger generations of singers (Bithell 1996) or about the dangers of reading the vitality of the stage culture as proof of a thriving "living tradition" (Bithell 1997), the distinctions between the different singing populations often turn out, on closer inspection, to be somewhat blurred. While some groups may now be composed of young singers who have learned their art at the *scole di cantu* or of older educated singers who have not grown up immersed in the rural traditions but have later come to recognize their value and potential, many include members who are themselves the direct inheritors of village traditions and the descendants of some of the most revered singers and poets of the past (see Bithell 2001). Moreover, even the most well-established groups, for whom performance has become a professional activity, do not operate exclusively in performance mode but often manage to function with one foot in the market and the other in the life of the local community. Many regularly sing the mass for weddings and funerals, usually at the request of friends; some can also be found singing *paghjelle* informally in the bars or at the fairs.

It is perhaps because Corsicanness belongs to, or is delineated by, the island as a whole that one does not find an "alternative" social strata such as one finds in "Celtic" areas of Britain (Glastonbury included). The island does not attract droves of incomers in flight from the rat race, eager to rediscover their Corsican roots and recreate their vision of a utopian Corsican existence. Nor have those Corsicans reluctant to relinquish the possibility of a trickle of Celtic blood in their own veins felt the need to give expression to their inheritance by sporting baggy jumpers, matted locks, and the sort of beard that "appear[s] to have declared itself an autonomous region" like the would-be Celts encountered by Stanley Stewart during his visit to the Lorient Inter-Celtic Festival (*The Sunday Times* 20 June 1999).

Corsicans do on occasion invoke their pagan roots in general or allude to the more arcane aspects of vocal technique associated with polyphonic singing, which is itself commonly referred to as having its origins "in the mists of time," but there is not the insistence on an elaborate and consciously constructed mysticism such as that popularly associated with the Celts. This is again in part because many of the types of ritual practices and beliefs that form the basis of Celtic mysticism do not, in Corsica, belong to a far distant past but to a surprisingly recent past that in some cases, as we have seen, continues to coexist with a more modern present. The passing of the "old" way of life is certainly viewed with nostalgia, but for many it still exists in the realm of personal memory. It is not distant enough to have become collectively sanctified.

Folklore groups do exist but, unlike the situation found in some other parts of Europe, traditional musical activity does not center on such groups. There remains a clear distinction both between folklore and the living tradition, and between folklore and the groups who "perform" traditional music.[31] Apart from a handful of artisans selling animal bells and goat's cheese at the fairs, it is, generally speaking, only in the context of the self-styled folkloric groups that one now finds the "traditional" costume of corduroy or velvet trousers and waistcoats and red and white checked shirts for men, and long skirts and headscarves for women, together with flags, guns, cowbells, and other accessories supposedly suggestive of the "traditional" way of life.[32] Even here, the wearing of a "national" costume has its raison d'être in the rules imposed by the folkloric federation in the context of which these groups had their origins in the middle decades of the twentieth century. In at least one case, it is seen as a regrettable but necessary compromise by the group itself.

Among the new generation of groups that have come into being from the 1970s onward, there is little attempt to cultivate a special "Corsican" image through their appearance. For concerts of predominantly traditional polyphonic songs, the singers typically wear black trousers and white or black shirts; for concerts featuring original *chansons* they are most likely to wear jeans and coloured shirts or T-shirts. The majority of the younger generation of singers wear their hair cropped close to their heads; beards, if worn at all, are similarly well-maintained. Their image is that of the average modern Corsican. Like the music they perform, their appearance is an expression of a contemporary reality as opposed to a museum-like reconstruction of a bygone era.

By comparison, the remaining folkloric groups are a literal anachronism, representing the tastes, fashions, and practical networks of a past age. The majority are, moreover, a part of *town* culture. People tend to join them because they appreciate the social outlet that such groups provide or because they enjoy dancing. The constitution often contains clauses referring to the society's commitment to keeping the traditions alive, but essentially people are there to have a good time. The typical musical repertory of these groups is similarly that of the towns—serenades, fishing songs, and barcarolles, redolent of languid summer evenings by the shore and relying heavily on an instrumental accompaniment—all a far cry indeed from the ruggedness of the a cappella polyphonic singing of the mountain dwellers.[33]

Aspects of my arguments for seeing members of the professional and semiprofessional groups in Corsica today as being integrated into what might be described, for want of a better word, as "normal" Corsican life as opposed to existing as a race apart, preoccupied with living up to a mythic past, can, of course, be applied to many of their counterparts in Celtic lands—I do not wish to suggest that Celts en masse be tarred with the same brush as the over-enthusiastic new convert, or that the majority of those "performing" their Celtic heritage should be seen as actors in a historical reconstruction. Indeed, meetings between ordinary Corsicans and ordinary Celts seem to be on the increase, thanks in part to the activities of the association Tutti in Piazza. Having inaugurated two new festivals, *A Festa di u Viulinu* (the first "edition" of which took place in 1997 in the village of Sermanu) and *I Scontri di Quatrigliu* (launched in 2000 in the village of Evisa), in 2002 the organizers combined the two initiatives to form *FestiBallu*, which took place over three days in the town of Corte (the size of the Viulinu gathering in particular having outgrown its original village location) and to which The Glencraig Scottish Dance Band and Irish musicians Seamus and Fidelma Bellew were invited as guest performers and teachers.

Another forum that promises regular contact between Corsican and Celtic musicians is the European Festival of Insular Cultures, currently in development within the Interreg III framework. As part of the preliminary exchanges, the group Caramusa (who include in their repertory traditional dance music as well as polyphonic songs) represented Corsica at the 2001 edition of the Gaelic Festival in Stornoway.

At the level of the musical fabric itself, intimations of acoustic links with Celtic culture now linger intriguingly not far beneath the surface of some of Corsica's musical output—partly, perhaps, as a result of a certain conflation between "world music" and Celtic music but also as a result of more permanent collaboration on the part of some Corsican musicians with others from France's Celtic fringe. A report of a concert given by the group I Muvrini in Calvi in 2001 enthuses: "The public was hypnotized by a sumptuous tour of song where 'word music' (sic), jazzy and Celtic in color, entered into a marriage with traditional polyphonies and well-known standards" (*Corse-Matin* 21 August 2001). While this perceived Celtic coloration undoubtedly derives from the incorporation of bagpipes and a hurdy-gurdy in the group's lineup (played by Loïc Taillebrest and Gilles Chabenat respectively), the resonances in themselves would appear to belong—not surprisingly—to a relatively recent manifestation of technologically enabled and commercially propagated "Celtic" style.

Meanwhile, the abiding sense among today's groups that an important part of their role is to safeguard indigenous forms of expression does, on occasion, have recourse to familiar imagery. The title of Canta's 1995 comeback album, *Sintineddi* (*Sentinels*, evoking the island's statue-menhirs), suggests that the group continues to see itself as guardian of traditional culture or at least of the insular spirit. These ancient stone sentinels had similarly been invoked in the context of I Muvrini's 1994 summer tour, which incorporated into its stage-set polystyrene models of the famous prehistoric statues found at the site of Filitosa, thus metaphorically associating the music with the earliest stages of the island's (pre-Celtic!) history and the deepest roots of its culture.

ACKNOWLEDGMENT

I am grateful to Dorothy Carrington for her kind and fascinating comments on an earlier draft of this chapter as well as for the inspirational example of her many published volumes on Corsica's culture and history. With her passing, the island has lost one of its most dedicated, energetic, and perceptive commentators.

NOTES

1. As Chapman notes, the Anglo-Saxons, upon their arrival in Britain, appear to have associated the megalithic monuments they found there with the Celts. Scholars writing in the eighteenth century then made a close association between the Celtic Druids and standing stones, "an association that is now firmly embedded in the popular imagination, and is thus truly part of the myth of the Celts" (Chapman 1992, dedication page).

2. Unless otherwise stated, English translations of non-English sources cited throughout the article are my own.

3. The existence of a specific "ethnic" group who can readily be defined as "the Celts" is, of course, also contested.

4. According to Carrington (1995, 4), the megalithic faith appears to have originated in the Near or Middle East, from whence it was carried around western Europe by missionary seafarers, reaching Corsica by the third millennium B.C.E.

5. Two works devoted specifically to a study of the *mazzere* are Carrington 1995 and Multedo 1994.

6. Speculation on the symbolic potency of the head is not entirely unscientific. Carrington (1984, 300) reports that: "Belief in the supernatural power of skulls survived in Corsica into the present century: in times of drought the members of a village would walk in procession with one or several skulls carried aloft on poles; the skulls were laid in a river bed and were thought to bring rain."

7. Further accounts of Boswell's involvement with Corsican affairs can be found in Daiches 1976 and Carrington 1984.

8. Having finally been granted the status of an autonomous *région* in 1970, in 1982 the island became the first *région* of France to elect a Regional Assembly. The assembly's powers, however, remain relatively restricted.

9. This perspective on latter-day intimations of Corsican-Celtic affinities is shared by the Corsican writer and anthropologist Jacques (Ghjacumu) Fusina, who comments with respect to the numerous resemblances reported by observers between Ireland and Corsica that "the analogies doubtless relate less to the landscape than to the particularism of the character of the two insular communities and to the tormented relationship which history has established with the nations to which they are respectively bound" (Fusina 1993, 143).

10. In 1951, the Corsican language had been excluded from the Deixonne law, which made provision for the inclusion of regional languages in education. Only in 1974 was this decision finally reversed. In accordance with a decree that "regional languages and cultures" might be taught on a voluntary basis, one hour's teaching a week in Corsican was initially granted. This was increased in 1982, at which time the writer and linguist Jacques

Fusina was made responsible for establishing and coordinating a Corsican syllabus for the Académie de la Corse (Fusina 1988). Further ground has been gained in recent years. See Jaffe 1999.

11. The question as to whether one can be both "Corsican," and "French," remains nonetheless a perplexing one for many Corsicans. See McKechnie 1993.

12. It is relevant to note that my own Celtic pedigree was of some significance to my Corsican acquaintances and a sense of shared experience and understanding certainly paved my way in some contexts. Meanwhile, those campaigning for greater use of the Corsican language on television had recently established a direct connection with Wales via the Welsh television channel S4C.

13. In the case of Corsica, this reputation has been unfortunately reinforced by recent events, culminating in the assassination of the French Prefect Claude Erignac in 1998. At the same time, it has to be noted that French state involvement in Corsican affairs has often been heavy-handed in its own right (witness the Bonnet affair of 1999).

14. For a detailed study of the various genres, see Laade 1981. My own Ph.D. thesis (1997) focuses primarily on polyphonic song types. In terms of recordings, a selection of pieces representing different genres of traditional music, taken from Laade's field recordings dating from 1958 and 1973, can be found on the CD *Corsica: Traditional Songs and Music* (Jecklin-Disco 1990). A more extensive set of examples, taken from Quilici's field recordings of the early 1960s and accompanied by detailed notes, can be found in the boxed set of three LPs *Musique Corse de Tradition Orale* (Archives Sonores de la Phonothèque National 1982). Interpretations of a similar range of traditional songs by contemporary singers can be found on the CD *Canti Corsi in Tradizioni: Canti, nanne, lamenti, voceri, paghjelle a capella* (Fonti Musicali 1989, conceived and directed by Mighele Raffaelli). Recordings of traditional polyphonic masses re-released on CD include *Corsica: Religious Music of Oral Tradition from Rusiu* (Unesco 1989; recorded 1975) and *Messa Nustrale in Sermanu* (Consul 1990; recorded 1977). Interpretations of songs from the polyphonic canon as a whole can be found in the output of numerous recent and contemporary groups (sometimes in combination with their own polyphonic compositions, thereby offering the listener a useful insight into the stylistic relationships between these two strands of musical activity): Examples of landmark CDs devoted almost exclusively to polyphony (sung a cappella) dating from the late 1980s and early 1990s are E Voce di u Cumune's *Corsica: Chants Polyphoniques* (Harmonia Mundi 1987), A Filetta's *Ab Eternu* (Saravah 1992), Donnisulana's *Per Agata: Polyphonies Corses* (Silex 1992), and Voce di Corsica's *Polyphonies* (Olivi 1993). More recent releases are too numerous to list individually but include a number of compilations featuring items from the polyphonic canon performed by a range of different

groups. Visitors to Corsica itself have ample opportunity to hear the current groups in performance, particularly during the summer months when many go "on tour" around the island as well as appearing at the various fairs and festivals: In July and August the local newspaper, *Corse-Matin*, carries daily listings of concerts, festivals, and other events.

15. I have examined elsewhere (Bithell 1996) the differences in detail between the style of singing and performance practice of the older singers still operating at a local level on the one hand and the younger semiprofessional groups with their more "modern" and cosmopolitan frames of reference on the other. Despite these differences, however, the style remains distinctively and recognizably Corsican, the degree of transformation being outweighed in most cases by the degree of continuity.

16. The popularity of lullabies—songs that were nonthreatening and heavy with nostalgia—is noteworthy.

17. Chapman has similarly noted how the propensity for pentatonic scales in much Celtic vocal music with its greater latitude in terms of the pitch of individual notes has the effect of appearing to those trained in the system of twelve-note harmony as "a kind of wild freedom, an emotional excess, or a lack of order and control," as a corollary to the more general perception of the "other" as inconstant, irrational and dramatic (Chapman 1994, 39).

18. A similar situation pertained in Wales where the prohibition of Welsh in schools was a major contributing factor to the loss of the language among my grandparents' generation.

19. See also the reference in the introduction to this volume and chapters by Reiss, Vallely, and others to the perceived similarities between Irish *sean-nós* singing and Middle Eastern styles of vocal ornamentation.

20. The fruits of Raffaelli's research and reflection can be heard, for example, on the disc *U Cantu Prufondu* (Ricordu 1993), which features a selection of traditional monodic songs sung by Mighela Cesari accompanied by Raffaelli on the *cetera* and other instruments.

21. Again, an obvious parallel can be drawn here with a similar ferment of activity in Wales during much the same period. Here, too, people reverted to Welsh forms of their name, in particular their family name, adopting the traditional practice of calling themselves "ap [father's name]" ("child of [X]").

22. Many people nevertheless continue to be generally known by the French version of their Christian name with which they are required to be registered at birth, which is subsequently used in all official contexts (including school registration) and to which everyone has therefore become accustomed. Their Corsican name remains a more formal one, a type of artist's signature that appears on discs, books, and so on while also being used in articles or books written in the Corsican language. This can lead to interesting confusions as an individual is known by two different names in differ-

ent contexts, but it is not always clear which name should be given preference in a particular situation. Family names, on the other hand, are always indisputably Corsican.

23. The concept and practice of music in Corsica remains inextricably bound up with politics. In my own experience, conversations about music almost invariably seem to revolve around political issues: Indeed, some of my original interviewees deemed it essential that, before we could even begin to talk about music, I should have a clear appreciation of the recent (or even not-so-recent) political history of the island. In this way, the central role played by the discourses and activities of the autonomist movement in a specifically musical revival became increasingly clear.

24. Salini comments on the fundamental and intimate links between cultural expression and the recognition of an independent national identity that accounts for the importance of cultural products to the autonomist movement: "A people exists only insofar as it possesses its own culture and . . . to the extent that it masters it" (Salini 1996, 193). For an account of the relationship between popular music and the nationalist movement in Wales during the 1970s, which would make interesting reading alongside my discussion of the Corsican case, see ap Sion 2002.

25. Algerian independence in 1962 had brought over 15,000 *pieds noirs* (French who had formerly settled in Algeria) to Corsica for resettlement, many being given fertile land on the east coast for cultivation. In 1975 a group of nationalists occupied the farm of a viticulturist (near Aleria) suspected of serious malpractice. The authorities responded by bringing in, by helicopter, 1,200 *gendarmes* and state security police who proceeded to stage an assault on the occupied buildings. Two of the police were killed and one of the demonstrators seriously wounded. Further demonstrations and confrontations followed.

26. Their position was finally contested when the *Consulta di i Cumitati Naziunalisti*, co-organizers of a reunion at Barcelona in the summer of 1983, made it known that, as far as they were concerned, Canta was no longer representative of nationalism in Corsica. Canta canceled its appearance at Barcelona and, a year later, the group disbanded (cf. de Zerbi and Diani 1992, 68).

27. A selection of songs by a range of groups involved in the *riacquistu* can be found on the disc *Canti di Libertà* (Ricordu 2000).

28. At this level, Canta's style might be seen to relate in some ways to that of nationalistically inclined troubadours elsewhere, such as Wales' Dafydd Iwan.

29. For an exploration of other factors that might be seen to account in part for the tenacity of *paghjella* singing, see Bithell 1996.

30. For a detailed discussion of issues relating to the "tradition-creation" debate, together with an analysis of a series of musical examples selected from the recent output of three different groups, see Bithell 2001.

31. In parts of Eastern Europe and the ex-Soviet Union, "folklore" does not carry the negative connotations that it now tends to have in Western Europe. During a recent visit to Georgia, for example, I was struck by the frequent use of "folklore" in the sense of "traditional" or "authentic." Corsica, on the other hand, very much shares a view of folklore as something inauthentic, derivative, and cheapened—a shallow reflection or a more willful travesty of the real traditions upon which it claims to be based.

32. Although McKechnie (1993) reports that, at the time of her fieldwork on the island, "amongst young nationalists, the keenest young men grew beards, wore waistcoats and dark wool 'Corsican jackets', symbols emblematic of their serious intent" (129).

33. A notable exception is the group *A Mannella*, featuring singers from the village of Sermanu (in the center of the island), which has always included a proportion of polyphonic songs in its repertoire.

BIBLIOGRAPHY

Angelini, Jean-Victor. *Histoire secrète de la Corse*. Paris: Albin Michel, 1977.

Ap Sion, Pwyll. "'Yn y Fro': Mudiad Adfer and Welsh Popular Song during the 1970s." *Welsh Music History* 5 (2002): 190–216.

Ardener, Edwin. "Social Anthropology, Language and Reality." In *Semantic Anthropology*, edited by David Parkin. London: Academic Press, 1982.

Berlinghi, Francescu. "Seconda, terza, bassu." In *Canta populu corsu*, edited by Ghjermana de Zerbi et al. Levie: Editions Albiana, 1993.

Bithell, Caroline. "Polyphonic Voices: National Identity, World Music and the Recording of Traditional Music in Corsica." *British Journal of Ethnomusicology* 5 (1996): 39–66.

Bithell, Caroline. "Issues of Identity and Transformation in the Revival of Traditional Song in 20th Century Corsica." Unpublished Ph.D. diss., University of Wales, 1997.

Bithell, Caroline. "Telling a Tree by its Blossom: Aspects of the Evolution of Musical Activity in Corsica and the Notion of a Traditional Music of the 21st Century." *Music and Anthropology* 6 (2001). www.muspe.unibo.it/period/MA/.

Bithell, Caroline. "A Man's Game? Engendered Song and the Changing Dynamics of Musical Activity in Corsica." In *Music and Gender: Perspectives from the Mediterranean*, edited by Tullia Magrini. Chicago: University of Chicago Press, 2003.

Boswell, James. *The Journal of a Tour to Corsica; & Memoirs of Pascal Paoli*. Cambridge: Cambridge University Press, 1923. Orig. publ., London: Dilly, 1768.

Campbell, Thomasina. *Southward Ho!* London: Hatchard, 1868.

Carrington, Dorothy. *Granite Island: A Portrait of Corsica.* London: Penguin, 1984. Orig. publ., London: Longmans, 1971.

Carrington, Dorothy. *The Dream-Hunters of Corsica.* London: Phoenix, 1995.

Casanova, Abbé Chanoine. *Histoire de l'église corse.* 4 vols. Zicavo: n.p., 1931–1938.

Chapman, Malcolm. *The Celts: The Construction of a Myth.* New York: St. Martin's Press, 1992.

Chapman, Malcolm. "Thoughts on Celtic Music." In *Ethnicity, Identity and Music: The Musical Construction of Place,* edited by Martin Stokes, 29–44. Oxford: Berg, 1994.

Chiari, Joseph. *Corsica: Columbus's Isle.* London: Barrie and Rockliff, 1960.

Daiches, David. *James Boswell and His World.* London: Thames and Hudson, 1976.

de Zerbi, Ghjermana. "Splendeur et misère du chant corse." In *Canta u Populu Corsu,* edited by G. de Zerbi et al., 11–27. Levie: Editions Albiana, 1993.

de Zerbi, Ghjermana, and François Diani, eds. *Cantu Corsu: Contours d'une expression populaire.* Ajaccio: Editions Cyrnos et Méditerranée, 1992.

Fusina, Ghjacumu. "A Strada di L'Avvene." In *Canta u Populu Corsu,* edited by G. de Zerbi et al., 139–47. Levie: Editions Albiana, 1993.

Fusina, Jacques. *The Corsican Language in Primary Education in Corsica, France.* Lyouwert / Leeuwarden: Fryske Akademy / EMU-projekt, 1988.

Geertz, Clifford. *The Interpretation of Cultures.* New York: Basic Books, 1973.

Hörstel, Wilhelm. *Die Napoleonsinseln Korsika und Elba.* Berlin, 1908.

Jaffe, Alexandra. *Ideologies in Action: Language Politics on Corsica.* Berlin: Mouton de Gruyter, 1999.

James, Simon. *The Atlantic Celts: Ancient People or Modern Invention?* London: British Museum Press, 1999.

Jaubert, L. *Étude médicale et anthropologique sur la Corse.* Bastia, 1896.

Jeoffroy-Faggianelli, Pierrette. *L'image de la Corse dans la littérature romantique française.* Paris: Presses Universitaires de France, 1979.

Laade, Wolfgang. *Das korsische Volkslied: Ethnographie und Geschichte, Gattungen und Stil.* 3 vols. Wiesbaden: Franz Steiner Verlag, 1981.

Laidler, Keith. *The Head of God.* London: Weidenfeld, 1998.

Lear, Edward. *Journal of a Landscape Painter in Corsica.* London: Bush, 1870.

Marcaggi, Jean-Baptiste. *Lamenti, voceri, chansons populaires de l'ile de Corse.* Ajaccio, 1926.

McDonald, Maryon. "The Construction of Difference: An Anthropological Approach to Stereotypes." In *Inside European Identities,* edited by Sharon MacDonald, 219–36. Oxford: Berg, 1993.

McKechnie, Rosemary. "Becoming Celtic in Corsica." In *Inside European Identities,* edited by Sharon MacDonald, 118–45. Oxford: Berg, 1993.

Mitchell, Timothy. *Flamenco Deep Song.* New Haven, Conn.: Yale University Press, 1994.

Multedo, Roccu. *Le mazzerisme, un chamanisme corse.* Paris: Editions l'Originel, 1994.

Pasquali, Iviu. *Pulifunie: Eri, oghje, dumane.* Petricaghju: Cismonte & Pumonti Edizione, 1993.

Pizzorni-Itié, Florence. "Les Enquêtes Thématiques Localisees." In *Cahier d'Anthropologie no. 4: 100 ans de collecte en Corse,* 57–97. Corte: Musée de la Corse, 1997.

Roosens, Eugeen E. *Creating Ethnicity: The Process of Ethnogenesis.* London: Sage, 1989.

Salini, Dominique. *Musiques traditionnelles de Corse.* Ajaccio: A Messagera / Squadra di u Finusellu, 1996.

Trosset, Carol. *Welshness Performed: Welsh Concepts of Person and Society.* Tucson: University of Arizona Press, 1993.

Turchini, Ghjiseppu. ". . . È . . . Cantò u Populu Corsu." In *Canta u Populu Corsu,* edited by G. de Zerbi et al., 194–97. Levie: Editions Albiana, 1993.

2

Celtic Australia: Bush Bands, Irish Music, Folk Music, and the New Nationalism

Graeme Smith

A higher proportion of the Australian population can claim Irish ancestry than in any other nation outside of the island of Ireland, with about 25 percent of the nineteenth-century settlers coming from Ireland, and Ireland resuming as a source of migrants in the second half of the twentieth century. In general and despite sectarian tensions, the history of Irish Australia has been one of social accommodation. In comparison with the United States, in particular, Irish emigration was relatively more ordered, prosperous, and better resourced and there was little significant cultural or socioeconomic division between Irish Australians and the rest of the population (MacDonagh 1987, 121–37). Irishness became one of the components out of which settler Australians constructed a distinctive national identity, and an identification with Irish history and culture has remained an important component of the politics of settler Australian identity formation. With its ability to move between Australian, Irish, and global perspectives, Irish music has been part of this, its sounds and meanings co-opted in negotiations of the shifting relationships among the claims on national identity by the original nineteenth-century settlers and their descendants, the postwar migrants, and the indigenous inhabitants.

This chapter describes two recent major moments in this process. The first is the development in the 1970s of a folk-rock bush band musical style, which embedded Irish traditional dance music into musical narratives of Australian national identity. The second is the popularization of the use of the Aboriginal *didjeridu* in Irish traditional dance music within a suprahistorical model of Celticity. In both these cases, Irish music has been a potent symbolic resource within the contemporary discourses of settler nationalism. In the first, it contributed to the imagination of a distinctive Australian national character and type. In the second, in a political climate full of doubts about the unitary basis of settler national identity, Irish music, along with its national and historical references, moved toward a protean Celticity, that allowed settler Australians to place themselves both in relation to the experiences of postwar non-British migration and to indigenous political claims.

THE BUSH BAND, NATIONAL IDENTITY, AND THE AUSTRALIAN LEGEND

During the 1970s a style of folk-rock referred to generically as the "bush band" developed and became widely popular. It drew explicitly on Irish musical identification, positioning it firmly within the contemporary politics of nation and identity. Bush bands combine a song repertoire of Australian vernacular ballads, the core song repertoire consisting of about thirty ballads popularized in the Australian folk revival, with Irish-style dance music, mostly Irish jigs and reels, supplemented by occasional tunes of similar style collected in Australia. They began in the pub rock scene, but acquired more general popularity through the staging of bush dances, where a caller would lead participants through various folk-style dances, drawn from the English folk dance movement, Irish *ceili* dances, Scottish country dances, and social dances from rural Australia. The format allowed a wide range of social uses, from riotous rock dances to cross-generational social occasions such as wedding receptions or fund-raising events. Whether as accompaniment for dancing or as music for listening to in sociable surroundings, bush bands promoted an image of lively Australianness. During the 1980s, a large number of such bands sprang up in response to public demand.

The instrumentation of the bush band is similar to the Irish-style group, with at least one melody instrument such as fiddle or accordion, with rhythm guitar accompaniment. Compared with most Irish traditional music groups that developed in the 1970s and 1980s, a more substantial "bottom end" is used, with electric bass and drum kits. The earliest versions of bush bands used improvised instruments such as tea chest bass, and an emblematic local invention known as a "lagerphone," though only the second of these survived the development of the band. It is an upright percussion instrument set with bottle tops struck and shaken, humorously projecting the improvisatory skills of the bushman that the bands celebrated (Smith 1994, 190–91). The musical format is fairly standardized, and to an ear used to Irish playing, some of the instrumental performance had more exuberance than finesse.

In creating its musical sound and in projecting this as distinctively Australian in the political and cultural circumstances of the 1970s, the bush band drew on a range of Irish musical resources spanning the history of Australian European settlement. Aspects of Irishness were evoked in the song repertoire, the tune repertoire, and in the performance style. The first of these to consider is the song repertoire. The nineteenth-century vernacular songs that make up the core of the bush band's song repertoire were collected and constructed into a canon by a radical nationalist intellectual movement in the 1940s and 1950s. In this period, inspired by similar movements in Britain and the United States, the left intelligentsia, the labor movement, and the Australian Communist Party were vigorously promoting a distinctively Australian radical culture centered on the concept of folk (Smith 1985). In 1958, historian Russel Ward published a book called *The Australian Legend* in which he argued that the distinctive Australian character was naturally democratic, socialist, and anti-authoritarian, and that this type had been created by the collectivist ethos of rural workers in the nineteenth century. Ward used vernacular song texts as part of the evidence for his argument (see Ward 1966).

For the purposes of this chapter, what is crucial is that this national type carried an image of Irishness. From the Irish convicts, some of whom were political exiles, to the gold rush adventurers and post-famine immigrants, to the bushrangers with Irish names, nineteenth-century Irish immigrants were identified as the source of the anti-authoritarianism, republicanism, and informality of manners associated with the distinctive Australian type, as well as with a determination to create a distinctive, independent Australian culture, free from deference to British models. Catholicism was ignored in this construction of Irishness, as was any residual identification with Ireland as a home place (Ward 1966, 46–57, 165–68). And while some of the songs that made up the canon were influenced by Irish song-making styles, most prominently a few songs from convict poets and broadside balladeers, together with the bushranger ballads, these were valued for their role in the construction of a national heritage and a distinctive Australian national type. When the bush bands performed these vernacular nineteenth-century songs they were thus performing a particular version of Australianness to which the nineteenth-century Irish immigrants were seen as having made a distinctive contribution.

By the 1960s the canon was being widely performed in the coffee lounges and folk clubs of the folk boom, generally by solo performers within the conventional singer-guitarist folk singer format who invested it with a "folk" sound. The performers in the early bush bands came from this context, but they modified the folk club format's insistence on the audience's attentive intellectual engagement with the music. Bush bands organized their relationship with and took control of their audience in quite different ways. They used powerful amplification, incorporated a strong rhythmic drive into performance, and encouraged dancing. They were thus able to break out of the folk clubs into a broader public arena. As the folk movement retreated into a cultish niche, the bush band went public, brash and popular. In this move they drew on a second Irish musical resource, the postwar virtuosic Irish instrumental music, which created the musical buzz of the bush band and seized the attention of the audience. In comparison with previous folk acts, bush bands greatly extended the theatricality of performance. Dobe Newton, the percussionist with the influential band The Bushwackers, said that before he started exploiting its possibilities, the lagerphone was "a sort of overgrown tambourine given to a vocalist if he or she couldn't play guitar." He turned it into a powerful, varied, and subtle percussion instrument, as well as a stage prop for dramatic rock-style stage antics.[1]

Any musical innovation depends upon establishing the right of the performer to command the audience's attention, and successful performers develop a range of strategies to achieve this. The inclusion of Irish instrumental music was crucial to establishing the musical credentials of the bush band. This was despite the fact, as has often been noted, that the musical style and certainly the dance repertoire characteristic of the bush band bore little resemblance to any preceding Australian style and so was blatantly at odds with its claims to historical representation (see, for example, Andrews 1988, Meredith 1986). The bush bands wrought a contemporary common-sense understanding of Australian folk music with the sound of Irish music as an integral part, and, as is common with such constructions, the sound was more a product of current circumstances than the past it purported to represent. As well, the Irishness that it incorporated and represented was itself a complex combination of past and recent histories and ideologies, both in Australia and Ireland. Crucial to this were the musical resources of a new wave of Irish immigrants to Australia who came as part of the massive migration program on which Australia embarked in the aftermath of World War II.

In general, these new Irish immigrants had little in common with established Irish Australia whose connections with Ireland were for the most part generations old and for whom Irish music played a marginal emblematic role among small groups of cultural enthusiasts. The new immigrants instituted new contexts for performance of Irish music, particularly Irish dance music, as the growing first-generation immigrant community staged Irish dances and sports events, re-creating in Australia the entertainment styles of rural Ireland. Initially they drew on the musical life of the provincial Ireland they had left and its forms of national identification. Later, they incorporated developments from the Irish musical rejuvenation movement of the 1960s, a movement that was also attracting the attention of young musicians in the folk movement (Smith 1990).

Mick Moloney has argued that this Irish musical movement had three major strands. The first was *Comhaltas Ceoltóirí Eireann* (the Irish Musicians Association), which, in the early 1950s, began to build a populist rural musical movement around dance music. The second was in the 1960s when composer Sean O Riada gave some genres of Irish music an aesthetically respectable concert format. The third was the ballad revival started by the Clancy brothers reforming of Irish popular national and regional song into the popular folk format of the ballad band style (Moloney 1982, 94–6). The Dubliners' extension of the Clancy Brothers' style then combined the hitherto irredeemably "cultchie"[2] instrumental dance music with proletarian sounding urban Dublin street ballads and rebel songs. For many young Australians on the folk scene, the Dubliners' reconstructed Irish music, shorn of sentimental and nostalgic songs, had the ring of authenticity. It seemed a true folk music, springing from a creative and unified lower class, and it was consonant with the image of the legendary Australian rural worker, the supposed originator of Australian folk music. Contemporary Irish models of performance were thus particularly attractive to Australian folk revival performers, and in the 1960s and 1970s, as LPs became increasingly available, performers in many styles and genres began to imitate and develop these models. In Australia, the impact of Irish traditional music was greatly enhanced by the growing community of Irish immigrants and their interaction with the local folk music movement.

As is often the case in contact between folk revival movements and musical styles that they admire, there were social differences to direct and inflect the terms of musical negotiation between the immigrants and the folk movement enthusiasts. Contrasting socioeconomic backgrounds set them apart, as did their family and community-centered social networks. Where the typical folk enthusiast was an Australian-born, tertiary-educated, white-collar employee, with politically radical views and little interest in religion, players from the Irish community were generally working class, employed in manual labor, socially conservative, and by Australian standards devoutly religious.

Crucial in bringing the two groups together was the local branch of *Comhaltas Ceoltóirí Eireann* formed in Melbourne in 1970. It was immediately successful among the Irish community, organizing regular *ceili* dances and concert evenings. Branches were also formed in Sydney, Brisbane, and Perth over the next decade. Because *Comhaltas* was a formal, open organization, in contrast to the domestic and semiprivate settings in which many immigrant traditional musicians mainly played, enthusiastic young Anglo-Australian musicians were able to listen and play in sessions with the most highly skilled players of Irish traditional music. To the relatively unsophisticated instrumentalists of the folk revival the highly developed musical techniques of some of the immigrant Irish traditional dance players were conspicuously brilliant. A group of folk movement players began to learn Irish dance music, and thus the music entered the bush band style. As well, the exposure to highly skilled instrumental players reinforced a growing interest in other kinds of instrumental music.

While both Anglo-Australian performers and Irish immigrants saw their preferred genres within a folk ideology, they had very different takes on what this might signify. For the Irish immigrant it was most often a project of conservative cultural maintenance that

had little in common with the romantic radicalism of the folk movement and its search for a viable contemporary form of performance.
There were, however, a few Irish immigrants influenced by the bur-
geoning Irish music movement of the 1960s who were able to move
between both groups and these were important in establishing initial contacts. Declan Affley, an Irish immigrant singer, formed the
Sydney-based band The Wild Colonial Boys, which was the first
band to attempt the stylistic fusion of the bush band. In Melbourne,
second-generation instrumental players such as Louis MacManus
and Anthony O'Neill became important bush band players, sewing
Irish dance music into the fabric of the bush band repertoire. Typically, these were children of musically dedicated postwar Irish immigrant families whose skill had been fostered in childhood in family and community organizations.

   The Irish sound of the bush band as it emerged in the 1970s was
the result of interaction between the postwar Irish immigrant community and the Anglo-Australian folk movement, rather than from
continuing or revived historical Australian music practice. If this is
the musical story behind the development of the style, why did it attract audiences? For this we need to look at the social and political
context. The popularity of the bush band rode on a revival of Australian nationalism in the context of the political turmoil associated
with Australia's involvement in the Vietnam War. The Australian
antiwar movement of the late 1960s and early 1970s revisited the
radical nationalism of the old left, with a significant section linking
this to a vocal nationalist opposition to the threat of U.S. imperialism
to Australian economic and political sovereignty (Frankel 1992,
60–63). Although bush bands and their repertoire espoused a relatively diffuse populism, their stance could accommodate political
positions ranging from hard-line Maoists to internationalist work-
erists to Labor Party republicans and the nostalgic nationalist ro-
mantics who probably made up the bulk of the audience. Bush
bands created an imaginative world in which this resuscitated radical nationalism could be enacted in the popular culture and politics
of 1970s radicalism. Irishness became the theatrical vehicle for this
politics of cultural independence, reinforced through the dynamic
power of traditional dance music within the bush band mix.

   The radical nationalists of the 1950s had been formed within the
populism of the popular front. This inspired the energy of the early
folk revival, and, for some, nationalism provided a way out of

Stalinism in the wake of the mid-1950s crises of international com-
munism. For the most part, the articulation of Australian settler radical nationalism was based on a narrative of the formation of a people out of and against the social structures of the British colonial
past. Within this, Irishness provided fertile ground for the articulation of Australian distinctiveness from various "English" characteristics. It was the musical core around which the whole cluster of supposedly distinctively Australian characteristics identified with the
Australian legend could be grouped: anti-authoritarianism, convivi-
ality, communalism, resourcefulness, steadfastness through adver-
sity, and loyalty to one's mates.

Yet this was an integrative and monolithic nationality, inherently
exclusionary and bounded, and the demographic changes conse-
quent on Australia's postwar migration program, together with
changes in the political status of indigenous Australians were ren-
dering it increasingly unstable. During the 1970s, under the impact
both of the rise of the new social movements and of new historiography, the Australian type identified by Ward with the naturally
democratic, anti-authoritarian outback worker was increasingly
read as male, white, and racist. The new-left revisionist attack was
lead by Humphrey McQueen's stylish Marxist polemic *A New Britannia*, and carried on by numerous feminist historians from the
1980s onward (see, for example, McQueen 1970; Dixson 1976). The
general questioning of the Australian legend's democratic credentials increased with the growth of the Aboriginal land rights movement and a new Aboriginal historiography (Reynolds 1982). This
challenged the existing white nation-building histories, radical as
well as conservative, with histories, from the perspective of the indigenous inhabitants, of invasion, massacres, and dispossession.

Linked with these historical critiques was the development of
multiculturalism as a national cultural model during the late 1970s
and 1980s. This was a response to the enormous demographic
changes brought about by postwar migration from continental Europe and Asia and it implied a far-reaching rethinking of the character and basis of Australian identity (Castles et al. 1992). For much
of the contemporary population issues to do with Australia's difference from Britain were increasingly irrelevant, and fewer had any
links with the historical experiences of the nineteenth-century settlers on which the Australian legend was based. Sharon Frost, of the
central New South Wales band Home Rule, described the dilemmas

such changes posed for Australian folk music: "In the 1950s, in the days before multicultural carnivales, when the Bush Music Club was formed, 'Australian' folk music seemed to have a straightforward character and identity. Now the folk movement in general is necessarily more self-conscious about what 'Australian' folk music might mean" (1992, 77).

The Irishness that was an important part of arguments about the creation of an Australian nation gained its symbolic value from its opposition to British identity. It was this that drew it into the bush bands' recreation of an Australian musical past. However, as musicians started to reposition the group performance of Australian folk music to accommodate the more complex politics of national identity associated with multiculturalism, Irish music ceased to be projected as the powerful core of Australian folk. Irish music was still played, but increasingly it was presented as the music of one of the ethnic streams that made up the rich tapestry of multicultural Australia rather than as the expression of a unified national character.

THE SECOND MOMENT:
THE DIDJERIDU AND CELTICIZATION

The second moment of interaction between Irish music and Australian constructions of nation and identity that I explore is the incorporation over the past decade of the *didjeridu* into Irish traditional instrumentarium and a generalized conception of Celtic music. On the face of it, the mix might be seen as merely another decontextualized exoticism, whether commercially inspired by world music market operatives or musically driven by talented musicians, confident in their skill and pleased to experiment with overlays of other sounds. However, while many such innovations have proved ephemeral and inconsequential, the use of the *didjeridu* in Irish traditional music has achieved more lasting significance. In Australia, in Ireland, and in the world generally, the sociomusical implications and connotative meanings of the musical sounds have amplified and consolidated the significance of the mix.

The *didjeridu* is a wide-bore wooden trumpet played by Aborigines in northern Australia. It is fashioned from a branch of a eucalyptus that has been hollowed by termites. The bore is cleaned out, and a broad mouthpiece and a slightly belled end shaped or enhanced.

Most instruments are about 1.2 m long with a bore of around 5 cm. It is played with a loose lip buzzing and continuous circular breathing, and produces a pulsing drone at around CC to FF, interspersed with an upper partial approximately a tenth above, and vocalized humming and articulated sounds. It has virtually no pitch variation, but produces a subtle range of rhythmic, timbral, and phasing-like effects. Some musicians may use improvised instruments, sometimes no more than a piece of PVC piping that can be cut to any desired pitch. In the societies where it is traditional, it is mainly used to accompany a relatively open public song repertoire. Archaeological evidence suggests a relatively recent (by Aboriginal standards) adoption took place sometime within the last thousand years (Yunupingu 1997; Barwick 1997).

In recent times it has been taken up by many other Aborigines as a symbol of pan-aboriginality and by settler Australians and musicians from around the world. Such non-Aboriginal users in particular have adapted it to many genres from personal alternative healing techniques to avant-garde and popular music creation (Neuenfeldt 1997; Homan 1997; Smith and Neuenfeldt 1998). A bewildering range of social and musical connotations are attributed to it, often raising issues of exploitation and appropriation along with cultural reconciliation and sharing.

The idea of placing the *didjeridu* under Irish tunes emerged in the late 1970s, first in Australia and soon after in Ireland. In most cases the instrument can be made to provide a continuous drone on the low D, which can be articulated with rhythmic patterns. Such an accompaniment was musically relatively simple, and, notwithstanding the striking exoticism of the instrument, it has gained a degree of acceptance among many traditional musicians on musical grounds. The *didjeridu* mimics the drone of the pipes, which many regard as the only fully legitimate accompaniment to the monophonic solo melody of Irish traditional dance musics. Drones and drone-based accompaniment style for Irish traditional music are increasingly valorized by current trends, particularly the open tuning guitar styles based on DADGAD tuning, commonly referred to as "Celtic guitar" and the bouzouki accompaniment techniques popularized and promoted by Donal Lunny's playing and record production. The syncopated rhythmic articulation of these styles is frequently imitated by *didjeridu* players. Such modern forms of accompaniment gain their power from the implied contrast with the piano vamping of the conservative *ceili* band tradition and similar chordal guitar styles. The rhythmic patterns generated by the *didjeridu*'s overtone in conjunction with vocalized sounds constitute the primary technique of *didjeridu* playing in traditional Aboriginal usage as well as in modern adaptations and developments, and these can mimic the accompaniment patterns used in bodhran playing.

However, as well as the musical properties that enable its incorporation into Irish traditional music-playing styles, the *didjeridu* carries a large symbolic freight, which gives this incorporation a range of meanings for various groups of users and listeners. The potency of these meanings is enhanced by the convergence of the political and social history and symbolic structure of non-Aboriginal Australian *didjeridu* playing with the recent Celticization of Irish music. The growth of indigenous political demands in the 1970s has already been mentioned. While the idea of Australia as a multicultural nation of immigrants was reasonably adequate to incorporate the social and cultural differences of Australia's diverse range of ethnic groups, it was quite inadequate to deal politically with the issues of indigenous Australia, and as well left many of the descendants of the nineteenth-century settler Australians feeling uncomfortably disconnected from their land and historical experience. The histories of the pioneering frontier were increasingly seen as a protracted war of occupation against the legitimate holders of the land, undermining the popular celebratory histories of pioneering and outback Australia. As well, increasing environmental consciousness was exposing the damage two centuries of European agriculture had inflicted on delicate Australian ecosystems. For many urban Australians the history of white rural past no longer provided an affective route to a grounded sense of national belonging.

Such issues increasingly confront musicians attempting to represent a national experience. Jan Wositzky, the "bush character" front man of the Bushwackers band, recalled a gig on an outback tour that included the Kimberley region in the remote northwest of Australia.

> We played for 400 blacks and they looked at us curious, a bit of polite clapping and the more we thundered away the quieter they became. The only conclusion I could draw from the crowd's response was the Bushwackers, calling ourselves "the real sound of Australia," was alien to this crowd. It was obvious to me that we didn't know the other side of the frontier. In white bush music, blacks had been written out apart from a few derogatory songs. (Quoted in Elliot 1998, 24)

Wositzky found the encounter between his fictional "real Australians" and the Aboriginal audience so unsettling that he subsequently abandoned the bush band project.

The first vigorous expressions of aboriginality in Australian popular music emerged in the late 1970s with Aboriginal rock bands, generally employing reggae and country-rock styles. Some commentators began to see such bands as promising a new, more authentic musical expression of national identity. Yet although bands such as No Fixed Address, Coloured Stone, and the Warumpi Band gained enthusiastic support from urban liberal intellectuals, they remained essentially Aboriginal bands, their music read as an expression of Aboriginal experience and so not available for the expression of a more shared national identity (Breen 1989; Castles 1992).

Their existence did, however, amplify the challenge to settler musicians to create music with an appropriate acknowledgment of indigenous settler relations. Some, like Paul Kelly and Ted Egan, used singer-songwriter styles to comment on indigenous history and politics. Others started to use the *didjeridu* within a number of musical genres, from progressive rock– and jazz-influenced performance to New Age music. Aboriginal rock groups, most of whom were outside the relatively small area of northern Australia from which the instrument comes, adopted it as an icon for pan-aboriginality; and it was adopted by settler musicians who were consciously seeking ways to ground their music in the landscape. At the same time, the *didjeridu* was achieving popularity as a meditational aid and in alternative therapy and semireligious personal experiments. A movement extending from amateur enthusiasts to professional musicians developed that was initially spontaneous and disparately individual, but during the 1990s more formal networks and organizations developed (Smith and Neuenfeldt 1998, 93–95). It was from this larger musical and social movement that the *didjeridu* moved into traditional Irish music.

The *didjeridu* was first used with Irish-style music in Australia by Stephen Cooney in Melbourne around 1980. Playing with the Melbourne-based group Poteen, Cooney started to use *didjeridu* as a backing for reels and jigs. Poteen had a shifting membership that usually included several Irish immigrants, one Scot, and several second-generation Irish Australian players. It based its sound on the model of Planxty and The Bothy Band. Cooney, already well established in Melbourne's inner suburban alternative rock scene, had heard the *didjeridu* in the Northern Territory where he became strongly attached to Aboriginal culture, making contact with and learning from well-known Aboriginal artist and player David Blanassi (*Meithal: Cooney and Begley*, 1988). Around the same time, he had heard the new Irish group sound associated with Planxty and found this, as well as the sociomusical ambience of the Irish music session scene, powerfully attractive. A number of other convergences of Aboriginal and Irish musicians around this period, such as the association of prominent Irish Australian fiddle player Louis MacManus with the Aboriginal rock group No Fixed Address, also aided the *didjeridu*'s crossover into Irish music.

Cooney moved to Ireland in the 1980s, where he established himself as a sought-after arranger, producer, and performer of Irish music. Working with the band Stockton's Wing, he introduced the *didjeridu* to Irish music in Ireland and the sound was picked up by other Irish groups to become an accepted inclusion in Irish music arrangements. Cooney understands his musical formation in terms of felt cultural affinities between Irish and Aboriginal groundedness. He reflects that he understands Aboriginal society better after being in Kerry, "because this is an Aboriginal society and a lot of the value systems are similar" (Moroney 1998). Such a statement resonates with the strong connection to place often felt to be part of Irish music.

As I have argued elsewhere, *didjeridu* playing by white players in Australia is implicated in claims to an unmediated relationship between the land and the individual. Such connectedness generally claims more than simple conventional associations with a localized musical symbol. The spiritual connotations of the instrument and its sound are linked to the very act of playing and its associated somatic experience, particularly the abdominal sensation of the resonant drone and the potential for psychotropic effects in the sustained circular breathing. The sound of the *didjeridu* becomes the sonic representation of the characteristic Australian landscape, and in producing this the player can feel directly connected with the earth (Smith and Neuenfeldt 1998, 55).

Such claims are not without their problems. Many Aboriginal players are wary that such claims to cultural access by settler Australians undermine their own politics of indigenous rights. However well intentioned, white uses or appropriations of Aboriginal culture are of little use to Aborigines. Others ask merely for acknowledgment and deference to Aboriginal cultural priority. But whether the playing is imagined as linked to Aboriginal culture, or to the land from which it has arisen, it circumvents traditional representations of the nation-state and its claims to organize the relationships of individuals to larger social structures and historical narratives. Similarly, though a historical link between the *didjeridu* and Irish music cannot be imagined, the convergence can be justified in terms of the ideals of identification of a music with a culture that predates modern nation making.

The meaning of the *didjeridu*'s incorporation into Irish music is amplified for Australians by the historic place of Irishness in the construction of settler identity, as was discussed earlier. As multiculturalism has elevated ethnicity to a primary category of social difference, then Irish or Irish Australian ethnicity is provisionally tried on by groups of Anglo-Australians who are otherwise excluded from claiming an ethnic identity. For them, the musical blending of Aboriginal and Irish musical traditions holds the promise of new grounds for racial and political reconciliation, as well as allowing them to imagine a history in which both the premodern Irish and the contemporary Aborigines participate in a generic tribalism. As each musical element is given a new context, its more disruptive and uncomfortable symbolic associations are removed. The association of Irish traditional music with modern, postindependence, Catholic Ireland has little appeal to the audience for Irish music in Australia. A general Celtic tribalism is far more appealing. Conversely, the Irish *didjeridu* deflates Aboriginal claims to unique cultural ownership of the instrument and allows settler Australians new grounds of identification with the instrument and through it with the land. The Australian landscape can become musically Celticized, the *didjeridu* offering settler Australian musicians the possibility of an authentic identification and personal grounding in the sounds of their land.

In Ireland, the *didjeridu*'s position in Irish music has been consolidated in a parallel process by its proposed analogy with the Bronze Age trumpets, and in fact the use of these as instruments was inspired by *didjeridu* playing. These bronze horns are striking archaeological artifacts of pre-Christian Ireland. Up to 1.5 m in length, with wide conical bore and an end or a side mouthpiece aperture, they have been found in various sites in Ireland. Usually dated from around 1000 B.C., many have been found in sites in Ireland, often apparently as votive offerings. Similar instruments have also been found throughout contemporary northern Europe. The Irish instruments are high status, perhaps ceremonial instruments of an aristocratic culture. In the mid-1970s, archaeologist Peter Holmes discovered that these instruments could be played using the *didjeridu* technique (Holmes 1979), and in the mid-1980s Irish musician Simon O'Dwyer incorporated them in live playing and recording. Beginning as a *bodhran* player, O'Dwyer started to play *didjeridu* around 1986, after hearing Steve Cooney's playing with Stocktons Wing, and subsequently traveled to Australia to develop his technique (Hummingbird 1998). Soon after he shifted his attention to the Bronze Age horns and incorporated them in the band Reconciliation, which also included Australian performer Phil Conyngham. The band traveled to Australia and established contact with noted Aboriginal player Alan Dargin (Macgowan 1997, 177–79). O'Dwyer manufactures his horns from historic models and emphasizes their decorative spikes to enhance the suggestion of primitive and fierce power (Hummingbird 1998).

Although the horn's position in Irish music was modeled on the *didjeridu*, once incorporated it invoked a deep imaginative and affective history for Irish traditional music. O'Dwyer claims that "Irish traditional music is receptive to the horns, not just because they are one of the very few native Irish instruments, but additionally because they add something to the music by way of sound and rhythm," (quoted in Casey 1994, 59) and because they make a direct appeal to "an element of the Irish psyche which still relates to its past." As O'Dwyer's comments indicate, Irish performers tend to believe that through their sounds, both the *didjeridu* and the Bronze Age horns directly address a collective and ethnic subconscious, and that this is felt too in the reactions of audiences (Casey 1994, 57–59). The perceived affinity between Irish traditional music and Aboriginal music thus contributes to the construction of a deep history for Irish music.

Currently this deep history takes the form of the recontextualization of Irish music as "Celtic," which involves a reformulation of the social and historical meaning of the music, as well as of the points of player and audience access. Typical of this recontextualization is the way the Afro-Celt Sound System formulates and presents their musical fusion of Irish traditional music with popular West-African styles (Afro-Celt Sound System, Real World, 1996). It relies on the construction of a deep Celtic musical identity to ground and explain its musical mixing. Here techno-dance producer Simon Emmerson further embroidered the fanciful "Atlantean" thesis of filmmaker and writer Bob Quinn of a North-African connection to *sean-nós* singing (Vallely 1999, 344). Emmerson suggested that his musical inspiration derived from the deep, in fact neolithic, connections imagined between Irish and African music, as he mixed Malian drumming with techno-beats and Irish traditional dance tunes. The promotional explanations that accompanied the release invoked stone monuments, trade routes, Celts and Africans in evocative but vague combination (Smith 1997; Vallely 1998, 37–38). Just as the music is given a non-Western and exotic genealogy, so the Celticity as a category of identification is constructed, neither race, nor culture, nor heritage, nor nation; but a direction for identification in which many Europeans, and most anglophone ones, can find some personal point of entry should they wish.

It is common to claim that musical sounds communicate in a direct way with the listener's consciousness. However, whenever such claims are made of *didjeridu*, bronze horn, and other Celticized musics, they are situated within historical, cultural, and social narratives that reach back beyond the modern era to invoke an earlier, premodern and more fundamental level of consciousness and experience. The constructions of society, time, and place that they evoke are all defined in contrast to the modern nation-state, whether Irish or Australian, and the claims that it makes over ethnicity and cultural identity. Just as the *didjeridu*'s drone contradicts the *ceili* piano and its representation of provincial Irish cultural nationalism, and the bronze horn reaches back beyond the legacy of European Judeo-Christian history, so the settler Australian *didjeridu* speaks of new universalist possibilities of relating directly to the land unhindered by differences of race or the history of the European invasion.

CONCLUSION

The two moments of interaction between Irish music and national identity in Australia discussed here emerged at different stages in the development of both Australian settler nationalism and Irish traditional music. In the first, the bush band was involved in constructing an Australian national identity drawing in part on Irish musical resources. Bush bands had little impact outside Australia, though within, they established themselves firmly within a narrative of national distinctiveness. The second moment of the *didjeridu* has had much greater resonance in the wider world of listeners and players of Irish music, paralleling similar reimaginings of the relationship between Irish music and both national and local cultures. In Ireland, as in Australia and elsewhere abroad, Irish traditional music has become part of a global popular music self-consciously playing with origins and identities. The previous terms of cultural identification for Irish traditional music within the geographical and social space of the nation are neither attractive nor adequate for this; thus ways are sought to reimagine Irish music free of and beyond Irish national experience. This broad process of creating an extranational mythopeoia for the music can be called Celticization, and the incorporation of the *didjeridu* contributes to its claims. Whether the *didjeridu* will continue to have a place in Irish music and thus generate more layers of musical and social meaning remains to be seen, but its entry into Irish music was the result of the parallel ways in which individuals in Ireland and Australia have been reimagining their relation to society, history, and the state in an increasingly globalized world.

ACKNOWLEDGMENT

An earlier version of this article appeared in *Perfect Beat*, vol. 5, no. 2, January 2001.

NOTES

1. Interview with the author, 10 February 1991.
2. *Cultchie* is a pejorative Hiberno-English term for a rural buffoon, which provided a cultural image of traditional Irish dance music for many urban or middle-class Irish people.

BIBLIOGRAPHY

Andrews, Shirley. "Why Not Appreciate Australian Folklore As It Really Was Rather Than How You Think It Should Be." In *Proceedings of the Third National Folklore Conference*, edited by Ron Edwards, 31–36. Canberra: National Folk Trust, 1988.

Barwick, Linda. "Gender 'Taboos' and Didjeridus." In *The Didjeridu from Arnhem Land to Internet,* edited by Karl Neuenfeldt, 89–98. Sydney: Perfect Beat Publications, 1997.

Breen, Marcus, ed. *Our Place, Our Music.* Canberra: Aboriginal Studies Press, 1989.

Casey, Conor. "The Use of the Didjeridu in Irish Traditional Music." M.A. thesis, Department of Social Anthropology, The Queen's University of Belfast, 1994.

Castles, John. "Tjungaringanyi: Aboriginal Rock." In *From Pop to Punk to Postmodernism: Popular Music and Australian Culture from the 1960s to the 1990s,* edited by Philip Hayward, 25–39. Allen & Unwin, 1992.

Castles, Stephen et al. *Mistaken Identity: Multiculturalism and the Demise of Nationalism in Australia.* Sydney: Pluto Press, 1992.

Dixson, Miriam. *The Real Matilda: Women and Identity in Australia 1788–1975.* Melbourne: Penguin Books, 1976.

Elliot, John. "The Continuing Adventures of the Bushwackers." *Australian Country Music Roundup* 5 (1998 March): 22–26.

Frankel, Boris. *From the Prophets Deserts Come: The Struggle to Reshape Australian Political Culture.* North Carlton: Arena Publishing, 1992.

Frost, Sharon. "Some Thoughts about Traditional Australian Music in the 1990s." *Australian Folklore* 7 (1992): 77–83.

Holmes, Peter. "The Manufacturing Technology of the Irish Bronze Age Horns." In *The Origins of Metallurgy in Atlantic Europe. Proceedings of the Fifth Atlantic Colloquium, Dublin, 30th March to 4th April 1978,* edited by Michael Ryan, 165–88. Dublin: Stationary Office, 1979.

Homan, Shane. "Terra Incognito: The Career of Charlie MacMahon." In *The Didjeridu from Arnhem Land to the Internet,* edited by Karl Neuenfeldt, 123–38. Sydney: Perfect Beat Publications, 1997.

MacDonagh, Oliver. "Emigration from Ireland to Australia: An Overview." In *Australia and Ireland 1788–1988: Bicentenary Essays,* edited by Colm Kiernan, 121–37. Dublin: Gill and Macmillan, 1987.

Macgowan, Fiona. "Out of Time, Out of Place." In *The Didjeridu from Arnhem Land to the Internet,* edited by Karl Neuenfeldt, 161–82. Sydney: Perfect Beat Publications, 1997.

McQueen, Humphrey. *A New Britannia: An Argument Concerning the Social Origins of Australian Radicalism and Nationalism.* Harmondsworth: Penguin, 1970.

Meredith, John. Letter. *Meanjin* 3, no. 45 (1986): 436–38.

Moloney, Mick. "Irish Ethnic Recordings and the Irish-American Imagination." In *Ethnic Recordings in America: A Neglected Heritage,* edited by Pekka Gronow, 85–101. Washington, D.C.: American Folklife Center, Library of Congress, 1982.

Moroney, Mick. "Local Heroes." *Irish Times,* 14 March 1998.

Neuenfeldt, Karl. *The Didjeridu from Arnhem Land to the Internet.* Sydney: Perfect Beat Publications, 1997.

Reynolds, Henry. *The Other Side of the Frontier.* Melbourne: Penguin, 1982.

Smith, Graeme. "Making Folk Music." *Meanjin* 4, no. 44 (1985): 477–90.

Smith, Graeme. "Irish Music in Melbourne 1950–1980." In *Irish Australian Studies: Papers Delivered at the Sixth Irish-Australian Conference July 1990,* edited by Phillip Bull, Chris McConville, and Noel McLachlan, 217–27. Melbourne: Department of History, Latrobe University, 1991.

Smith, Graeme. "Irish Meets Folk: The Genesis of the Bush Band." Iin *Music-Cultures in Contact: Convergences and Collisions,* edited by Margaret Kartomi and Stephen Blum, 186–203. Sydney: Currency Press, 1994.

Smith, Graeme. "WOMADELAIDE 97." *Arena Journal* 8 (1997): 17–22.

Smith, Graeme, and Karl Neuenfeldt. "Romancing the Drone: The Contemporary Didjeridu in Victoria." *Overland* (May 1998): 53–55.

Vallely, Fintan. "Gucci Paddy." *Graph* 3, no. 2 (1998): 37–41.

Vallely, Fintan. "Sean-nós." In *The Cork Companion to Irish Traditional Music,* edited by Fintan Vallely, 336–45. Cork: Cork University Press, 1999.

Ward, Russel. *The Australian Legend.* Melbourne: Melbourne University Press, 1966.

Yunupingu, Mandawuy. "Yidaki: A Foreword." In *The Didjeridu from Arnhem Land to the Internet,* edited by Karl Neuenfeldt, vii–viii. Sydney: Perfect Beat Publications, 1997.

FILMOGRAPHY

Meitheal: Cooney and Begley. Dublin: Hummingbird Productions. Shown on RTE 1, Ireland, 17 March 1988.

3

Diasporic Legacies: Place, Politics, and Music among the Ottawa Valley Irish

Johanne Devlin Trew

For some, the Ottawa Valley is simply a place; for others it is a state of mind or an affair of the heart. A basic geographic definition is easy, as a river runs through it. The Ottawa River is one of the great rivers of North America, if not the world, and it was a major part of the *voyageur* canoe route, the main highway through this rugged hill country to the west of Canada for early explorers, fur traders, and settlers. Later, the railroad and today's Trans-Canada Highway followed the same route, up the Ottawa to the Mattawa River, then west to Lake Superior. The center of the valley, then, is clear, but defining its boundaries has proven to be problematic due to local perceptions regarding which areas belong to the valley and which remain outside. Roughly speaking, it is the land that follows the length of the Ottawa River from Lake Temiscaming to its mouth at the St. Lawrence River, bordered on the Ontario side by the Opeongo hills and by the Gatineau hills on the Quebec side.

Traveling through the Ottawa Valley, one has a sense of coming face to face with history. The impact of the past can be seen and felt all around. While its dramatic history is filled with incidents of extreme hardship and tragedy, the overriding impression one receives is that of a triumphant survivalism associated with its strong men of the past: the *voyageurs*, the *coureurs du bois,* and the lumbermen. Unused and often dilapidated pioneer farm buildings and fencing stand adjacent to modern houses and barns, icons to first settlers and the lifestyle they carved out of the bush. Many pioneer log cabins remain inhabited and plaques bestowed by the Century Farm Program are prominently displayed.

Because of its relative isolation until recent times, the Ottawa Valley has developed and maintained its own unique traditions and culture. Three predominant groups—the Irish, the Scots, and the French Canadians—settled in the region during the past two hundred years, in patterns that little respected current provincial borders, and the region became well known for its rich singing, storytelling, fiddling, and step dancing traditions. Today, "Old time" fiddle and step dancing contests are annual events in many centers in the valley such as Pembroke, Mattawa, Montebello, and Lanark.

The Irish influence in the valley is very strong. In the Upper Ottawa Valley during the nineteenth century, for example, 54 percent of the population of the counties on the Ontario side of the river were of Irish origin, the largest concentration of people of Irish origin in British North America. In Carleton County this figure was over 77 percent, with four of its townships (March, Goulbourn, Huntley, and Marlborough) showing figures of over 80 percent. In Pontiac County on the Quebec side of the river, the Irish population during the same period was approximately 70 percent of the total. To contrast this, it is interesting to note that in the cities of Toronto, Boston, Philadelphia, and Baltimore, the Irish never made up more than a one fourth of the population, and New York City's Irish population peaked in 1855, reaching 35 percent (Lockwood 1988). It is not surprising, therefore, that the culture of the Ottawa Valley has a predominantly Irish flavor. The case of the Ottawa Valley Irish demographic is the opposite to that for most of Canada; approximately two thirds of the Irish immigrants to the region were Catholics as opposed to Protestants.

IRISH EMIGRATION TO CANADA

Much of the literature concerning Irish emigration has been based on myth and romanticized history. In order to embark upon an informed discussion of the Irish Diaspora, a brief look at the facts of the emigration question is required. Most Irish emigration to Canada occurred after the Napoleonic wars, from 1815, climaxing during the 1840s to a figure of 97,000 in the year 1847 and thereafter beginning to decline because "the Canadian authorities applied a head tax on emigrants to defray the costs of caring for them. The result of this tax was to direct Irish emigration to the United States during the remaining years of the nineteenth century" (Grace 1993, 37). The famine migration lasted until 1854, after which time the number of Irish immigrants to Canada decreased dramatically.

What was the status of the people who left Ireland? As historian Donald Akenson (1993) states, "The emigrants were not the truly poor, the near-starving, for such persons did not have the resources to leave Ireland. Those who emigrated, however poor they may appear to our modern eyes, were, by definition, in command of surplus economic resources—enough in any case to allow them to reach a seaport and to pay passage away from Ireland" (37). It is also important to note that these emigrants chose to leave and were not the pathetic exiles denied their homeland that they are sometimes depicted to be.[1] Irish emigrants were for the most part already anglicized. Only 4.9 percent of the Irish population in 1851 could not speak English and only 23.3 percent of them could speak Irish. They were reasonably well educated in mid-nineteenth-century terms, due to the establishment of the national school system in 1831. In educational terms, this put them well ahead of countries like Italy and Spain and on a par with France.

Approximately two thirds of the Irish who settled in Canada were Protestants while the remaining one third was Catholic. The information for these figures was garnered from nineteenth-century and early-twentieth-century Canadian census data. Unfortunately, after 1941 the Canadian census lumped all the peoples of the British Isles into one category, "British," so little demographic evidence is available on the Irish as a distinct ethnic group from that point in time. In the United States, the demographic evidence for Irish immigration is almost nonexistent. As Donald Akenson reports, not until the census of 1969–70 was a question asked about the ethnicity of the individuals enumerated and no question about religion was asked either. This paucity of demographic data has led to a number of invalid assumptions. For example, while it is generally assumed that the Irish Diaspora of the United States is majority Catholic, studies conducted since 1975[2] refute this notion, putting Protestant Irish at between 54 and 58 percent of the total. Reasons for this as suggested by Akenson rest primarily on the fact that the Protestants, for the most part, arrived earlier, and have therefore produced more descendants (1993, 219–20).

HOMELAND AND DIASPORA

The concepts of "homeland" and "Diaspora" are tied to identity, history, and place. The concept of homeland has four essential components: it is a place; there are people who live there; these people exert control over the place by demographic or other factors (e.g., land ownership); and the people have a sense of this place, having bonded with it. Cultures whose economies are tied to the land have a stronger bond with place than those whose economies are not land dependent (Nostrand and Estaville 1993). The urge to bond with place may originate in animistic religion where it was believed that spirits inhabited the landscape (Roark 1993). But the Bible also reinforces the idea that all peoples should have a place; eviction or exile from place (e.g., as from the Garden of Eden)—a recurring theme in the Old Testament—is portrayed as a devastating event, a deterioration of the social order (Smith 1996).

The reinforcement of group identity is the impetus for bonding to a homeland; however, it is clear that such a bond must be with the people residing in an area as much as with the place itself. To have a homeland is to be rooted to a place. The very use of the term *roots* implies stability; thus, the general and unquestioned assumption prevails that the deeper one's roots, the better off one is likely to be (Sarup 1994). Homelands may also be imagined or mythic. A mythical motherland or fatherland may be invented to serve the cause of nationalism, for example. The invention of a mythic homeland is particularly important for groups that have been severed from their place of origin by exile and emigration but it may also be equally important for people still resident in their land but unable to acknowledge their history due to political trauma. As Bhabha and Bennett (1998) put it: "To survive, strictly speaking, is to continue to live after the cessation of some thing, event, or process; it demands an articulation or bridging of the moments 'before' and 'after' a discontinuity—and the courage to live through the flux of that moment of trauma, cessation, or loss. Simply to forget trauma is to be amoral and amnesiac, but to remember trauma alone is to refuse to turn cessation into continuance."

Inventing a mythic homeland is one way of turning, in Bhabha and Bennett's terms, a cessation into a continuance. In Ireland, for example, the invention of the myth of the motherland was developed as a result of Ireland's political colonization. The motherland

bridged the period between ancient bardic Ireland and the establishment of the Irish Free State (Kearney 1984). The German concept
of Heimat, as portrayed in the film of the same name[3] has provided
the German people—historically and culturally disenfranchised after World War II—with an alternative tolerable view of homeland
(Morley and Robins 1993). This has been part of the "quest for a new
German past in the post-Cold War world" as in West Germany
"memory was sealed off in post-traumatic oblivion behind the 'Zero
Hour' of 1945" while in East Germany, "the government enshrined
courageous Communist anti-Fascists and omitted other victims
from its memorials" (Koonz 1994).

The concept of Diaspora stresses the linkages between emigrant
groups and their place of origin as "the Diaspora invokes an imagined geography, a spatiality that draws on connections across oceans
and continents" (Keith and Pile 1993). This imagined space, akin to
Homi Bhabha's concept of cultural in-between or Edward Soja's
"third space" (Soja 1989), is where identity negotiation takes place,
the result being the production of hybrid cultural forms. These
forms express both the linkages and the distinctiveness of the
settler/origin groups stretched over this imagined geography. Music and dance are especially powerful expressions of this link/sepa-
ration as it is particularly in these nonverbal practices that people
can more easily accept cultural hybridity and pluralism (Stokes
1998). "New hybrid cultures are building upon history as the carrier
of meaning in the Diaspora present" (Alund 1996, 99).

But in Diaspora politics, elements of fundamentalism and exclusion are legitimized by history: experience of fear and oppression;
conditions of exile (e.g., slavery, famine, discrimination, etc.); the impossible fantasy of a return to the place of origin; and the redemptive power of suffering (Gilroy 1993). The use of the word *Diaspora*,
with all its associations of painful, forced dispersion, and longing for
the homeland, implies conditions that no longer exist, if indeed they
ever did; and it may lead to assumptions or claims that are not valid
such as the homeland's claim of the Diaspora communities without
their knowledge or consent.[4]

The overwhelming presence of the Diaspora Irish in the Ottawa Valley region has been fundamental to the development of a distinct identity. Many generations after the arrival of the first settlers, the population continues to celebrate its Irish roots. Making or claiming the
valley as an Irish place through the transfer of old-world traditions has

been fundamental to the maintenance of Irish identity because in practice their history is being imagined or reconstructed in the present. Keith Basso has stated that the Apache view of history is that of a well-worn path or trail:

> Beyond the memories of living persons, this path is no longer visible—the past has disappeared—and thus is unavailable for direct consultation and study. For this reason, the past must be constructed—which is to say, imagined—with the aid of historical materials, sometimes called "footprints" or "tracks" that have survived into the present. (Basso 1996, 31)

Due to its relative isolation and its position as a border region, there has been little interest in the Ottawa Valley from outside, and as a result, valley people have had to be self-reliant in the recording and transmission of their local history and culture. Much of this has been accomplished by oral means, leaving a heritage of tracks or footprints that can be examined, demonstrating how their employment in the present continues to construct a past in which valley identity is anchored.

PLACE-NAMES

The definition of "placeness" by the process of place naming is one way of putting a cultural mark on the landscape. "This process of identification is one essential marker of cultural activity. It forms the basis for the elaboration of spatialization for it allows the differentiation of both places from space and places from each other" (Shields 1991, 48). In this way, place-names become an important cultural symbol and can be a significant indicator of the presence of an ethnic group in a region. However, there is also a certain element of power politics at play in that it is the people of influence who generally assign the names. In the Ottawa Valley, for example, the larger towns tend to bear Scottish or English place-names (e.g., Lanark, Perth, Renfrew, Calabogie, Pembroke, Pakenham), while many of the smaller villages and rural areas bear Irish names (Antrim, Mayo, Westmeath, Shamrock, Killaloe, Maynooth, Cormac, Letterkenny, Donegal, Mount St. Patrick, Brennan's Hill, Clontarf, Ryanville, etc.). This, to some extent, demonstrates the lower economic position of the Irish in the region, relative to the English and Scots settlers, and points to their predominance in the rural areas.

But the naming of places extends to more than villages and towns. Landmarks, trails, farms, lakes and streams, churches, bridges, and forests all are named over time. Many of these names attest to events associated with the particular place. In Ireland, the tradition of *dinnseanchas* (place-name lore)[5] shows a connection between people and the land. Irish places often retain the names of families who lived there, even when they have long disappeared from the area. Other place-names have historical or even mythical significance.

This is much the case with the Ottawa Valley as well. Farms and homesteads tend to be known by the names of the early families that settled there. Settlement roads are also often named for early settlers. But places such as Ghost Hill on Highway 148 in Pontiac County have been named for the ghost sightings reported at that location since the early 1800s. Keith Basso's assertion of the ongoing power of the present-day use of place-names in the case of the Western Apache people doubtless holds true for other peoples as well: "that whenever one uses a place-name, even unthinkingly, one is quoting ancestral speech" (Basso 1996, 30). In place naming, early settlers often attempted to re-create the familiar topology of their former homelands in an attempt to recover a lost relationship with their place of origin, an act that no doubt served to facilitate the process of bonding with the new territory. "The evocative power of the place name provides a key to the shared social memory of a landscape whose collective meanings were part of a unifying repository of community knowledge" (Nash 1994, 240).

Places of worship were very important to the Irish immigrants, as were their cemeteries. Gravestones of first settlers usually bear the name of their place of origin in the "old country." Holy wells, also common to Ireland, are scattered throughout the country. Other visual evidence of Irish settlement is evident in the number of Irish pubs and small hotels of the region such as one in the village of Douglas, Ontario, which has the notoriety of hosting the biggest and best St. Patrick's Day celebration in the valley. So many people from all over the valley congregate for the celebrations here that it is next to impossible to find a place to park your car within a mile or two of town. In Douglas, the "Paddy's Day" celebrations last for the best part of a week. The event is viewed more as a valley celebration than as an Irish celebration. Rather than simply being a remembrance of things past, the view from the valley is that St. Patrick's Day is the celebration of a culture that is very much alive and flourishing.

POLITICS AND "RECREATIONAL VIOLENCE":
THE ORANGE ORDER

Although Orangemen were active in Canada since the early 1800s, it wasn't until 1830 that a Grand Lodge was established to coordinate Orange strongholds in Newfoundland, New Brunswick and Ontario, and most particularly in the Ottawa Valley, including its Quebec territory (Senior 1972). Many in Upper Canada (Ontario) did not look favorably upon the activities of Orangemen in the region during the 1820s, no doubt due in part to the civil unrest they incited.[6] Despite the opposition, however, the Orange Order became firmly established in Canada. The case of the Order in Newfoundland is most interesting in that there were few Irish Protestants resident in the territory. Protestant-Catholic disputes flourished there, however, between the West Country English, who adopted Orangeism, and the Irish Catholic population. "Ironically, the Irish Catholics of Newfoundland found themselves in a land where Orangemen lived, but where Protestant Irishmen did not" (Houston and Smyth 1988, 746–47).

But it is in Upper Canada (Ontario) that Orangeism has had the most influence in a political sense. Its success was partly due to its establishment just at the time of the massive Irish immigrations to Upper Canada in the 1830s. The Order functioned as an immigrant association as well as a political one, thus becoming a focus for community and family social life. In addition, in Canada the Orange Order was not only associated with the working class; influential businessmen and politicians were among its members.[7] Wherever groups of Protestant Irish settled, the building of Orange Lodges soon followed. Houston and Smyth have shown that it was the spread of Irish Protestant migration, not anti-Catholic sentiment, that was the chief influence in the rapid spread of Orangeism in Ontario. "Our geographical analysis reveals that the variability in growth of the Order was a function of the simultaneous advance of Orange ideology, and the unfolding of Ontario's demography and settlement history" (Houston and Smyth 1977, 24).

The numerical strength of the Orange Order in Canada during the nineteenth century was considerable. In 1881, a total of 1,400 lodges were operational in the country; approximately 1,000 were located in Ontario. One of the most interesting aspects of Houston and Smyth's geographical study is their finding that not only were Orange Lodges to be found in older settled areas but they were quickly established in the frontier areas of Ontario. Orangeism acted as a conservative defense of social, moral, and political ideologies, and was regarded, by its proponents, as both the hallmark and the defense of the British Empire in North America. It articulated and sustained the destiny of Ontario, beleaguered by French Canadian Catholicism and American republicanism, and its role on the frontiers of the province was that of a garrison (Houston and Smyth 1977, 4; see also Shields 1991).

In the Ottawa Valley, Orangeism spread with the arrival and settlement of Irish Protestants. Soon after their arrival, Orange Lodges were established in many centers such as Almonte, Shawville, Quyon, and Bristol, among others. As well as functioning as meeting places for lodge gatherings, Orange halls became the focus of community activity, serving as the venue for local dances, parties, and in a few cases, even the teaching of step dancing. Valley settlement patterns show that Protestants and Catholics generally settled in small homogeneous communities throughout the region. However, these communities were never far apart, and there is a history of strained relations between the two groups as was the case in the Eganville area. According to Joe Quilty of Calabogie:

> I hear a lot of talk about the Orange and the Catholics having their battles, fighting over this and that and the other thing. . . . I think up in Eganville they had bad problems up there. One side up there was Protestant, on the other side of the river, and on this side of the river where the big church was, was Catholic. And I guess they used to have battles up there like you wouldn't believe back in the old, old days. . . . They missed the boat; they should have mixed them all up at that time and we would never have had a problem instead of putting the Protestants over there and the Catholics over here.[8]

Catholics were not welcome in Protestant areas; there was often a policy of exclusion in effect. Clarendon Township in Pontiac County, Quebec, including the town of Shawville, was one such area. Ottawa Valley historian Joan Finnigan, described the area this way:

> It was a hundred percent Protestant. You weren't allowed to go if you were a Catholic. . . . You couldn't buy land. . . . You see, Pendergast, he came as the Crown land agent with the absolute determination not to allow a Catholic in . . . because he didn't want the strife he had experienced in Ireland. You could not get land from him if you were a Catholic so it was a hundred percent [Protestant]. . . . There was a quiet

subterranean agreement that you would never sell to a Catholic . . . you knew that you would be ostracized if you did.[9]

Murt Fahey, a Catholic from down river at Luskville, Quebec, recounted to me the following experience of a visit to Shawville during the early 1930s:

> Well, the first time I went to Shawville, I was working at Baileys [a prominent family with a number of local businesses] and they had a pipe and drum band and they were hired to play for the Shawville Fair. So, of course, I was driving one car and I stayed overnight. . . . I went to the barber shop in the morning and called in to the barber and I told him [it was my] first time in Shawville. . . . I said, "You've a nice clean town." What I meant about being clean was, in Aylmer there was a lot of paper on the sidewalk at night and I didn't see that in Shawville. He took it another way. He said, "Yes we have a pretty clean town. We've only had two Catholics in town. We got rid of one last summer and we're going to get rid of the other one pretty soon." And I said, "Good for you." The razor was too damn close to my neck.[10]

ORANGE PARADES

Throughout the valley, the Protestant Irish communities marched in their parades. Catholics did not attend parades and usually kept a low profile on "the glorious twelfth" (of July). But, as one informant, Bruce Armitage, described, this was not always the case.

> They had the Orange Parade in Quyon [Quebec] and apparently, they were having their dinner in the hotel and they left all their banners outside on the sidewalk. And there was this guy called Madden—he was a Roman Catholic. . . . He tore the banner that was outside . . . ripped it up . . . and there was hell. Then they were looking for him, they were going to kill him. And he hid in a rain barrel. . . . Oh, they would have killed him . . . and they couldn't find him. Now whether he was breathing through a straw or what, I don't know, but that's how he got away.[11]

The day's events usually began with the local Orange parade followed by a family picnic where there were political speeches, games for the children and music and dancing for entertainment. The following excerpt from an interview with Bruce Armitage describes the

festivities that took place in the Onslow, Quebec, area during the
1940s and 1950s.

> TREW: Would the people around here have been mostly Protestant?
>
> ARMITAGE: Well, right around would be, yeah. . . . And like from
> here back. But out that way—we called it the swamp—there was a lot
> of Irish Catholics in there. O'Reilly and Farrells but we were all good
> neighbors. Like it made no difference. But still, on the twelfth of July,
> everybody went out and hooray for King Billy, the hell with the Pope
> and all that, you know. But then, the rest of the year, we thrashed with
> the Catholics and we all got along. . . . I remember the night, usually,
> before the twelfth—the eleventh—they would go to the lodge and they
> would practice and we could hear the drum from here. And the night
> before, everybody'd get to bed early that night to get up for the Orange
> Parade. . . . You see they had their lodges everywhere. We had one back
> here on the hill, it was called Onslow no. 34. . . . And then there was
> one in Beechgrove, no. 70, and there was one out at Bristol and all those
> places, they had their lodges. So they would organize on the twelfth of
> July. They would organize to have the picnic at a certain place and they
> would all congregate there. . . . And then there would be a parade and
> they would parade and play the drum and march and all the banners
> and everything.
>
> TREW: Did they have a horse and a King Billy[12]?
>
> ARMITAGE: Oh yes. Yes, indeed. And then they would come back
> after the parade. Then there would be seats set up and there would be
> speeches and all that kind of stuff and there'd be lunch available on the
> grounds if you wanted to. Oh, it was a day off. It was a day to look
> forward to. . . . We always went. . . . It always rained the twelfth of July
> but oh, they would march and the water running out of their boots. It
> didn't matter.
>
> TREW: Did any of the Irish Catholics or French-Canadians show up
> at it?
>
> ARMITAGE: No, no, no, no. Not a one, not a one. Not a one. . . . Oh
> yeah, 'twas a big thing.[13]

Parades are not simply an innocent celebration or festivity.[14] As Larsen
(1982) points out in her study of the July 12 celebrations in the Northern Ireland town of Kilbroney, "the Twelfth is a statement not only
about social order but about the area subject to that order. Processions
and marches are means of asserting control over territory" (289). In
other words, parades are a means of laying claim to place. Writing
about Orange and St. Patrick's Day parades in Victorian Toronto, Peter
Goheen explains how parades there were linked with power:

Parades claimed privileges in certain streets where prestige accrued by monopolizing their use for the passing minute or hour. The public space they chose to occupy lent recognition to the sponsoring organization and helped legitimize its existence. The intention was to associate with the power and to appropriate the status therein represented. (1992, 342)

In the newly formed communities of nineteenth-century Ontario, including the Ottawa Valley and its Quebec territory, "Orange parades were the expression of the power and control of a self-convinced charter group whose duty it was to preserve and defend the very foundations of the state" (Houston and Smyth 1977, 7). The extent of the claim is indicated in the parade routes chosen that focus on the major arteries rather than simply the Protestant areas. The participation of influential community leaders and politicians in the parade and in the subsequent speeches at picnic grounds afterward reinforces the legitimacy of this claim on place.

There is no longer an Orange Parade in every valley town but rather a shared regional parade, which is rotated among a number of valley communities from year to year. Certain areas, however, have maintained their own local parade held on a different day from the main one. So while the religious and ethnic strife brought over from Ireland has greatly dissipated in recent years, even the smaller local parades still manage to attract significant participation. Clearly, many individuals retain an awareness of their ethnic origins and an interest in their traditions. A step dancer, John Langford, described the recent festivities in Pontiac County, Quebec:

> Yeah, they're still active down there [in Quyon]. It's been a big area for years on that. It's starting to get a lot of the older ones are dying off and the young ones don't seem to want to get into it the same. They'll have a parade here [Shawville] . . . and then they'll go to another, say, at Carleton Place, on July 12th and have another big do. I went down and danced last year for them in Quyon. They had a big do and a supper. . . . A man told me they were having their own do there but they invited others to come, like from other places, and they did have quite a crowd. Anyway, we danced in the evening for a bit, put on a little show there.[15]

While the Orange Order is still active in the valley, its presence has diminished sharply over the last thirty years. Many people feel that it is definitely on the way out. This opinion has likely been reinforced in recent times by the significant (and overwhelmingly negative) coverage over the last four years that the Canadian Broadcasting Corporation (CBC) radio and television have given to the Orange Order's protests at Drumcree.

Increasingly, the sons of Orangemen are choosing not to join the Order. Bruce Armitage, whose father was an active member of the Lodge, chose instead to join the Masons.

> Well, I guess the Orangemen had their purpose, maybe, but I think it's done now here. We don't need it here. Maybe we never needed it. . . . It just created animosity. Kept them from inter-marrying. . . . The Orange Lodge was a fighting force. They were fighters to fight the Catholics.[16]

TRADITIONAL MUSIC IN THE OTTAWA VALLEY

In the Ottawa Valley, the predominant form of traditional or folk music is what is commonly referred to as "old-time fiddling." Other musical traditions also exist, particularly in the urban centers of Ottawa-Hull, where the presence of recent (first generation) immigrants to Canada has ensured the survival of a variety of ethnic musics. There is, however, little interest in or awareness of valley music on the part of these immigrants or of urban residents in general. The Irish and Scottish communities in Ottawa, for example, regularly host cultural events where the music played is similar to that currently being played in Ireland and Scotland, featuring a variety of instruments such as the whistle, bagpipes, and accordion.

Not much is known about Ottawa Valley music prior to the 1920s but the general assumption is that the fiddle tradition was brought over to the Ottawa Valley by the Irish and Scottish immigrants to the region. Since these groups, the Irish in particular, formed the large majority of the population, the fiddle tradition quickly became the predominant music tradition of the region. The fiddle's popularity throughout the region is no doubt also attributable to its portability. Joe Quilty explained:

> I think the fiddle was so popular because in the first place, it came from the old country where people played them over there, the Scottish and the Irish and whatever. They brought them out here and they blended in here real well because you could cart them around so easily. . . . The

fiddle was an instrument that you could carry under your arm. Lots of
people didn't even have a case for them; they put them in a pillowcase
and off to the neighbours and play some tunes. . . . It was a great instrument for parties.[17]

The same fiddler, remembering his childhood, remarked that the
fiddle played a particularly important role in the extreme isolation
typical of valley communities prior to the Second World War.

The fiddle was an essential household accessory for social activity.
As Joe Quilty pointed out:

A lot of these people had fiddles in their homes that didn't even play.
They'd have a fiddle sitting—it might be in a box or it might be sitting
up on the sideboard or hanging on the wall 'cause somebody down the
road might come in that could fiddle and away they'd go and have
some music.[18]

Still today, the fiddle appears to hold a special place in the hearts
and minds of valley people. Over and over again, I heard of people
who collected fiddles and of others who simply wanted to own one,
even though they couldn't play it. I recorded this exchange between
two fiddlers at a house party.

Do you know where I could get a cheap old fiddle for somebody that
will never learn to play but wants one? . . . He's probably looking for
one hanging up in somebody's attic, though, because he'll never play
it. He just wants a fiddle to call his own.

Well I just love a guy like that, you know.

He's an old-time dancer, not a step dancer, but a round dancer, and
he grew up with the fiddle music. He hasn't got a note of music in
him.[19]

Most valley people, even those not involved in musical activities,
appear to be well aware of the valley's fiddle culture. While it is
common in the valley to be knowledgeable about the genealogy of
families in one's own locality, that awareness frequently extends to
knowledge of particular talents or character traits belonging to those
individuals. Musical talents are understood to be fairly common
among valley people and this is often explained in terms of their
heritage. Joe Quilty put it this way:

Yeah, it's a way of life, I guess. . . . Some of the fiddlers around here before my time were great fiddlers too. Like up around Mount St. Patrick, I guess there was some Mulvihills up around through there. Sheedys. All Irish, eh, and they could play like you wouldn't believe. McKeown—there was a McKeown around here. There's still some of his relatives that live over around Spruce Hedge across here somewhere. I never heard the man but they say he was something else. So it's really a history of this part of the country right here, the fiddle.[20]

As the excerpt above makes clear, the musical culture of the valley is seen as the natural expression of their heritage. And while it is part of their everyday life, it also connects them to their past.

OTTAWA VALLEY STYLE

Carleton University's Linguistic Survey of the Ottawa Valley (Pringle and Padolsky 1981; see also Pringle and Padolsky 1983) has revealed that there are ten English-language dialects in the valley, the predominant ones being Southern-Irish-Hiberno-English and Ulster-Hiberno-English. Musical dialects are as diverse in the valley as linguistic dialects. Ottawa Valley fiddlers are, in my view, musical chameleons. Diversity is the normal condition of the music and perhaps its richest component. It is embraced by Ottawa Valley players much as it is with musicians from other multicultural countries who have similarly compound identities. To quote musicologist James Robbins, "Cuban musicians and writers on music stress diversity and multi-ethnic heritage as the major factor in the richness of their musical culture" (Robbins 1994, 195).

Probably the most striking aspect of Ottawa Valley playing is the ability of the musicians to absorb and blend diverse styles and repertoire. That a good valley fiddler is a musical chameleon is manifested in a number of ways:

1. The fiddler plays the same tune in two or three different styles, the style he chooses depending on the situation (e.g., fiddle contest, group playing, individual playing).
2. The fiddler plays each tune according to what he feels is its most authentic interpretation, with successive tunes then being played in radically different styles by the same player.

3. The fiddler plays predominantly in one style/repertoire when playing alone and reserves the playing of other styles/repertoire for playing with others.
4. The fiddler commonly composes tunes in various styles.

There is a reverence in the fiddling community for players who not only have an extensive repertoire of tunes but also for how many styles they can play and how convincingly this is executed. When I asked fiddlers if they thought there was an Ottawa Valley style of fiddle playing, they were almost all quite convinced that there was. Descriptions of it varied tremendously from specifics of bowing and tone production to linking it more with the repertoire played. One fiddler told me that while this identity was very definitely there, he could not see it himself because he was a part of it. He likened it to not being able to hear your own accent.[21]

Particular fiddlers who best exemplify Ottawa Valley style were mentioned over and over again by the fiddlers, dancers, and piano players interviewed. Those most frequently cited were Bob Ranger, the late Reggie Hill, the late Jerry Lafleur, the late Dominic Curley, the Daly brothers of Quyon, and the late Doherty brothers of Wolf Lake, Quebec. Graham Townsend described a visit he made to Wolf Lake in the late 1960s to hear the Doherty brothers play.[22]

> I went up there with Andy Lusk and a bunch of us on about a three-day rip as we would call it. I didn't want to play 'cause I wanted to hear Johnny and Andy [Doherty] play. And they played all these tunes. They played old tunes that I had never heard. All the old, old Valley tunes. That is an Ottawa Valley style but again, it's taken from the Irish people.[23]

The largest consensus of opinion about Ottawa Valley style was that there was an "Ottawa Valley sound." Many described it in terms of the overall presentation; the importance of rhythm and tempo (e.g., timing) was often mentioned.

The sound is why they say they have an Ottawa Valley style. And I think it's got a lot to do with the sound. How it's presented, how the music is presented.[24]

Some musicians felt that the Ottawa Valley style has become the contest style of playing. A player from the Canadian Maritimes suggested that fiddlers from around Canada have adopted the Ottawa Valley "contest" sound through exposure to it from years of com-

peting at the Pembroke and the Canadian Grand Masters fiddle contests. These fiddlers, in turn, have passed the sound to other players
in their home regions.

From my conversations with musicians and fans alike, the predominant theme that emerged was that timing or danceability was
the most important element of the music. If there is a distinct Ottawa
Valley style, it is danceability that makes it recognizable, particularly
noted in the playing of jigs, the tune type most associated with Irishness. Even when the music is performed in a listening context, the
influence of the dance is still the most important factor in its performance. Many players talked about having to imagine dancers on
the floor in order to get the right feeling or timing in their playing.
The creation of this imagined space necessary to performance accentuates concepts of space and movement as fundamental to the
production of this music. It also highlights the role of old-time fiddle music as dance music and in doing so, links it to the social context of community old-time dances, which are on the wane. Since
community dances are a prime venue for the creation of communitas, preserving the danceability of the music is one way of preserving the old time, preserving the link with the past, and maintaining
communitas.

PERFORMING IDENTITY: FIDDLE
AND STEP DANCING CONTESTS

The fiddle and step dancing contest[25] is the main annual cultural
event of Ottawa Valley communities. These contests operate in a circuit, with each host community having its own designated weekend.
The contest circuit in the Ottawa Valley begins with the long weekend—the third—in May at a contest in Perth, Ontario, and generally
finishes with the Pembroke contest on the Labor Day weekend at the
beginning of September. Besides the actual contest itself, other events
are often included in the contest weekend program such as social
breakfasts, "old-time" dances, and church services. Many community groups will take advantage of the fiddle contest weekend to
stage other complementary events. Local merchants might organize
a sidewalk sale, for example, or there might be a parade or street performers, and community interest groups might host a charity supper.
Fiddle contest organizers are usually only too willing to cooperate

with their local chamber of commerce and other local groups to make the contest a truly all-community event.

The first regular annual contest established in the valley was at Pembroke, Ontario, in the mid-1960s. It ran for a few years and then, due to organizational reasons, ceased for a number of years. It started up again in 1976 and has continued ever since. Many other regular annual contests in the valley have started up in the years following Pembroke's second wind and most have been quite successful. While the smaller valley contests tend to attract a largely local audience, the larger contests such as Pembroke attract thousands of people, many from distant parts of North America.

As public events, fiddle and step dancing contests portray the dominant ideology or ethos of how valley people ideally see themselves, which includes such personal characteristics as adaptability, self-reliance, charity, industriousness, neighborliness, and equality—all traits perceived as having developed from their pioneer past. This ensemble of traits represents an ideology that I define here as "old-time community." It forms the basis of the organization of public events and as such, it is ever present in the public discourse and cannot be ignored. Even those who disagree with this "old-time community" image are trapped by it as they are forced to define their own views against it or in opposition to it. The contests operate to provide the symbolism and the occasion for the expression of competing versions of identity.

At all the contests I attended there was a noticeable sense of togetherness, of all of us present belonging to something. This was achieved or "managed" in a variety of ways, owing much to the role of the Master of Ceremonies (MC).[26] For example, the MC regularly made announcements about other community activities and events throughout the contest, thus promoting the community and the place, and was also continually joking on stage with members of the audience and contestants alike, relating humorous anecdotes about them in a familial manner, thus co-opting the assembled audience into the "family," so to speak. On one occasion as a contestant left the stage after playing, for example, the MC told a joke to the audience in which he substituted the contestant's name for that of the joke's protagonist. He also made frequent allusions to a shared past, to the ethnic origins of the community, notably telling many "Irish" or "Paddy" jokes and also talking about the many trips to Ireland made by himself and various community members. References to place and to the past are also expressed in the MC's many anecdotal valley stories, usually humorous and having a rural theme, relating tales of valley farmers, woodsmen, fiddlers, and dancers, past and present. In this way, stage talk operates to link the event and its performances to a perceived shared and idealized past (Bealle 1993).

The MC's banter on stage provides a frame of cultural clues around the aesthetic performance. The open-platform style of stage also accentuates the role of the MC as there is no backstage area for setup and tuning, so the pace of the event relies heavily on the MC's interaction with the audience, giving him more time to provide the cultural framework to the performances. The perception of a shared past, place, and purpose as endorsed by the MC promotes symbolic unity and contributes to the development of communitas (see Davies 1998; Trosset 1993).

Fundamental to what I call the Ottawa Valley ethos is that social bonds among people are more important than status, as is evident from the informality of their public events, the use of personal rather than positional identities in public, and in the way that competitiveness is continually downplayed by the relaxed atmosphere and the transparency of contest structure and organization. Contests are an occasion to strengthen community bonds, allowing, as they do, for the expression of various interpretations of community identity. Fiddler Brian Hébert has eloquently articulated how the performance of the music expresses valley ethos:

> I think attitude's as important as the playing part. Because you have to accept, not only the music, but the way it's presented, the fellowship that goes along with it, the attitude that goes along with it, the way people present themselves, the lack of competitiveness. I mean you have to take that as part and parcel too. . . . I've seen people move to the area with one attitude and after four or five years, or even three years, a whole different attitude, a whole different person. They've accepted the culture, the music and the attitude of how the music is played, how important it is to the people, and how unimportant it is as a business or as a way to compete.[27]

CONCLUSION

While the Ottawa Valley population is today made up of numerous ethnic groups, the hegemonic valley culture and identity is Irish.

This is due to the overwhelming numbers of Irish—particularly Irish Catholics—who settled in the region during the nineteenth century. So apart from groups whose identity remains staunchly Scottish, many others have adopted or even claimed Irish identity and culture.

Yet while the foundation of valley culture may be Irish, as can be seen in the environment, folklore, politics, language, music, and dance, the question of identity is much more complex. It is important to appreciate the difference between a sentimental pride in one's origins and real patriotism or nationalism, which is now invested in the new country, the country that is indeed home. The experiences of five generations in Canada has considerably influenced what was once an Irish population and identity. Marriage with other ethnic groups, absence of contact with the "old country," and the very different realities of life in a climate and landscape uniquely Canadian have contributed to the development of an emerging new Canadian identity. A sense of place is a key component of valley identity. As Joan Finnigan suggested to me:

> I think [valley identity] has a lot to do with geography. Certainly, in the beginning, you know, I've called it a metaphoric island because it really was an island. In the early days, the mountains—the Gatineaus and the Opeongos—made it into the little watershed of the Ottawa River and its twenty-six rivers and it was somehow closed. It's still a little closed. And then the network of clans were like veins. The river was the massive artery and the twenty-six rivers running in were the arteries. And then the network of clans was sort of like veins running through the Valley. . . . I think there's a feeling of real pleasure in saying, "I'm from the Valley." . . . And I think a lot of people outside not only envy the fact that you're Irish . . . but also . . . that they aren't as rooted. It's the rootedness that's so wonderful. A closeness to the landscape. . . . I think it has something to do with how the land allows you to ally yourself with it and to belong to the natural world.[28]

The Ottawa Valley retains a strong Irish character, particularly evident in its oral traditions, but their setting is distinctly Canadian. The legends, folklore, and customs of the valley are rooted in a tradition of orality that the Irish emigrants brought with them, but in the new world context, they express an indigenous Canadian folklore still in its infancy.

NOTES

1. This is not to understate the effects of the famine in Ireland on the emigrants. Even prefamine Irish immigrants to Canada would likely still have had family members in Ireland during the famine years. Famine narratives collected in Canada from people of Irish descent attest to the strong impact of the famine on their families and communities. See McBane 1996–1997.

2. Akenson cites a set of studies conducted during the 1970s by the National Opinion Research Center of the University of Chicago; another conducted by the Gallup organization during the 1980s concerning religious affiliation; and The National Survey of Religious Identification, 1989–1990, conducted by the Graduate Center of the City University of New York (1993, 21, 302).

3. *Heimat,* film series for television, by Edgar Reitz, 1984.

4. In her inaugural speech on December 3, 1990, Irish President Mary Robinson uttered the now-famous proclamation, "There are over seventy million people living on this globe who claim Irish descent. I will be proud to represent them" (cited in Akenson 1993, 15).

5. The Irish word *dinnseanchas* comes from the preposition *de* in its form *dinn*, meaning of, off, or from, and *seanchas,* meaning tradition, lore, or storytelling. *Dinnseanchas* is translated by the word *topography* in English. In early Ireland, it was the responsibility of the poets to collect and preserve place-lore. The *Dindshenchas* was a twelfth-century collection of place-lore that consisted of about three hundred poems in which each had the title of a place-name with the text of the poem relating the story of the origins of the name. See Ó hÓgáin 1990.

6. Examples of Orange unrest were the Ballygiblin riot near Perth, Ontario, in the Ottawa Valley in 1824 and another riot in 1827 in the city of Kingston.

7. Pennefather 1984 outlines the importance of Orange political connections. In the twentieth century, a number of Ontario and Saskatchewan Premiers were known Orangemen as well as numerous Federal and Provincial MPs. Orange political influence in Ontario extended into the 1980s.

8. Joe Quilty, interview by author, 26 September 1996, Calabogie, Ontario. Tape recording.

9. Joan Finnigan, interview by author, 8 December 1996, Hartington, Ontario. Tape recording.

10. Murt Fahey, interview by author, 24 October 1995, Luskville, Quebec. Tape recording.

11. Bruce Armitage, interview by author, 18 October 1995, North Onslow, Quebec. Tape recording.

12. King William of Orange is invariably depicted in Orange iconography riding a white horse. See Jarman 1997 for further discussion.

13. Bruce Armitage, interview by author, 18 October 1995, North Onslow, Quebec. Tape recording.

14. For analyses of the meaning of parades, see Cottrell 1998; also Jarman 1997.

15. John Langford, interview by author, 17 September 1996, Shawville, Quebec. Tape recording.

16. Armitage, interview, 18 October 1995.

17. Quilty, interview, 26 September 1996.

18. Quilty, interview, 26 September 1996.

19. Joe Quilty and Bob Buck at house party, interview by author, 13 August 1996, Calabogie, Ontario. Tape recording.

20. Quilty, interview, 26 September 1996.

21. Dawson Girdwood, interview by author, 10 October 1995, Perth, Ontario. Tape recording.

22. Andy Lusk recorded some of the Dohertys playing on this visit. Dennis Alexander kindly provided me a copy of this tape.

23. Graham Townsend, interview by author, 5 December 1995, Barrie, Ontario. Tape recording.

24. Webb Acheson, interview by author, 19 October 1995, Mink Lake, Ontario. Tape recording.

25. Even though the term *competition* is occasionally used on publicity brochures for these events, *contest* is the usual term employed by organizers, contestants, and fans alike.

26. The MC at 90 percent of the Ottawa Valley fiddle contests over the years has been Art Jamieson, currently Reeve of Beechburg, Ontario, a village near Pembroke. Many informants have reported that although other MCs do a pretty good job, there is no one the equal of Art Jamieson, and his engagement at a contest is definitely a factor in attracting more people to the event. Jamieson has become so popular in recent years that he has even been invited to contests in Western Canada.

27. Brian Hébert, interview by author, 12 December 1995, Pembroke, Ontario. Tape recording.

28. Finnigan, interview with the author.

BIBLIOGRAPHY

Akenson, Donald Harman. *The Irish Diaspora: A Primer.* Belfast: Institute of Irish Studies, The Queen's University of Belfast, 1993.

Alund, Aleksandra. "The Stranger: Ethnicity, Identity and Belonging." In *The Future of the Nation State: Essays on Cultural Pluralism and Political Integration,* edited by Sverker Gustavsson and Leif Lewin, 79–106. London: Routledge, 1996.

Basso, Keith H. *Wisdom Sits in Places: Landscape and Language among the Western Apache.* Albuquerque: University of New Mexico Press, 1996.

Bealle, John. "Self-Involvement in Musical Performance: Stage Talk and Interpretive Control at a Bluegrass Festival." *Ethnomusicology* 37, no. 1 (1993): 63–86.

Bhabha, Homi K., and David Bennett. "Liberalism and Minority Culture: Reflections on 'Culture's In Between.'" In *Multicultural States: Rethinking Difference and Identity,* edited by David Bennett, 37–47. London: Routledge, 1998.

Cottrell, Michael. "St. Patrick's Day Parades in Nineteenth-Century Toronto: A Study of Immigrant Adjustment and Elite Control." In *A Nation of Immigrants: Women, Workers, and Communities in Canadian History, 1840s–1960s,* edited by Franca Iacovetta, Paula Draper, and Robert Ventresca, 35–54. Toronto: University of Toronto Press, 1998.

Davies, Charlotte Aull. "'A Oes Heddwch?': Contesting Meanings and Identities in the Welsh National Eisteddfod." In *Ritual, Performance, Media,* edited by Felicia Hughes-Freeland, 141–59. London: Routledge, 1998.

Gilroy, Paul. *The Black Atlantic: Modernity and Double Consciousness.* Cambridge, Mass.: Harvard University Press, 1993.

Goheen, Peter G. "Parading: A Lively Tradition in Early Victorian Toronto." In *Ideology and Landscape in Historical Perspective: Essays on the Meanings of Some Places in the Past,* edited by Alan R. Baker and Gideon Biger, 330–51. Cambridge: Cambridge University Press, 1992.

Grace, Robert J. *The Irish in Quebec: An Introduction to the Historiography.* Quebec: Institut Québécois de Recherche sur la Culture, 1993.

Houston, Cecil, and W. J. Smyth. *The Orange Order in Nineteenth Century Ontario: A Study in Institutional Cultural Transfer.* Toronto: University of Toronto Press, 1977. (Dept. of Geography, Discussion Paper No. 22)

Houston, Cecil J., and William J. Smyth. "Orangemen in Canada." In *The Untold Story: The Irish in Canada,* edited by Robert O'Driscoll and Laura Reynolds, 743–52. Toronto: Celtic Arts of Canada, 1988.

Jarman, Neil. *Material Conflicts: Parades and Visual Displays in Northern Ireland.* Oxford: Berg, 1997.

Kearney, Richard. *Myth and Motherland (Field Day Pamphlet, no. 5).* Derry: Field Day Theatre Company, 1984.

Keith, Michael, and Steve Pile. "The Place of Politics." In *Place and the Politics of Identity,* edited by Michael Keith and Steve Pile, 1–21. London: Routledge, 1993.

Koonz, Claudia. "Between Memory and Oblivion: Concentration Camps in German Memory." In *Commemorations: The Politics of National Identity,* edited by John R. Gillis, 258–80. Princeton, N.J.: Princeton University Press, 1994.

Larsen, Sidsel Saugestad. "The Glorious Twelfth: A Ritual Expression of Collective Identity." In *Belonging: Identity and Social Organisation in British*

Rural Cultures, edited by Anthony P. Cohen, 278–91. Manchester: Manchester University Press, 1982.

Lockwood, Glen J. "Eastern Upper Canadian Perceptions of Irish Immigrants, 1824–1868." Ph.D. diss., University of Ottawa, 1988.

McBane, Michael. "Irish Famine Stories in the Ottawa Valley." *Oral History Forum* (1996–97): 16–17, 7–25.

Morley, David, and Kevin Robins. "No Place Like Heimat: Images of Home(land) in European Culture." In *Space and Place: Theories of Identity and Location,* edited by Erica Carter, James Donald, and Judith Squires, 3–31. London: Lawrence and Wishart, 1993.

Nash, Catherine. "Remapping the Body/Land: New Cartographies of Identity, Gender, and Landscape in Ireland." In *Writing Women and Space: Colonial and Postcolonial Geographies,* edited by Alison Blunt and Gillian Rose, 227–50. New York: Guilford, 1994.

Nostrand, Richard L., and Lawrence E. Estaville. "The Homeland Concept." *Journal of Cultural Geography* 13, no. 2 (1993): 1–4.

Ó hÓgáin, Daithí. *Myth, Romance and Legend: An Encyclopaedia of the Irish Folk Tradition.* London: Ryan, 1990.

Pennefather, R. S. *The Orange and the Black: Documents in the History of the Orange Order, Ontario and the Canadian West, 1890–1940.* Toronto: Orange and Black Publications, 1984.

Pringle, Ian, and Enoch Padolsky. *A Historical Source Book for the Ottawa Valley.* Ottawa: Carleton University, 1981.

Pringle, Ian, and Enoch Padolsky. "The Linguistic Survey of the Ottawa Valley." *American Speech* 58, no. 4 (1983): 325–44.

Roark, Michael O. "Homelands: A Conceptual Essay." *Journal of Cultural Geography* 13, no. 2 (1993): 5–11.

Robbins, James. "What We Can Learn When They Sing, Eh? Ethnomusicology in the American State of Canada." In *Canadian Music: Issues of Hegemony and Identity,* edited by Robert Witmer and Beverley Diamond, 193–202. Toronto: Canadian Scholars' Press, 1994.

Sarup, Madan. "Home and Identity." In *Travellers' Tales: Narratives of Home and Displacement,* edited by George Robertson, et al., 93–104. London: Routledge, 1994.

Senior, Hereward. *Orangeism: The Canadian Phase.* Toronto: McGraw-Hill, 1972.

Shields, Rob. *Places on the Margin: Alternative Geographies of Modernity.* London: Routledge, 1991.

Smith, Jonathan M. "Ramifications of Region and Senses of Place." In *Concepts in Human Geography,* edited by Carville Earle, Kent Mathewson, and Martin S. Kenzer, 189–211. Lanham, Md.: Rowman & Littlefield, 1996.

Soja, Edward W. *Postmodern Geographies: The Reassertion of Space in Critical Social Theory.* London: Verso, 1989.

Stokes, Martin. "Imagining 'The South': Hybridity, Heterotopias and Arabesk on the Turkish-Syrian Border." In *Border Identities: Nation and State at International Frontiers,* edited by Thomas M. Wilson and Hastings Donnan, 263–88. Cambridge: Cambridge University Press, 1998.

Trosset, Carol. *Welshness Performed: Welsh Concepts of Person and Society.* Tucson: University of Arizona Press, 1993.

4

Policing Tradition: Scottish Pipe Band Competition and the Role of the Composer

Jerry Cadden

If the motivation in our music were to come from searching for the groove instead of searching for the trophy, I think our place in the world of music would be much healthier.

—Craig Colquhoun, bass drummer, 78th Fraser Highlanders Pipe Band (ON)1

There's a big difference between winning and them letting you have it.

—Nat Russell, Pipe Major, Victoria (AU) Police Pipe Band

Throughout more than a century of history and "tradition," the Scottish pipe band has been an evolving ensemble, though the pace of change until the 1980s has seemed (outwardly) very slow. The accretion of drummers to groups of pipers in the British Army Highland regiments in the late nineteenth century marked the first instance of a regulated ensemble (pipers having been mustered into the army some one hundred years earlier), but an aesthetic of musical composition and unified performance did not exist until much later. Ironically, real integration and concern for concerted musicality is a direct by-product of music competition, in all its contention and restriction. Only when bands began to be adjudicated against one another did the need arise to quantify, and, thus, *control* music. Pipers' and drummers' attempts to work within the rigid framework of competition forced an adherence to a central idea of tradition, but those attempts also provided a spark for the musical creativity that defines what community members think of as the "forefront" of the genre.

119

Music competition is a complex phenomenon, having qualities of both aesthetic competition (rather like a "juried" art exhibition) as well as qualities more at home in a more physical arena. Analogies to sport are frequent in Celtic music competition, with perennial crowd favorites and trainspotter logs and league tables being compiled by both competitors and fans alike. In practical terms, all music competitions share certain categories that can be empirically judged: technical proficiency, intonation, rhythmic precision. The categories outside empiricism, however, provide the most interesting field of study: ideas such as "ensemble"[2] are thrown about with abandon in this gray area, always bumping into other equally poorly defined ideas such as "musicality" and "effect." In this chapter, however, I am mainly interested in competition as an institution central to the globalization of the Scottish pipe band and in the way it is used to control innovation, to police "tradition," and to mediate a cautious engagement with other kinds of music, in particular those of the Western European art and popular music traditions, and those of Celtic world more broadly conceived.

BEATING STANDARDS, STANDARD BEATINGS

My interest in this community has focused on the relationship between pipers and drummers, pipe tunes and drum scores, and the ways in which composition of these two elements has varied from generation to generation and from band to band, driven always by the competition circle. Conventional wisdom holds that the two types of music involved, melodic and percussive, can (and most often do) exist separately. Roles in early pipe bands were clearly defined—composing pipers were responsible for the musical direction of the band, composed pipe tunes in relative creative isolation from drummers, and dictated a secondary mode of composition for drummers. In its strictest sense, this relationship formed the practice of writing "standard beatings" for side (or snare) drum.

Pragmatically speaking, standard beatings for drummers enabled ease of teaching and facilitated adding more than one band together to play as a "massed band." Importantly, the practice fostered the composition of a common store of musical knowledge from which to draw for composing percussion scores to nonstandard tunes. Since the overwhelming majority of pipe tunes were (and still are) composed in "common," or "symmetrical," meters—2/4, 3/4, 4/4, and 6/8[3]—the regular 8-measure phrase structure means that structural markers in the pipe tunes tend to happen at roughly the same points in phrases in each tune, making the corpus fertile ground for regularization in percussion scores.

As soon as I began to do fieldwork within the community I noticed, however, that this model not only no longer obtained, but also was often used as a rhetorical basis for how *not* to proceed in composition. With an eye toward history, composers can certainly reference older styles but most actually see this as a yardstick of how far their compositional technique has evolved. For example, lower grade bands—bands often made up of younger players or older novice players—still use a modified system of applying a standard drum beating to a pipe tune. Parade sets of marches, played one right after another in groupings of three or four tunes, use standard metrical drum beatings almost exclusively.[4] One way in which higher grade bands musically distance themselves from each other and from those in the lower competition grades is by either composing their own "standard beatings" (one 4/4, one 6/8, etc.) for their parade sets, or by composing a special new drum score for each military march they play.

From its inception as a military ensemble, the Scottish pipe band has occupied a dual position as military (and later, civil ceremonial) ensemble and musical ensemble. In addition to finally being molded into a visual and sonic icon for a nation and its public face, the ensemble has been forced to accommodate both these roles when creating musical material. The military heritage (which still exists, though in ever-narrowing circles for budgetary reasons) demands precision and standardization, while musical concerns drive toward creativity and innovation. However, owing in part to the military heritage of many early pipers and drummers and their role in the foundation of the modern pipe band movement, the community has struck a sort of compromise between rigidity and flexibility that is at the very core of the music's characteristic sound and function.

A generally conceded date for the first "official" pipe band in the British Army is 1854, though such pay records as exist in regimental museums are contradictory on the precise meaning and timing of "pipe band." By way of explanation, pipes and drums had existed as functionary instruments in the Highland regiments of the British army since at least 1677. However, anecdotal and archival evidence suggests that pipes were either paid as solo instrumentalists or as a group of pipers for official functions, and drummers were meant to beat reveille and mess calls, as well as battle orders and retreats.[5] Pipers were officially added to the army's payroll in September 1745, with each independent company raised by Duncan Forbes, Laird of Culloden and Lord President of the Court in Session, comprising one hundred men with a piper and a drummer.[6]

We know little of the early history of duties of these musicians other than a supposition from late-nineteenth-century duties. Scholars can deduce that, even at this time, government authorities were well aware of the power of the Highland bagpipes to serve as a sonic and visual icon for national pride or as a fomenter of unrest, if only from the famous quote attributed to Sir Walter Scott: "Twelve Highlanders and a bagpipe make a rebellion."[7] In addition to being useful tools for marking daily time in a regiment and sounding battle calls, the Highland pipes (and later, pipe bands) came to symbolize the Scottish regiments' famous hallmarks: pride in country (Scotland, and, by extension, the United Kingdom), fierceness in battle, and devotion to the Crown.

Pipe bands as an entity, being a late-nineteenth-century phenomenon, coalesced almost in tandem in their military and civilian forms. Though scant records exist, there is evidence of pipe band competitions in the upper Midwest of the United Sates as early as 1864,[8] marking the phenomenon as both extremely rapid and as an intercontinental development. It was from the military, however, that early methods of composition and ensemble formation for pipe bands took their cue, both because of the widespread military experience of pipers and drummers at that time and because of the pseudo-military ceremonial function early (and, to an extent, modern) pipe bands serve. Separation between composing for pipes and composing for drums was set up as a function of early "standard beatings" for snare drum, and continues as a norm to the present day.[9]

Drum "standards" formed the early core of the modern pipe band drumming repertoire. Having numerous practical functions, these broadly interchangeable percussion pieces complement the early history of the pipe band as an ensemble that played a corpus of "traditional" tunes at various mandated times of the day in a military setting. In this setting the function of the pipe band was different from its civilian incarnation. Rather than concentrating on a limited repertoire in preparation for an also limited number of competitions, military bands had a vast repertoire of pipe tunes associated with specific military events and the daily sonic cycle of the regiment. In addition, the Highland Regiments were often called on to perform in "massed band" settings, arguing for introduction of pan-regimental standardization both in pipe tunes and in the drum settings meant to accompany those pipe tunes.

Perhaps the earliest model for true standardization in repertoire was initiated by the Scottish Division of the British Army in the 1930s. With the publication of *The Army Manual of Bagpipe Tunes and Drum Beatings, Book 1* in 1934,[10] the foundation was laid for the model of pipe band composition that was to form the modern idiom, with all its complexities and shortcomings. On this groundwork was laid a foundation for teaching students, solidifying competitive practices, and fostering and continuing the participation of ex-military musicians.

Pragmatism is the watchword for this compositional style. Simply stated, when one gathers different military bands from throughout the Scottish Division into a large massed band performance (or, indeed, civilian pipe bands for a closing massed bands ceremony at a modern Highland games), the sheer numbers of performers and the dearth of rehearsal time makes "instant ensemble"[11] necessary, a feat that would be impossible without some preordained repertoire that is assumed to be held in common across the performing groups. The assertion cannot be made that this divide between composing for pipes and composing separately for snare drums has "harmed" pipe band composition, but the point can be made that this long history of separate realms makes recent developments (since the mid-1980s) all the more revolutionary.

In order to understand how the system of snare drum standard beatings works in pipe bands, one merely has to look at the structure of both the pipe tunes and the drum beatings side by side. While the bagpipe repertoire is remarkably diverse and contains a large number of musically interesting compositions, certain patterns can be easily observed across the board. When analyzed for structure, one immediately sees that important musical moments occur in the same position of each phrase, giving the music the highly symmetrical look and sound of much of the Western European folk dance music to which piping tunes are closely related. This broad similarity is particularly true of the gracings that adorn pipe tunes and serve as separators for adjacent same-note melodic patterns.[12] These patterns of secondary notes provide rhythmic support for the melody, tying it directly to a rhythmic structure that can be exploited in percussion writing.

This feature of Scottish traditional music's phrase structure (also true of much of Irish traditional music) allows for the interchangeability that is a hallmark of the repertoire of standard drum beatings. With structural norms governing the inner architecture of pipe tunes, percussion scores that provide support to the structure, rather than the specific tune, can be easily composed. Indeed, drummers in the pipe band community note that scores matching the time signatures for even newly composed pipe tunes can be substituted for the newly composed drum scores and can be played as a sort of last resort; the architectural similarities between phrases in new composition are as prevalent as those in so-called traditional tunes.[13] Though the standard settings survive today as drum scores for massed band marches in various time signatures, a standard drum beating in 6/8 will correspond to a double jig (also in 6/8) in important musical ways.

It is important to remember that musicians never see the music presented as a connected "grand staff." The standard beatings are printed, distributed, learned, and played without regard to the melodic content that will accompany them, and the pipe tunes are played with the assurance that these standard settings (or settings very like these) will accompany the melody. Uniform compatibility of structure within the repertoire is the assumed factor that makes the system work both musically and practically.

The standard snare drum beatings system revolves around time rather than melody, making it is possible to play these standard beatings with any tune of a corresponding time signature. A 6/8 march beating can, in an emergency, serve for a snare drum accompaniment to a jig in 6/8, as can a 2/4 march beating for a 2/4 hornpipe, and so on. Correspondences between like time signatures include measure pairings, structural nodes in the phrases, and formulaic endings. It is therefore ironic that most of what outside musicians might call "the musical aspects" of performance (dynamics, rests, phrasing) come from the side of the band that began its labors under the extreme sanction of a system of "standards."

Throughout this standard beating system, pipe band drummers, though seemingly operating in a fixed system, have always been responsible for musical expression—insertion of the dynamics, accents, and phrasing—which are difficult or impossible to accomplish with the constant-pressure bagpipe. One final feature that helps to move the standard beatings system into a position where it can be understood as the basis for modern pipe band drumming composition is the practice of *forte* and *piano* sections within pipe band marches. The terms used for these sections correspond to their meanings in Western classical music ("loud" and "soft," respectively), but each section has a special application. Within pipe band composition and playing there certainly exists a practice of writing dynamic expression into the musical score. However, hearkening back to military applications, not all players play at the once, both creating a barrier of rank between the leading drummer and the drum corps and forcing a soft/loud dichotomy on the music.

Traditionally, this divide was caused by and/or resulted from a difference of ability in the leading drummer of the military pipe band (called the drum major or drum sergeant, denoting actual military rank) and his drum corps.[14] In order to accommodate this difference in ability (i.e., to "thin" the drum sound that results when players of varying abilities play in unison), the leading drummer in this system plays certain parts in the "piano" section of the phrase (the first time through a "part") alone. The entire corps plays the rest of the music with him, in unison. The "forte" section, by contrast, though a simple repeat of both the pipe tune and exact drum score of the part, utilizes all the drummers playing in unison throughout. Though the resulting effect resembles the terraced dynamics of the Baroque period in Western classical music, it still does provide a rudimentary move toward a fully realized use of dynamics as used in modern pipe band music. Modern performance practice features both a residual idea of piano and forte sections and the characteristic lead drummer/drum corps dichotomy.

In the modern pipe band, the split between lead drummer's part and the corps parts is more nuanced and used more for musical effect than in the formulaic way of the military march repertoire. Though the leading drummer still plays the entire drum score as in the military tradition, the corps parts do not follow strict guidelines. Composers write a series of "chips" or "seconds"[15] denoting where the entire drum corps should play, most often for rhythmic accent or dynamic effect. Individual composers' compositional styles have as much to do with choice of placement for chips as with actual rhythmic content, with drummers sometimes being able to discern a score's author by listening to chip patterns, or being able to "play the seconds" to a certain score from musical instinct (i.e., by knowing the composer's musical history and his style of chip writing).[16]

In an interesting corollary, the visual military image of the pipe band takes its cue from musical concerns in this respect also. Drum majors in pipe bands have two different modes of marching when leading bands (though, in reality, drum majors are little more than "window dressing,"[17] with the leading piper being responsible for setting tempos and directing tune changes). During the "piano" section, or first time through each part, the drum major marches in a fairly subdued manner, holding his mace down and close to his body, almost cradled in the crook of his left arm and barely swinging to the beat of the music. In direct relationship with the music, the drum major uses the forte section for each march part to be visually "louder," utilizing tosses, spins, walk-throughs,[18] and other flourishes to add impact to the band's performance.

One of the characteristics that practitioners of the form look for in order to assess a drum major's ability and awareness of the music going on behind him or her is the knowledge of when to flourish and when to "be quiet." Though evidence is only anecdotal and modern performance practice does not hold to this rule, the modern practice of drum majors linking themselves closely to the musical sound is a vestige of the standard beating and piano/forte military system; though modern drum majors may perhaps have never led a drum corps, the military rank system was set up with the drum major and the drum sergeant both having definite military rank. A drum major, the highest-ranking drummer in the regiment, would have at one time played with the corps. Once a military drum major achieves the rank of major, duties shift, in the main, away from musical performance to administrative duties, with the drum major marching in front of the band, but the connection with musical practice is retained and passed on to civilian practice and competition in much the same way that compositional norms and performance practice have been.

NONSTANDARDS

The most innovative model of composition in pipe bands today, however, is a model of compositional integration used to some degree by the Victoria Police Pipe Band of Melbourne, Australia, and to a much greater degree by the Shotts and Dykehead Caledonia Pipe Band (referred to as the "SDCPB"). Rather than take as read the time-honored methodology of writing music that isolates one half of the ensemble from the other, present-day (or "modern" composers, both those of a younger generation and those from previous generations with forward-leaning musical styles) prefer to take all aspects of a unified musical aesthetic into account when they compose. It is clear from conversations with Robert Mathieson and Jim Kilpatrick, the leading piper and drummer in the Shotts band, that this methodology is a conscious effort to link Scottish traditional music with more "modern" forms of music—ironically, in this case, forms such as common practice Western classical music and Western-influenced popular music.

The Shotts compositional model is deceptively simple, practically speaking. Mathieson and Kilpatrick utilize their long-standing musical collaboration to "second-guess" what the other will write in certain circumstances, and not only compose with this in mind but also "try out" musical ideas on each other, searching for advice as the competition season's tunes are written into the lineup. During the project of publishing their music, in which I was involved, Mathieson's observations about this process were invaluable, helping me to gain insight into what I had thought were some salient features of his compositions—percussive use of melodic grace note patterns, syncopation, rhythmic melodic writing—finding that these elements of the tunes were actually elements of Kilpatrick's drumming style transferred to a melodic line for bagpipes.

The compositional methodology has proven so successful in competition in the past decade that it is now utilized as a theoretical groundwork for solo and band recording projects as well. As this approach to pipe banding has developed over the last six years (under the watchful gaze of the fieldworker), it has become nuanced into an approach not only for musical choices but also for choices about ways in which Scottish traditional music can be made to "pay its own way." Tunes that were once just written for "medley slots" are now composed with an eye toward integration with the other half of the ensemble (pipes or percussion), toward how the ensemble adjudicator will feel about the tunes, toward tie-ins with any future albums, and toward a larger and ongoing "Scottish" marketing effort.

It is interesting that the SDCPB won the World Championships in 1997 and lost in 1998 to the only other band with a musical "identity" at the moment, the Victoria Police Pipe Band (a band that was still operating, in the main, under the older "separate" model of composing pipe and drum scores).[19] For the dissertation project, a conjunct investigation of some aspects of the Victoria Police band strengthens my basic premise that shades of innovation are cautiously weighed each year against a requirement for tradition: The Australians have managed to be one of the most musically aggressive voices for change in the genre in the past decade, but have always simply "changed." In other words, rather than take a cautious attitude toward change and "newness" in musical competition, the band has played some radically new—and very crowd-pleasing—music in recent years, only to finish a perennial third or fourth place in the World Championships.

Composition in the pipe band community is a balancing act between moving away and "staying put." The two composers with whom I've worked most closely are certainly not the only composers writing new music for pipe band, but their special methodology allows them a rarefied place in the current pipe banding community. Though I've concentrated on their music separately in my other work, their approach to "ensemble" and the ways in which that approach informs their writing both reaches back into past practice and broadens the genre in new directions, with both musical and competitive success and failure. Indeed, by paying special attention to the musical possibilities in an oft-neglected area of the competition medley, the slow air that always occurs in the middle of the tune-grouping, the composers and the band have managed a redefinition of musicality within the band community.

In discussions within the pipe band activity, one finds that Mathieson and Kilpatrick are both most often thought of as composers of something other than airs, for different and very specific reasons. Pipe band music has its own canon that, while akin to the canon of Western classical music, seems to include more extramusical factors than its classical counterpart. Both composers are central to this canon, but each for different reasons that point toward the same goal—competitive success.

Kilpatrick's position as a composer is more "traditional" than Mathieson's, as well as more mythic. Known most readily for his scores for solo competition, Kilpatrick's fame depends to a great extent on his own success as a solo competing artist and as a leader. Kilpatrick scores circulate as broadside ballads and folksongs once did, becoming a sort of musical currency handed around as degenerating photocopies of handwritten manuscript rather than as printed editions. None of the scores has ever been actually "authorized" as official and sanctioned, and, therefore, "legal," though Kilpatrick himself has provided some copies of some scores to friends, colleagues, and students. The most obvious reason for this lies buried in the competition structure, and particularly in the traditional MSR. Although competing pipe corps might conceivably enter a competition and all be playing the same traditional march, strathspey, and reel, the custom drum scores are highly personal and particular to a specific band. Not only might the propriety of the drum score and the nuance within it have a great influence on the outcome of the competition, but these factors might actually win or lose an MSR competition in the top competitive grade, hence an air of near-secrecy.[20] To that end, Kilpatrick (and his colleagues at the top of the drumming ranks) are most known by average players and learners as composers of long-form competition marches and reels. Competitors at all levels have a perception of his music as "winning," certainly strengthened by Kilpatrick's own overwhelming presence as a solo player for the last twenty years, as well as his reputation for being particularly sensitive to musical line and melody.[21]

Conversely, Mathieson's place in the canon is assured in the main by a phenomenon that closely parallels American radio's Top 40 system. His own abilities as a leader of winning pipe bands and as a successful solo recording artist come into play to an extent, but the largest factor here is the sheer availability of his compositions, both sonically and materially. With three books of compositions and three solo albums, all currently in print and selling well, Mathieson does not suffer from (nor benefit from) the supply-and-demand theory in the way that Kilpatrick does. Young players and lower-grade pipe bands, however, are steady and voracious consumers and programmers of Mathieson tunes, though some of his contemporaries speak of Mathieson's success in terms of overexposure and ubiquity.[22] Mathieson's popularity is most apparent when pipers are warming up alone, before forming into bands: His reels and jigs are known "finger-wigglers," showing off a player's technique while at the same time having catchy melodies and heavy syncopation.

Thus both composers bring different sets of public perceptions to the genre of the slow air—a tune type not only not known for its flash and accessibility but also not known for being an area of innovation or even "concern." Slow airs played in competition often seem to be merely placeholders, separating a moderately paced first half of the competition medley from a much faster closing section. Musical interest seems to wane, in both audience and competitors, making slow airs often seem to be musical "throw-aways." Airs hold an esteemed place in other genres of Scottish traditional music, as well as in other Celtic musics (most notably the Irish tradition). In the pipe banding activity, however, airs seldom garner much attention.

With perhaps one exception, composers that were interviewed in the course of this research speak of writing the tune (melodic line) of a new composition in its entirety, either straight onto manuscript or after "improvising" on a practice chanter or set of smallpipes until the tune has formed in their ear. They do not, however, often think of harmonies while composing the original tune; in other words, harmony is not an initial or structural factor in composition, but, rather, a performative aspect. The compositional process and structure of Mathieson's airs mark them as members of a growing number of tunes in which harmony and percussion orchestration were paramount at the time of composition.

ENSEMBLING

This new direction toward full integration is important as one of the few truly "new" occurrences in piping composition in the last twenty years because of the way in which the composers write "ensemble" into the music. In the pipeband community, musical ensemble has a nuanced meaning that comes under constant scrutiny and definition each competition season. Rather than speaking of the instruments or players themselves as a collective entity (in the traditional sense of ensemble), the term has musical meaning both for the members as musicians and for the adjudicators who police the aesthetics of the activity that almost reaches into the indefinable.

In order to ascertain just how a new compositional model can effect major changes in this community, ensemble itself must be examined. Judging in pipe band competitions treats ensemble as an important component of a competing band's total score, even having a separate adjudicator for the category.[23] Percentage of the final score allotted for ensemble judging seems negligible: Two piping judges account for 50 percent of the total score, one drumming judge a further 25 percent, and the ensemble judge contributing 25 percent. However, in a move that has been copied round the pipe band world, the RSPBA (the Royal Scottish Pipe Band Association) stipulates that, in the event of a tie, the ensemble judge casts the first tie-breaking vote.[24] According to my fellow musicians, this simply indicates that all adjudication and competition in pipe banding revolves, at its base, around musicality and "The Music," rather than competition. The concept of ensemble, though, is entirely problematic, both from a musicians and an adjudicator's standpoint.

In determining that another category was needed to clarify placings in competition, the Music Board of the RSPBA originally envisioned ensemble as something that might denote coherence and musicality.[25] The Association quickly became aware of the difficulty of quantifying musicality, however. In truth, in the thirteen years I have been involved with pipe banding as a performing musician, band administrator, and researcher, not one satisfactory definition of ensemble judging has ever presented itself, making the term *ensemble* a loaded one for players and a controversial one for adjudicators and governing bodies. Technical execution, including such factors as note errors, intonation in the pipe corps, rhythmic precision in the snare drum corps, and tuning and setup[26] of the snare drums, is adjudicated by the piping judges and the drumming judge. These judges also evaluate intercorps precision—in effect, whether all the pipers and drummers are playing together as two separate groups or as a unified whole. Finally, the drumming judge considers the propriety of the scores the leading drummer has composed or chosen to accompany the pipe tunes. This seems to be exhaustive coverage of the musical activity, leaving little for the ensemble judge to consider in awarding his score.

Ensemble is a complex idea precisely because of its problematic position in competition. The ensemble judge is charged with evaluating a number of aspects of performance, though none exactly matches a Western classical idea of technical "togetherness." One of the most interesting is the notion of evaluating the performance as a "total package." Not only is technical "togetherness" a small aspect of ensemble consideration, but aesthetic concerns also enter the broader picture here. Construction of tune groupings is listened to closely for unity and flow (a logical movement from one tune type, key signature, or time signature to another), for fit within a tradition, and for other such inexact variables as difficulty, originality, and musical content. Finally, the ensemble judge also considers the other corps that has no direct judge of its own: the "midsection" of tenor drums with bass drum, considering both tone and intonation of these drums as well as the way in which they "knit" the two other corps together musically. When the duties of an ensemble judge are put on paper, they seem a nearly impossible task; in fact, after every major championship, legions of pipers and drummers discuss the vagueness of this area of judging in "beer tents" and, more recently, on the Internet. Ensemble as a concept gives the modern pipe band genre its special character but also continues to lend it a negative aura of mystery and judging secrecy that helps to drive the competitiveness of the form.

Ensemble as a concept is also crucial to understanding the success and influence of the SDCPB and its peer, the Victoria Police Pipe Band of Melbourne, Australia, during the competition seasons of 1997 and 1998. Both of these bands competed at the highest levels of the genre, with the SDCPB winning the World Championship in 1997 and the Victoria Police band winning in 1998. Close followers and musicians within the activity thought of the bands certainly as aggressive rivals, but also as two bands with similar musical voices, sometimes even referred to as "ensemble bands."[27] Both bands approached the problems of defining ensemble differently but achieved the same end result: competitive success.

The SDCPB traversed the 1996–98 major championship circuit with a string of successes that other bands certainly envied: thirteen wins in fifteen championship competitions. One consistent factor across all the competition successes was a growing sense that top pipe bands were developing a theory of the meaning of ensemble in competition. Though the Shotts pipe corps had matured into as consistent a group as the drum corps had always been, fans and other musicians noted a growing concern with original composition in both the pipe tunes and drum scores chosen by the SDCPB's leaders for competition.[28] Starting in 1996 and fully in force in the 1997 competition season, Mathieson began to program only original tunes in his competition medleys, with the exception of the two traditional strathspeys. Interestingly, this most Scottish of dance forms is not considered an area for new composition where competition is concerned. In speaking of strathspeys, Mathieson claims that a leading pipe major could never program originally composed (i.e., modern) strathspeys in a competition medley, the medley's "modern" feel notwithstanding.[29] Mathieson's compositional style is particularly well suited to medley composition, and the SDCPB is known as a "medley band."

The 1997 competition season marked the beginning of a commercial rise for both Mathieson and Kilpatrick's careers as musicians and a fully realized Shotts "treatment" of the ensemble ideal. Since all tunes (except the strathspeys) were composed by Mathieson, all were written in collaboration with and contemporaneously with Kilpatrick's drum scores. Mathieson's 2/4 polka "The First Fifty," composed in honor of the fiftieth anniversary of the "open era" sanctioned world championships, is a prime example of Mathieson's metaphorical use of ensemble, while feeding in to his musical ideas of the term. The polka, the lead-off tune of the competition medley, was printed on the inside back cover of the official program for the championships—breaking an unwritten rule in pipe banding that holds that a certain mutual "anonymity" should be enforced between competing bands and the governing association.[30]

Though the SDCPB was successful with this medley and its reliance on interplay between musical elements, "ensemble" in this case was seen as a more all-encompassing idea during this competition season. Many followers of the form noted that the 1997 incarnation of the SDCPB marks the first incarnation of a marriage of musical and nonmusical ideas of ensemble in the pipe band arena. In addition to close musical collaboration, the band entered the fray with a number of extramusical tie-ins. While commercialism and marketing had, by 1997, begun to become common factors in Grade 1 pipe bands' public identity, the Shotts summer of 1997 push was seen as unprecedented by attendees to the championships and by fellow competing musicians. In addition to the tie-in between Mathieson's tune choice and the RSPBA's official program for the event, the community noticed the conflux of Mathieson's album launch and R. T. Shepherd's heavy sales promotion of it. In some ways, Mathieson told me later, he was interested in an "Americanization" of the pipe band form.[31] (When pressed it became apparent that he actually meant a combination of "North Americanization" and "modernization.")

He sees these terms as a set of parallel lines of commercial and artistic possibility. Though Mathieson remains involved in the high political circles of the local Scottish organization (the RSPBA, in this instance, is very "local"), he sees the genre as in desperate need of modernization, coming from within the bands themselves and moving outward into the organization (and the activity) as a whole. From the standpoint of the players and leaders of the SDCPB, the various tie-ins perceived by the public were not necessarily meant to influence competition at all, but, rather, to move away from the standard thinking in Scotland that a band such as Shotts and Dykehead can rely on its history and tradition to remain a vital participant in the pipe band community.[32] By moving the band as a "product," not as a somewhat mythically successful musical group, into the public eye, Mathieson sought access to the same audience achieved by peer ensembles, most particularly the Simon Fraser University Pipe Band and the Victoria Police Pipe Band, both of which competed at the same level as the SDCPB and both of which were perceived as "new" and "vital" by virtue of their foreignness and popular appeal.

COMPLETE PACKAGING

The story of the Victoria Police Pipe Band is somewhat atypical and a comparison to Shotts and Dykehead reveals the problematic aspects of crafting a single unified model of the modern pipe band genre. Much of my own opinions about pipe band music relies to a great extent on public reaction to uncover what practitioners of the music considered to be unusual or "groundbreaking" in the form. Invariably, the two bands most often pointed to were the SDCPB and the Victoria Police.[33] Unlike Shotts and Dykehead's long history of winning championships, the Victoria Police band was a relatively new ensemble, without a single win at a major championships in Scotland until 1998. Logistics played a major role in this: Raising money to bring a group of pipers and drummers from Australia to compete in Scotland is prohibitively expensive, making a once-yearly trip to the World Championships a singular event—and cutting down dramatically on the band's chances to win major championships in Scotland.

Pipe Major Nat Russell was born in Northern Ireland and served as Pipe Major for the Royal Ulster Constabulary's pipe band in

Belfast, competing successfully in Grade 1 until he emigrated from Northern Ireland to Australia. Russell became leader of the regional police force's pipe band at the request of Commander Roger Reid, an influential figure in the Australian pipe band scene.[34] According to Russell, his goal from the outset was to assemble a prize-winning pipe band and return to Scotland to win the World Championships.[35] Though this seemed a rather pointed comment about music competition, I was to learn that Russell had a complex view of both traditional music and its incarnation in diasporic communities as well as the specific role of the pipe band in Scotland and abroad. Though success in competition was certainly a goal, this success was, because of the Victoria band's geographical location, commercial and financial from the outset.

After one season of competing in Grade 2, the Victoria Police Pipe Band became a perennial entry in the prize list at the World Championships. Russell likened the situation to the "always a bridesmaid, never a bride" cliché, though the band was consistently within reach of the title. Interestingly, the pipe banding community views the now-defunct[36] Victoria Police band as one of the most consistently entertaining recording bands in the history of the activity. The band had from the beginning of its rise to prominence cultivated its dual personality as a solid competitor as well as a "product" to be consumed through recording.

The musical personalities of the SDCPB and the Victoria Police band are both closely related and strikingly different. On the one hand, Russell consciously crafted the sound of his band to rely on tone and technique in the piping section, producing a more "traditional" image than Shotts and Dykehead's characteristic and overt "newness." However, Russell also cultivated a system of band camaraderie and interactivity that gave the band's public image a sense of unity, as if the sound, musical character, and presence of the band were one—for the pipe band community, this indicated "ensemble" in every sense of the word. Both bands were seen to be near the front of the form, leading the music in ways that might indicate a closer adherence to some unity principle than was either "traditional" or practical, a utopian ideal of pipe banding.[37]

The Australians had a musical "team" of sorts, as well. Though not melded together as a band by co-composers in both corps as were Shotts and Dykehead with Mathieson and Kilpatrick, the Victoria band had as pipers and composers two of the most innovative

writers for pipe band in the 1990s, Mark Saul and Murray Blair. In
the eyes of the community, the sound of the Victoria Police band was
the sound of Saul and Blair playing off each other as composers in
the competition medley, combining the tunefulness characteristic of
Mathieson's output with what was perceived as a greater degree of
technical difficulty.

The band's commercial face as a recording unit, however, became
paramount during its last competitive season. "Ensemble" was to
play a role not only in the band's Scottish tour, but also in its con-
current album release and concert in Motherwell, Scotland. The 1998
release of the band's third album, *Masterblasters*, was timed to coin-
cide with the concert and the championship competition, permeat-
ing the year's activities in much the same way as Mathieson's successful solo release and the SDCPB's win the year before. Issues of
marketing and product placement fed into the public perception of
the concert itself,[38] with the band utilizing a "multimedia" format
that was until that time almost unheard of in pipe banding. Far from
being a "traditional" concert (either in terms of programming traditional music or in terms of following past norms for concert format),
the *Masterblasters* concert had the aura of a rock concert. Amplified
backing tracks written and recorded by the band's composers overlaid the music, T-shirts and albums were on sale in the lobby, and the
unease of the "traditionalist" faction in the audience was apparent.[39]

The technical facility for which the band was rightly famous was
astounding to many seeing the band for the first time, with the
group playing concert versions of the fast tunes that were part of
their recorded reputation. Russell did, however, program the band's
complete competition repertoire of MSR sets and competition medleys, providing, in his estimation, a firm grounding in the tradition
of the music to go along with the "newness."[40]

The concert was a commercial success, if not a complete critical
success. Most of the negative reaction was along staunch traditionalist lines. The backing tracks and "world music" instruments that
helped give the band its musical character (and were an integral part
of the compositions) were seen as "detractors." In rehearsal the next
day, the band was concerned that the reception of their concert
might have a negative impact on their competitive success, but the
implications of the "world tour" approach were apparent. Re-
hearsals at the band's perennial home in Scotland, Glasgow's Glen-
hill Hotel, were overrun with curious musicians and well-wishers,

eager to gain insight into the workings of the band and hone their own rehearsal and playing techniques.

The crucial moment for the history of pipe banding lies in the fact that both these bands were successful at the World Championships in their respective "complete package" years. *Complete package* is a term that has come to mean something nearly analogous to ensemble. Bands that are making a move from asserting their competitive dominance in ways other than technical prowess in the competition circle—by a combination of developing a marketing strategy, a distinct musical voice, or a unified public persona—are said to be "complete packages." Though one cannot say that all pipe banding has turned (or will or can turn) to this model, it is instructive to note that not only have these bands been the most successful in recent years[41] but that other top Grade 1 bands are beginning to move in the same artistic direction. Recording projects are consistently moving away from strict competition material and toward more eclectic offerings, and bands are promoting recordings and souvenir merchandise on Web sites and at competitions. None of this activity is specifically judged on the competition field by the ensemble judge, but all of it enters the public arena as part of the genre's reception history, as part of the ensemble perception of the community.

Civilian pipe bands themselves contain perhaps the most striking clue that this is a music about boundaries, definition, competition, and rules: The most successful pipe band of the "open" era was the Strathclyde Police Pipe Band under Pipe Major Ian McLellan. The history of major championship wins was dominated by various police and military units until the 1990s, with many of the rules of competition concretized during the years between 1950 and 1980. The analogy between policing and pipe banding is a necessary one, both because of the civilian band's debt to the military and the police, and because of the reliance by the form on rules and regulations to make music happen "properly."

The RSPBA has as part of its constitution Rule 1.4: "To devise and operate a proper system of Pipe Band Contest Rules."[42] The phenomenon of musical competition practically insists, however, that these rules will need to address as many nonmusical components as musical ones. Music competitions as varied as *Comhaltas Ceoltóirí Eireann*, Drum Corps International, and the British Federation of Brass Bands make multiple allowances within their contesting structure for elements that make no sonic contribution but are deemed crucial for the proper presentation, and, thus, adjudication of music.

CONCLUSION

Creativity and musicality exist in the framework of competition almost at their own peril. In the realm of the Scottish pipe band, the goals seem more about the maintenance of tradition that the invention of tradition. Though the early codifiers were concerned with putting something on paper to install a perceived level playing field for increasingly diverse participants, the arena of music competition steadfastly refuses many "innovations" as a means of shoring up what traditional music "is," how it "sounds," and why one partakes. Though rules don't necessarily hinder music, the process is not uncomplicated, nor is it "one way," or entirely exclusionary, as I have tried to demonstrate in this chapter. In the Scottish pipe band world, one that continues to thrive in the British postimperium, music competition sets up a standard of near-global reach to judge what is "good" or "well played," and a discourse within which musicians can maintain, police, and reaffirm what "tradition" might mean. It also provides a controlled context within which this same sense of "tradition" might engage with a broader and self-consciously "modern" sense of the world in which it is embedded.

NOTES

1. Quoted from *Piper and Drummer*, November 1996, in an article discussing ensemble technique and "the music between the notes."

2. In most cases, the word *ensemble* doesn't mean "Is there one?" in the physical sense of "a body of players" in competition, but, rather, the way in which the music coalesces into a pleasing, appropriate, or even "proper" sound.

3. Time signatures of 9/8 and 12/8 are also frequently used in jig composition. While these signatures are sometimes asymmetrically divided in Western classical music, they fall neatly into Celtic music's ideas of rhythmic symmetry.

4. Pipe bands in North America most often use a sort of *urtext* set of standard beatings (that of the Pipers and Pipe Band Society of Ontario) as their

model, codifying even more concretely the unchanging "feel" of military marches.

5. Francis Collinson also rightly conjectures that, in regiments raised for the Crown in the Highlands such as *Am Freiceadan Dubh* (The Black Watch), a number of pipers would have been mustered in among regular recruits, making the presence of pipe (and fiddle) music for recreation a certainty. See Collinson 1975.

6. Collinson 1975, 166.

7. Attributed to Scott and supposedly appearing in an unpublished letter to J. W. Croker in 1829.

8. Records of the Detroit St. Andrews Society Highland Games record this date as their first games, with competitions in Ontario (1865) and the Chicago area (1869) following soon after.

9. It must be noted, however, that, in the modern competition scene, new compositions for the percussion section are written at all levels and for every new season. I use the term *norm* in this instance to denote the still-separate function of most writing for pipes and for drums.

10. This first volume was followed by *The Army Manual of Bagpipe Tunes and Drum Beatings, Book 2* in 1936. Both were British government publications.

11. As will be noted by any musician who has ever performed in a massed band setting, I speak here not necessarily of "good" or "musical" ensemble (in the words of my fellow pipe banders), but, rather, of simply having a greater majority of musicians playing the same thing at the same time.

12. Grace notes, or "gracings," function differently in Scottish Highland bagpipe music than they do in the Western classical tradition. While gracings in pipe tunes can certainly be considered adornment of the melody, they also serve a practical function: A constant-pressure instrument such as the Highland bagpipe can neither play "rests" nor differentiate between two adjacent melody notes of the same pitch. The gracings serve to provide the mentioned rhythmic structure and to allow a pipe to play discreet melody notes—an A followed by an A, for example.

13. Perhaps one of the most striking differences between Irish traditional music and Anglo-Scottish traditional music is the perception of what "traditional" means in the provenance of tunes. Though Irish traditional music has a parallel internal history of both tunes with credited authors and tunes with unknown composers, the overwhelming majority of tunes in the pipe band community's understanding of "traditional" tunes have named authors and have been published in government or privately published collections since their composition, the "Trad." composer listing notwithstanding.

14. Interview with Ian Millar, April 1993. A native of Aberdeenshire in Scotland, Millar was then playing as a drummer in the University of Chicago Pipe Band.

15. Reference to corps unison parts as "seconds" bears a striking resemblance to the terminology used for harmony parts written for pipe tunes. Piping "seconds" are sometimes considered afterthoughts of composition, and certainly "secondary"—the main musical idea (the melody or the leading drummer's score) exists in a position of primacy, with harmony and unison drum corps "seconds" enhancing musical effect but not being necessary for a "basic" performance.

16. Interview with Blair Brown, a very successful young solo drummer and corps drummer with the 78th Fraser Highlanders Pipe Band, Milton, Ontario, April 1999.

17. Interview with Peter Duffield, English ex-patriot and former drum major of the University of Chicago Pipe Band, August 1995.

18. A specialized move common to the British military, a walk-through is the use of a drum major's mace in a highly modified version of a walking stick motion. Rather than spinning or tossing the mace, the drum major brings it down to his right side in his right hand and executes a stylized four-count move that keeps the point of the mace in one place on the ground as the drum major "walks through" (around) it.

19. In dramatic developments in the 1998–1999 off-season for pipe bands, the Victoria Regional Administrator banned the Victoria Police Pipe Band from having civilians in its ranks (a practice accepted in the United Kingdom), forbade the band to use public funds for competing in Australia, forbade its raising money privately to go to Scotland to compete in August's World Championships, and is under negotiations with the Police Musical Unit to require all police musical ensembles to contribute a to-be-decided percentage of their outside musical income from nonpolice jobs to the Treasury. This has effectively killed the band's ability to be a force in musical circles, though it still exists as an ensemble.

20. Obviously once a score is played once in competition, this "secrecy" is compromised. But the importance lies in the fact that top grade bands guard against overexposure of drum scores, for, while teaching and composing and setting a good musical example are all aspects of pipe banding, the end goal is still competitive success.

21. As discussed in chapter 4, there is impending change: Kilpatrick is currently producing a book of drumming instruction and scores with the aid of computer music typesetting technology.

22. In formal and informal surveys of Highland Games in the American Midwest, Ontario, and Scotland, Mathieson compositions have heavily outnumbered any other composer in both solo "kitchen piping" and band competition since 1996—the publication date of the his second collection, *About Time Two*.

23. All detailed analysis of rules and regulations in Scottish competitions is based on *The Royal Scottish Pipe Band Association: Constitution and Rules* (*RSPBA* 1993).

24. *RSPBA* 1993, 29.

25. Interviews with the MacAllister brothers, members of the founding dynasty and former pipe majors of the Shotts and Dykehead band, March 1997.

26. Setup of Scottish snare drums for solo playing or for a corps performance remains one of the most mysterious and even secretive aspects of band performance. Though some attempts are being made at a set of procedures or aesthetic "rules," bands still go through a system of trial and error, adjusting tension of better (top) heads and snare mechanism height and tension, both in a search for a "proper" sound and, in an indirect way, in an effort to emulate the sound of experienced Grade 1 drum corps.

27. Group conversation among bystanders at a prechampionship rehearsal in the Shotts band hall, August 1997.

28. In speaking of the practice of "ensemble" in pipe banding, most musicians concern themselves with the competition medley, not with the more traditional MSR tune grouping. Though ensemble judges are present in both competitions, originality and musicality are more easily discussed in an arena that is known for original composition rather than "heavy" traditional tunes.

29. Typesetting conversations with Robert Mathieson, July 1996. In answer to a question about his reason for not composing many strathspeys (the smallest in number of the genres in his compositional output), Mathieson replied that the good ones had already been written and that there were so many good ones to choose from it was a waste of time to compose more.

30. The tune appears on page 84 of the program, with the following inscription: "We are grateful to P/M Robert Mathieson of Shotts and Dykehead Caledonia Pipe Band for specially composing this tune to mark the occasion of the 50th Anniversary World Pipe Band Championships."

31. Interview with Robert Mathieson, August 1998.

32. Interview with Robert Mathieson, August 1998.

33. Opinions varied, of course, reflecting a broad range of personal tastes and even nationalistic bents. Crucial to my own theories about pipe banding, a third band was often mentioned but then discarded as a band that doesn't figure into the top prize picture: the McNaughton's Vale of Atholl Pipe Band, a consistently innovative ensemble from north-central Scotland. In other words, though the Vale of Atholl band was seen as an interesting group of forward-thinkers, the bands that were explained as having influence were bands that could *win.*

34. Russell was later named to the post of Director of Music, putting him in charge of all musical ensembles under the control and funding of the Victoria Regional Police; in this capacity he was not only responsible for the administration of the pipe band (in which he served as leading piper) but was

also the commanding officer of various brass bands, pop and jazz ensembles, and vocal ensembles.

35. Interview with Nat Russell, August 1998.

36. In one of the most shocking turns of events in the recent collective memory of the community, the regional policing authority chose to completely reevaluate the band's duties after the 1998 competition season. Though the band had finally brought the championship to Australia after a decade of consistently good competition, the controlling authority banned the ensemble from raising money for travel and from competing with civilian pipers, effectively killing the program. A pipe band still exists in Melbourne, but the assembled stars of the Australian piping and drumming world that played in the band till its demise have moved on to other bands (even other continents) in pursuit of competitive opportunities.

37. It was often said in the course of my research that one could play in a band like the Simon Fraser Pipe Band (also consistent world champions and prize-winners) with enough hard work and dedication, whereas the SDCPB and the Victoria Police band were able to knit together in such a way that they managed to outdistance themselves from the competition musically.

38. The Glasgow Skye Association Pipe Band sponsors a concert at the Motherwell Civic Center each year on the Tuesday night before the World Championships. The event is timed to attract the greatest number of pipe band aficionados from around the world, and is seen as either a "good" thing for a top band to do (to increase exposure and to help foreign bands acclimate to jetlag and Scotland's weather before the championship) or a "bad" thing (making judges and audiences familiar with or weary of the band's music before the big day or sapping the band's energy for competition)—a dichotomy that is not unusual in traditional music circles.

39. Russell later told me that the programming of the concert had been a calculated risk: The band wanted to play music that expressed the musical identity of the group (with electronic backing and with the Aboriginal *didjeridu* prominent in many arrangements), but they were also aware that the adjudicators that they would play for in the championship contest would be in attendance as well and might not appreciate the eclectic and decidedly nontraditional flavor of the music.

40. Interview with Nat Russell, August 1998.

41. Since these two competition seasons, the Simon Fraser University Pipe Band, a musical antipode to the SDCPB and the Victoria Police band but perhaps the most "complete" complete package band in competition today, won the World Championships in 1999 and 2001, with the SDCPB taking the title in 2000.

42. *RSPBA* 1993, 1.

BIBLIOGRAPHY

The Army Manual of Bagpipe Tunes and Drum Beatings, Book 2, 1936.

Cannon, Roderick. *The Highland Bagpipe and Its Music.* Edinburgh: John Donald Publishers, Ltd. 2002. Orig. publ., 1988.

Collinson, Francis. *The Bagpipe: The History of a Musical Instrument.* London: Routledge and Kegan Paul, 1975.

Mathieson, Robert. *About Time Two.* Glasgow: ISA Music, 1996.

Mathieson, Robert. *Taking Notes.* Glasgow: ISA Music, 1997.

RSPBA. The Royal Scottish Pipe Band Association: Constitution and Rules. Rev. 1993. Glasgow: Royal Scottish Pipe Band Association, 1993.

5

Tradition and Imaginary: Irish Traditional Music and the Celtic Phenomenon

Scott Reiss

The phenomenon of "Celtic" music has made a remarkable impact in the music business in the past decade. But what is Celtic music? Is it the traditional music of Ireland, Scotland, Wales, Brittany, and other nations that share the heritage of the ancient Celts?[1] Or is it something separate, that might be understood as *interacting* with those traditional musics and the communities that produced them? This chapter is concerned with Ireland and the relationships between "Celtic" music and Irish traditional music.

Many critics contest the use of the term *Celtic* because it erases the boundaries between Irish, Scottish, Welsh, and Breton traditional musics. This criticism is both right and justified. Most Irish traditional musicians, and those people connected to the traditional music community, do not recognize Celtic as a musical category, referring to it as a "noncategory" or "the C word." The conflation of Irish, Scottish, and other styles enacted by the phrase "Celtic music" contradicts the local, regional, and national associations embodied in the music and its performance.

But this creates a paradox: Celtic music embraces those traditional musics whose proponents reject Celtic as a category. At the same time, the Celtic label is used more and more frequently as an identity marker in the commercial world within Ireland, to promote both goods and services (as in the many Celtic book stores, Celtic dairies, or even, as I saw on the side of a truck in Dublin, 'Celtic Movers'). The phrase "Celtic music" is sometimes used to include traditional music, particularly in commercial locations like the Celtic Note record shop in Dublin, which has an excellent collection of Irish and

Scottish traditional musics as well; or the periodical *Irish Music*, which often conflates the terms "Traditional" and "Celtic." Martin Hayes, a recording artist and fiddler from Co. Clare currently living in Seattle, has a travel story that illustrates this eloquently: "If somebody sees my fiddle case on an airplane, say, and asks me what I play I say 'Celtic music.' If I were to say Irish music he likely wouldn't know what I was talking about" (personal communication).

Notwithstanding the rejection by insiders in the tradition, the existence of Celtic music as a global category cannot be denied. But the difference between it and the various traditional musics that constitute its core can and should be drawn. My focus primarily on Irish traditional music provides a grounding in a living, and thriving, tradition in exploring Celtic music as an internationally recognized category. My view is that the two categories are separate, but overlapping. I examine the dynamic relationship between "Celtic" music, understood as media-driven and existing within a virtual community, and the community-based traditional musics of Ireland.

SOCIAL CONTEXT, COMMUNITY, AND SYMBOL

Irish traditional music is a social phenomenon as much as a musical one. The music is preserved, transmitted, shared, and developed in musical/social gatherings, at dances, pub sessions or informal playing occasions, as well as through a network of competitions and schools. But there is no absolute consensus in Ireland as to what traditional music is, or rather, what its boundaries are. To some Altan are traditional, but Anúna are not. To others Noel Hill is, but Sharon Shannon is not. To still others, Tommy Peoples is, but Martin Hayes is not. And for many, the simple act of participation in commercial music (which is, after all, what makes the aforementioned performers familiar to many listeners thousands of miles away) is problematic.

Traditional music defines not a single community, but multiple communities with overlapping senses of identity. What these communities share are the commonly held forms of songs (whether in Irish Gaelic or in English), dance tunes, and instrumental slow airs (often associated with *sean-nós* songs.) In my initial fieldwork I asked many people in Ireland "Where does the tradition reside?" and the response was overwhelmingly "In the tunes." But how the tunes are performed, configured, shared, and transmitted sets the boundaries for traditional music as it is constructed by various groups of people. Fintan Vallely's description of the basic social configuration of the music neatly sums up the views held by many musicians today: "'Traditional music' communities are normally either local, or united by a common aesthetic, a 'feel' for the interrelationships of players with their sources, audiences and their local history" (1997, 47).

This "feel" is also recognized in the style, the way of playing the music: "The interpretations of that 'way'—the *nya*, as it is known—are what carve up traditional music itself into its different interpretive camps" (Vallely 1997, 150).

Local styles have historically distinguished the playing of musicians from different regions in Ireland. Local and regional styles have suffered the effects of the media since the 1920s; people were no longer sonically isolated, but could hear the music of other areas on the radio or recordings. Some distinctive regional styles can still, however, be recognized, and these distinctions are important to the identity of many musicians.

The communities of singers, dancers, and instrumentalists are fluid, their boundaries permeable. Nevertheless, the individual communities are bonded by activities they share: dances, sessions, festivals, schools, formal and informal gatherings. Competitions also delineate a specialized community within traditional music and dance. The *fleadh cheoil* (literally "feast of music") and *feis cheoil* ("festival of music") are two types of events held locally, regionally, or nationally that sponsor music and dance competitions. The competitions create uniform structures within which music and dance are performed and judged. All these groups participate in the Irish traditional music community, yet each has a distinct identity.

Community is, according to Anthony Cohen (1985), both defined and bounded by symbols:

> The community itself and everything within it, conceptual as well as material, has a symbolic dimension, and . . . this dimension . . . exists as something for people "to think with." The symbols of community are mental constructs: they provide people with the means to make meaning. In doing so, they also provide them with the means to express the particular meanings which the community has for them. . . . [The boundaries of community are] symbolic receptacles filled with the meanings that members impute to and perceive in them. (19)

The boundaries of different traditional music communities in Ireland are set in tunes, in styles of playing, and in dance types. For Vincent Griffith, from Feakle, East Co. Clare, a farmer by trade and fiddler by passion, slides and polkas[2] are symbolic boundaries of the musical community in Cork and Kerry, and they are not part of the Clare tradition: "We don't do them here in Clare. We don't like what they play and they don't like what we play" (personal communication). Within these boundaries resides the *nya*, the "common aesthetic," the "interrelationships of players with their sources, audiences and their local history" (Vallely 1997, 150).

Playing traditional music in Ireland defines a certain construction of Irishness. It enacts a culture of orality, an awareness of heritage and lineage, and an aesthetic of spontaneous creativity. Dance tunes, songs, and airs are shared in a convivial space such as a pub or a private home. In its original usage, before the term became associated with social dance events the *ceili* was an informal gathering, a tradition in which neighbors came together to share food, drink, talk, music, and stories (Breathnach 1971; Glassie 1982).

The theme of sharing, or making offerings, or as Glassie calls them, "gifts," is central to the *ceili*. In Glassie's description of *ceili*s in Ballymenone in the north of Ireland simple gifts are offered and exchanged: gifts of food (often cakes or breads,) gifts of drink (usually tea in this context), gifts of music and dance, and gifts of speech. Collectively, these gifts are referred to as *entertainment*, a term whose meaning of reciprocity and bonding goes far beyond the commodity form that we associate with it.

Sessions in pubs are a relatively recent phenomenon, becoming increasingly common since the folk revival of the 1960s. Today they stand as the quintessential forum for sharing traditional music in Ireland and the Irish Diaspora. The pub session is an arena in which symbols, both concrete and aural, define the boundaries of the traditional music community. If we think of the pub session as a *ceili*, certain boundaries of the Irish traditional music community become clearer. Sessions are often a weekly event for an informal group of musicians to converge at a local pub and "have some tunes." The session is a ritual of sharing in which the values of the community are enacted.

Throughout a session there is an exchange of "gifts." Chat is the first level in Glassie's hierarchy of gifts; talk moves into the realm of entertainment when it passes from formulaic greetings and falls into the free-flowing rhythm of chat. Chat is a device of inclusion; the words spoken by each person in the group constitute this small community's boundary. Drinks are bought, instruments taken out, but still the gifts are verbal. Wit and verbal virtuosity are highly valued. Eventually someone starts a tune. Almost immediately two or three others are playing along, then all, if there are more. The "gifts" have gone from verbal to musical; each is freely given and gratefully received.

One of the layers of symbolism in the performance of Irish traditional music is a putative link to the past. The belief that the music issues from a source located in an undefined antiquity is deeply embedded in the construction of Irish culture held by insiders and outsiders alike. It is revealed in the ubiquity of the term *ancient* used to describe Irish traditional music, from the eighteenth- and nineteenth-century collections by Edward Bunting, George Petrie, and others[3] to contemporary descriptions of the music. Embedded in the word ancient are layers of meaning and symbolic implication. Implied is an unquestioned authenticity in a static source, a point of origin from which all Irish traditional music issues. It conjures the image of a "Golden Age" of Irish culture, a pure and ideal past, and the subsequent struggle to assert or preserve Irish cultural identity.

The "authentic source" referenced by the word "ancient" is the imagined ancestral base of lineage so valued by all branches of the Irish traditional music community. Traditional musicians often say they have received something from musicians before them and feel a sense of obligation to "give something back to the tradition." Source need not always be primeval. Peter Woods captures this in his book *The Heartbeat of Irish Music*: "His playing had in it echoes of the time the old man who taught me had talked about, when the whole country was alive with pipers; and hadn't Doran's family links back to those times, wasn't he descended from the Cashs, themselves horse dealers and pipers?" (Woods 1997, 35).

What musicians give back is their own creativity. In this way the tradition coheres and continues through the belief in lineage; and that lineage creates a symbolic boundary for the traditional music community. Ciaran Carson (1996), both poet and musician, puts it eloquently:

All great musicians recognize their ancestry and pay respect to it, and they know the thing is bigger than the sum of individuals: it progresses

in a multiplicity of exponential steps and fractal variations; and step-
ping on a butterfly way back there in the past will have an unforeseen
chaotic implication for the present or the future. Because a note was
bent back then, the whole tune has taken on another bent or warp or
woof, and sometimes, someone will put in another bend that gets back
to the source, just as the flooded Mississippi breaks its banks and takes
a straighter, faster course between its hitherto meanderings. (61)

Carson evokes the fluidity of the tune, its ephemeral nature, its
power to embody what Cohen (1985) calls "symbols of the 'past,'
mythically infused with timelessness" (102). The past is a resource
with the power of myth. The Irish "ancient" is beyond rational
scrutiny; it exists out of time and is a symbol both for heritage
and an ideal, a lost Golden Age that, whether used to refer to the
time of one's grandparents or to the ancestral Celts, is just out of
reach.

DECLINE, RENEWAL, AND REVIVALS

This return to source is a trope of identity and continuity. It has
served to periodically revitalize traditional music in Ireland. The belief in the link to an original authentic source has perhaps been at
least partially responsible for the remarkable durability of this music. Irish traditional dance music has undergone repeated cycles of
decline and renewal. There have been periods during which the future of traditional music was in question, but it has persisted
through a repeating pattern of renewal, either through the efforts of
individuals or groups in Ireland or through unexpected influences
coming from outside.

With the process of renewal comes transformation. In the eighteenth century, as the social conditions for sustaining the tradition
of the Bardic harpers ebbed and the harpers and their music became extinct, the harp itself went through various changes and became a parlor instrument for middle-class and aristocratic women.
Tunes were also collected from the early eighteenth century onward, rendered into music notation, and published, often also for
parlor use. Although the instrument, the playing style, and the social class in which it was situated changed, the harp, an iconic symbol of Irish culture, did survive through a process of renewal and
transformation.

At the end of the nineteenth century, *Conradh na Gaeilge* (the Gaelic League) was established to revive interest in the Irish language and reinvigorate a perceived decay of traditional culture. The mission of the League was "the regeneration of the contemporary nation . . . by a return to its creative source in the evolving Gaelic civilization of its past" (Hutchinson, quoted in Meyer 1995, 29), an explicit reference to redemption through a reunion with its source. The Gaelic League used traditional dance and music in its conventions, in part to draw participants as well as to symbolize authentic Irish culture. The League's interest in Irish set dancing served to promote it, but also, in an attempt to discern the "authentic" from the "imported" forms its standardization of the sets deliberately excised some sets from the repertoire.[4]

In the 1920s and 1930s, traditional music and dance suffered the ravages of emigration and condemnation by the church. This time revival came in the form of technology: radio and the gramophone helped reignite interest in traditional music in rural Ireland. Recordings of Irish musicians in England and recordings of Irish immigrant musicians by American companies served to revitalize interest in the music at home. Even today one can hear the same medleys of tunes played in much the same manner as Sligo fiddlers Michael Coleman, Paddy Kiloran, and James Morrison. But interest in and respect for traditional music ebbed again in the late 1930s and 1940s with the decline of recordings of traditional music and the Public Dance Halls Act of 1935, which forbade the informal house dances and "crossroads dances" that had until that time been the primary site of social dancing. In 1951, *Comhaltas Ceoltóirí Éireann* was established. Dedicated to the promotion of traditional music and dance, it did much to restore traditional music to respectability and continues its mission to the present day.

Despite the efforts of *Comhaltas* and *Conradh na Gaeilge*, traditional music and dance were largely ignored by most of the Irish population throughout the 1950s. Radio programs by archivist Ciarán MacMathúna and piper and folklorist Séamus Ennis helped promote traditional music, but the audience for it was still a very specialized one. It was the 1960s when two phenomena brought the traditional arts to the attention of the general public. The first of these phenomena was embodied in a figure who reconciled several cultural dichotomies. Seán Ó Riada, a composer who first gained fame as a film score writer, formed the first traditional ensemble that was not a *ceili* band, Ceoltóirí Chualann, in 1960. The ensemble consisted of two fiddles (one of whom doubled on concertina), flute, pipes, button accordion, singer, bodhrán, and harpsichord![5] Ó Riada bridged the gap between high and low art[6] with his formal presentation of informal music, and the gap between written (classical) and oral (folk) traditions with his written-out arrangements for Ceoltóirí Chualann. Ó Riada's influence was dramatic and lasting. He had succeeded in making Irish traditional music accessible and acceptable to a majority of people in Ireland. In doing so with the creation of the traditional band, however, he changed the face of traditional music, which had been, except for the *ceili* band, an essentially solo tradition.

The second phenomenon of the 1960s that fueled the popularity of traditional music was the folk revival. An international phenomenon, the folk revival of the 1960s brought Irish ballad groups like the Clancy Brothers with Tommy Makem to a large international audience. The concept of singing Irish songs in harmony was another innovation, like the concept of the band. Ceoltóirí Chualann spawned other groups; first the Chieftains, with overlapping membership between the two groups. Then in the 1970s groups proliferated, led by Planxty, the Bothy Band, and De Dannan.

The symbolic boundaries of traditional music have changed with each of these processes that contributed dramatically to its survival. A view of any of these historical moments would reveal a different "Irish traditional music," the norm being solo musical performance and crossroads and house dances before the 1930s, larger *ceili* dances and *ceili* bands (not excluding solo performance) from the 1930s to the 1960s, bands and vocal groups (not excluding any of the above) from the 1960s on. The construction of traditional music in each historical moment is different and reflects its own current social and musical conditions.

The cycle of decline and renewal demonstrates the power and resilience of Irish traditional music. But the phenomenon of renewal is also deeply enmeshed in a dynamic process that has occupied a central position in the life of music in Ireland for literally hundreds of years, the relationship between tradition and innovation.

THE TRADITION/INNOVATION DEBATE

Traditions, although they represent a cultural continuity, are somewhat paradoxically fluid within that continuity. That fluidity usually precipitates a condemnation of the "influences of change" by the "voices of stability." This process has been ever-present in Irish culture, or in the words of Nicholas Carolan, director of the Irish Traditional Music Archive, "[it] has been going on as long as there has been human occupation in Ireland which in round figures is about 8,000 years, and I'm sure that there were people in the megalithic stone age complaining about the innovations of people of the neolithic stone age and saying 'Why don't they play it the way my father played it?'" (in Ó Súilleabháin et al. 1995, episode 1). But it seems to have intensified in this decade. One camp impugns the kinds of innovation that we have seen since the mid-1980s as "destroying the tradition" while the other side holds innovation to be necessary to its survival.

This kind of polarization is common in cultures undergoing intense social change, a characterization applicable to Ireland throughout the tumultuous twentieth century, indeed throughout much of its history. In times like these symbols of the past attain particular power as "communities have to drop their heaviest anchors in order to resist the currents of transformation" (Cohen 1985, 102).

The internal impetus from unprecedented prosperity in 1990s Ireland, the so-called Celtic Tiger, coupled with the opportunity presented from outside by the sudden expansion of Celtic music as a vital category in the global music market may account for the surge in artistic experimentation by musicians trained and steeped in Irish traditional music. We have already seen that traditional Irish music, as seen through the lens of time, takes on different forms. Instruments have been adopted. The bodhrán, now so strongly associated with Irish traditional music that it is sold by the thousands to tourists along with cheap pennywhistles, was not a customary traditional instrument before Sean Ó Riada adopted it in the 1960s. And the bouzouki would have seemed completely exotic, before the 1970s.

These accumulations of traditional forms are simply signs of a healthy tradition adopting to novel socioeconomic conditions. It is only when one point in the continuum is idealized and the term *traditional* is limited to that form that the tradition becomes "invented" in Hobsbawm's sense, "to inculcate certain values and norms of behavior by repetition, which automatically implies continuity with the past" (Hobsbawm 1983, 2). This link to the past is activated by reference to "ancient Irish music," an authenticating trope often used to validate a claim of heritage. Denial of change participates in the redemptive myth that authenticity issues from a pure source located in antiquity. But many of Irish traditional music's forms today—pub sessions, instruments like the bodhrán and bouzouki, bands, harmonic accompaniment—have been innovations within living memory.

Yet the debate over innovation rages. Two events in the mid-1990s have catalyzed and focused this debate: the seven-part television production *A River of Sound* in 1995, and *Crosbhealach an Cheoil*: The Crossroads Conference, an arena for the exchange of views from many perspectives on the subject of "Tradition and Change," presented in 1996. Mícheál Ó Súilleabháin, composer, pianist, creator, director, and professor at the Irish World Music Center at the University of Limerick, stands out as the pivotal figure on one side of the debate, the voice of innovation. Ó Súilleabháin was the creator of *A River of Sound* and a keynote speaker at *Crosbhealach an Cheoil*.

A River of Sound, broadcast on RTE (*Radio Telefís Éireann*), the national television network, is little known outside Ireland.[7] Yet its impact on the traditional music communities in Ireland was incendiary, much more so than, to take an obvious comparison, *Riverdance*. The theme running through it is that traditions are never frozen, but always fluid, invoked by the symbolism of the title *A River of Sound*. Blacking (1986) uses similar symbols when speaking of musical change, referring to cultures as "floating resources which people invoke and reinvent in the course of social interaction" (4). The message is created as much in this medium by the choice of aural and visual images as by the actual verbal content. Many times the music underlying the speech is Ó Súilleabháin's own, accompanied by images of him at the piano surrounded by his student orchestra alternating with black and white photos and old scenes of traditional musicians and dancers. The alternation of images and sounds creates a peculiar disjuncture, one in which a linkage between traditional and classical music is engaged. The relationship between classical music and Irish traditional music is an issue of great historic import. It is a particular interest of Ó Súilleabháin's, who has written and spoken extensively on three figures: Turlogh O'Carolan, Sean Ó Riada, and fiddler Tommy Potts, who "all shared an interest in the mediation of European art music and Irish traditional music" (Ó Súilleabháin 1994, 342).

These and other images—of the Chieftains performing in Japan with Japanese musicians, of the kora and other West African instruments being played with Irish traditional instruments, of blues riffs improvised on harmonica and rock bands backing traditional tunes—are powerful markers when juxtaposed with black and white images of players and dancers of a bygone era. While he treats the music and its heritage with utmost respect, Ó Súilleabháin's message in some ways suggests an inevitable move away from older forms of the tradition. The river image again referred to suggests an almost evolutionary view when he says "traveling back up stream will help us to find parts of ourselves which may lie hidden." But he also implicitly refers to the renewals of tradition throughout the twentieth century when he says "the musician reworks once again the balance between tradition and innovation. In this way the sense of what tradition is is both affirmed and challenged" (Ó Súilleabháin et al. 1995, episode 1).

Crosbhealach an Cheoil: The Crossroads Conference was held in April 1996, the year after *A River of Sound* was broadcast. The conference, subtitled "Tradition and Change in Irish Music," was organized by an independent committee of five concerned and respected scholar/musicians and included forty-two speakers. Many questions were asked in the introduction to the conference booklet, including "Does all this [the shift in venue of live music from home to pub and concert stage, the popularization of Irish 'folk' music, the economic emphasis on commoditized music, and the media focus on just a few 'stars'] devalue the notion of community in music? Is Traditional music part of any community life at all anymore? Are these changes inevitable?" (Vallely 1996, 2). Many views were presented on these and other topics.

But it was the keynote speeches that set the combative tone and attracted some media attention. The broadcast of *A River of Sound*, "with its authority of an educational overview, [had] caused severe differences of opinion ranging from elation to distress" (Vallely 1996, 3). The (obvious) choice of Mícheál Ó Súilleabháin to represent "one pole of the debate" was bound to draw the fire of those who were still stinging from *A River of Sound*. Tony McMahon was chosen to represent the other "pole." As it turns out McMahon had been interviewed and appeared in *A River of Sound*, making an eloquent statement about music not properly being a commodity, but rather "something which changes the chemistry of the moment in the individual heart which makes the day that degree or two brighter, which precipitates that shaft of blue from the bottom of the stomach up to the top of the head" (Ó Súilleabháin et al. 1995, episode 2).

A report in the periodical *Irish Music* described the encounter between Ó Súilleabháin and McMahon as "Fencing at the Crossroads" (O'Hara 1996, 6). The *Evening Herald* had previewed the encounter between McMahon and Ó Súilleabháin as "a terrible and vicious debate." By the accounts of people who were there and the report in *Irish Music*, Ó Súilleabháin was determined not to let the discussion deteriorate into rancor and bitter recrimination: "Part of the function Tony and I have this evening is not to be dogmatic, nor . . . to try and hint that we have all the answers. It's to try and stimulate discussion" (Ó Súilleabháin, quoted in O'Hara 1996, 6). But it was not to be. In addition to expressing his deeply felt views on the "principle of care and the principal of respect for a music that was a gift from previous generations" (7), McMahon spoke of the "butchering" of Irish traditional music and "joy-riding with traditional music."

Blacking has characterized the tradition versus innovation debate in musical communities as a conflict between the "purists" and the "modernists or syncretists" (1977, 3). In his analysis the purists refuse to relinquish the "dead weight" of "traditional routine" and the syncretists are "unaware of the superficiality of merely fashionable changes" (1977, 3); that both failed to take into account different varieties of musical change and to link them to changes in other sectors of society. But in Ireland traditional music is seldom "routine" or "dead weight" in this time of tremendous vigor within the community. Nor does it seem that innovation is "merely fashionable change." There seems to be some sort of "fundamental change, not just surface change" (Ó Súilleabháin, quoted in Crowley 1997, 129) occurring, but the variety of that change still seems to be in question.

From the perspective of an outsider, the debate is further complicated by musicians' own self-definitions. Often, musicians whom I encountered who seemed very innovative staunchly defended their identities as "traditional musicians." One of these was Niall Keegan, a flute player living in Limerick and on the faculty of the Irish World Music Center there. What I heard in Keegan's improvisations was the language of jazz: blue notes, chromatic melodies, even modulations to a different key! But when I asked him, he denied using jazz, explaining "I don't really play jazz. It's traditional Irish music. It's just a different aesthetic. It just expands it [the tradition] a little."

When I pressed him on another occasion he admitted that he liked jazz and listened to it, but again denied having any "great understanding of it." When I said I clearly heard the jazz influences and that I had heard other people describe his style as "jazzy" he said: "When I change a tune I think I'm upholding an aesthetic of variation" (personal communication). For Keegan it is a responsibility of the performer in a music that values improvisation to continue to push the limits of the musical language. To do so does not take the performance outside the boundaries of the tradition.

Another musician who seems to push the envelope, but more with style than improvisation, is Martin Hayes. A professional fiddler currently living in Seattle, Hayes grew up in Feakle, Co. Clare, where he learned the East Clare style of playing. His playing seems to distill the tune to its most basic elements, slow it down, state the tune in a streamlined, elegant way. In his economy of notes and relaxed, legato style he seems to reinvent traditional Irish fiddling. But in our conversation he downplayed the innovative nature of his playing and emphasized his mission to discover the ever-elusive essence of a tune. He seeks out musicians who give him inspiration. These include both well-known musicians whose qualities like the "emotional power of Joe Cooley" or the "evocative eeriness of Podraig O'Keefe" (personal communication) he engages in his own playing. He also seeks out older unrecognized players in whom he sometimes finds "more primitive organic types of melody, less sophisticated, more earthy, more rooted." And he tries to absorb all that he can here, in any tradition, not to create fusion, but rather always to "go back to my reference point which is the melody, the ideas of the people in the music, what it's all about, and if what other people do can be of service to that, I enroll it, absorb it into it." On the subject of innovation, he says "I am trying to walk that very narrow line between pushing the boundaries innovatively and staying completely within the tradition."

So it was with many musicians I heard and met. Extremely creative musicians need to "push the boundaries innovatively," yet there is still a sure identification with traditional music. The debate between innovation and tradition will not affect traditional music in Ireland. Nor will innovation in and of itself, since, as we have seen, innovation is as much a part of Irish traditional music as it is of any healthy tradition. The symbols embodied by innovation are, however, sufficient to ignite the emotions of members of the community since "the boundary as the community's public face is symbolically simple; but, as the object of internal discourse it is symbolically complex" (Cohen 1985, 74). Innovation creates multiple symbolic boundaries. But still the tradition remains as the center of concentric circles of performance and identity. The crux of the issue lies in what Blacking called the "varieties" of musical change. From the inception of bands, concerts, staged performances, and recordings Irish traditional music has been presented and transmitted outside the domain of social space. This is a fundamental change. The commercialization of Irish traditional music is another fundamental change. As long as these two things are peripheral to the social aspect of the music the cultural identity it represents will remain intact.

Tony McMahon, at the end of his presentation at The Crossroads Conference played a cut from the CD version of *A River of Sound* composed by Mícheál Ó Súilleabháin and Donal Lunny. It was a fusion piece incorporating orchestral as well as Irish traditional and African instruments. His attitude was apparent when he called the piece "Hiberno jazz scrubbed clean of roots, ritual and balls." The audience applauded both the piece and the comment (O'Hara 1996).

CELTIC MUSIC AS VIRTUAL COMMUNITY

Assuming that Celtic music is not the same as Irish traditional music, and that it does, in some sense, exist, and that "Irish music" is included in the definition of "Celtic music" by outsiders of the Irish tradition, the question arises as to how to consider the relationship between Celtic music and Irish traditional music.

We have seen that the symbols that define Irish traditional music communities are drawn primarily from the social meanings inherent in the music making. The boundaries of those communities are both social and sonic. Celtic music exists in a different location entirely; not in a social community, but wholly in the realm of sound and image. Celtic music is not shared, but it is exchanged. Its space is not personal and acoustic but public and mediated. Celtic music only exists after it is produced and marketed; it has no existence outside its commodity form. Traditional music exists on its own, wherever people decide to share it, to play, sing, or dance together, whether or not it is commoditized. The community in which Celtic music resides is the virtual community. It is born in the studio and lives on

CDs and tapes, on radio and TV, in the movies, on the Internet and on stage.

The boundaries of Celtic music are extremely vague. Both the most radical and the most mainstream expressions of traditional music are included under the "Celtic" banner. Both the Afro-Celt Sound System, a group combining instruments, players, and styles from Ireland and West Africa, and button accordion player Joe Burke can be found in the Celtic bins of the record shop. These boundaries are kept open and flexible primarily for commercial reasons, causing no small amount of consternation to traditional artists who reject the Celtic label. On the other hand the same flexibility allows other artists freedom and latitude to experiment, to define their own sonic space.

Most of these experiments can be categorized in relation to traditional music as either extensions, fusions, or departures. Extensions add layers to the traditional tune such as bass and rhythm section, which in turn can give the music a rock or country beat. Most of the early bands from the 1970s could be considered extensions of traditional music. Ensemble playing itself, dating from Ó Riada's Ceoltóirí Chualann, could be considered an extension of the solo tradition. Sharon Shannon performs with a crack (no pun) backup band that can give her a rock, country, or pop backing, while she plays the tunes pretty much as she would play them on a neighbor's porch. She says, "if it was possible for the listener to listen to my accordion playing alone, with all the backing taken away, you'll hear it's very rooted. It's true to the tunes and doesn't break any of the rules of traditional style. It's the backing that makes them sound different" (O'Connor 1997, 6–7). It is her band that makes her performances extensions of tradition.

Fusions are combinations of Irish traditional music and musics from other cultures. Andy Irvine was perhaps the first prominent musician to introduce cross-cultural influences, in this case Balkan rhythms, into his music. The Afro-Celt Sound System, as their name suggests, performs a fusion of Irish and African musics. Their first release, *Sound Magic* (1996), includes two pipers, Celtic harp, whistles, accordion, the West African *kora* (gourd harp) and talking drum, two vocalists, one Irish and one African, no less than three keyboards and synthesizers, and a host of guests. The result is a fascinating variety of grooves with a percussive, distinctly Afro-pop flavor. Only the sound of the Irish instruments, particularly the uilleann pipes and whistles, and the occasional use of an Irish tune give any hint of the "Celt" in the Afro-Celt mix.

Kíla, on the other hand, use pipes, whistles, fiddle, bouzouki, clarinet, sax, guitar, bass, and a large collection of percussion (particularly African) and percussive (hammered dulcimer) instruments to create an intercultural sound including Irish, Middle Eastern, and Eastern European influences despite their all-Irish lineup. Their second CD, *Tóg É Go Bog É* (1997), in particular captures a distinctly African flavor on the title song and "Gwerzy," and an uncanny Russian flavor on the waltz "Dusty Wine Bottle."

Departures could be described as music labeled Celtic that have left the domain of Irish traditional songs or tunes entirely. *Celtic Legends*, a collaboration between Jeff Johnson, a keyboards player, and Brian Dunning, a flute, pipes, and accordion player, is an example of the Celtic departure. This CD, released in 1997 on the Windham Hill label, has much of the distinctive New Age sound for which that label is famous, but the music is completely divorced from Irish traditional music. The only link is the text of the CD booklet, which recounts the legends of Taliesin and cúChulainn (sic). The titles of the musical pieces are drawn from these legends.

Music intentionally created as Celtic is often produced with definite sound characteristics in mind. It has been associated with New Age and World Music by the record industry and fans. It can be linked to both these genres by both sonic and extramusical features. Using the primarily vocal groups Clannad and Anúna as examples, we can easily hear the New Age components of the Celtic sound: heavy reverb; a soft, sibilant texture that makes the sound seem like it emanates in waves. Musical attacks are never sharp or sudden; the "envelope" of each sound is very broad. Much of the music categorized as New Age has these characteristics. These sound characteristics call up various images that are encoded in words like: ancient, mystic, magic, enchantment, tides, well—all of which are used by the music industry to consciously create imaginary associations with Celtic music. Of these, only "ancient" is often associated with Irish traditional music and its imaginary. The "New Age Celtic Twilight sound, evoking magic, mystery and mysticism" (Curtis 1994, 26–27) became the standard for the industry that has burgeoned in the second half of the 1990s.

One of the first stages in the construction of Celtic music by the recording industry was the inclusion of Irish traditional music within the label world music, which was actually invented in 1987 by music business executives to capitalize on the growing interest in African music (Taylor 1997, 2). Irish traditional music was one of those "folk" musics to be included. This link is a possible factor in some Irish musicians going in the direction of cross-cultural fusions. The sounds of *djembe,* congas, *didjeridu,* and other "world" instruments is not uncommon in Celtic music. These sounds both delocalize and situate the music in an exotic imaginary.

So if the boundaries of Celtic music are in question, the questions become "What is it?" "When did it start?" and "Where is it situated?" Arjun Appadurai (1990) provides a useful model of postmodern "landscapes": broad and somewhat fluid categories of human action and interaction on a global scale in which he enumerates "five dimensions of global cultural flow" (6):

1. Ethnoscapes: movements of large numbers of people ("tourists, immigrants, refugees, exiles, guestworkers . . .").
2. Technoscapes: global configuration of technology (mechanical and informational) and the speed and ease with which it crosses "various kinds of previously impervious boundaries."
3. Financapes: currency markets, stock exchanges, commodity speculation, the speed with which huge amounts of money are moved.
4. Mediascapes: "both the distribution of the electronic capabilities to produce and disseminate information (newspapers, magazines, TV stations and film production studios . . . and the images of the world created by these media."
5. Ideoscapes: "also concatenations of images [which are] often directly political and frequently have to do with the ideologies of states and the counter-ideologies of movements explicitly oriented to capturing state power."

These landscapes provide us with a matrix for locating Celtic music and beginning to understand the dynamics of the "virtual community."

Ethnoscapes, the movements of large numbers of people, open the conceptual door to categorizing diverse local groups under a general banner. The world music industry has a way of conflating styles to make many musics fit into one bin in the record store. So initially Irish, Scottish, and their diasporic musics became "Celtic," soon to be followed by Breton and eventually Galician musics. The inclusion of Celtic under world music also encourages cross-cultural fusions.

The global technoscape, fueled by the resources of the finanscape, makes possible the production and distribution of tens or hundreds of thousands of CDs and videos with the capability of exceeding live performance possibilities through overdubbing, layering, and sampling sounds, and other sophisticated production techniques. The mediascape is then brought into play to disseminate the products or information about them through broadcast, print, computer, and film media. These sounds and images then congeal in the ideoscape through which Celtic music is constructed. The "virtual community" consists of the performers, audience, and all the people whose jobs are involved with the production mechanisms of the global landscapes.

The concept of ethnoscapes provides us with a lens through which we might view the subtle play of constructed community. The Irish American musicians of the Diaspora influenced and reinvigorated Irish traditional music. Ireland's own periphery sustains the core, becomes the center, in the 1920s and 1930s. Throughout the second half of the century, Irish, Scottish, Breton, and eventually Galician musicians reconfigure their music by sharing and combining their musical languages and vocabularies, largely through the medium of recorded music. A community begins to emerge, a community without place. The world music industry then conflates styles to make many musics fit into one bin (Celtic music) in the record store. Ethnoscape, the movement of large numbers of people, opens the conceptual door to categorizing diverse local groups under a subsuming banner, and the music industry seals that door. The diasporic movement is ultimately transformed into a movement of disembodied participants by medium and label.

The global technoscape makes possible the production and distribution of many thousands of CDs and videos. The Internet now can further disembody the products through instantaneous transmission. The mediascape disseminates the products to consumers throughout the world. These sounds and images then congeal into the artistic ideoscape of Celtic music. The "virtual community" consists of performers and consumers; the absence of personal contact is the primary distinguishing feature between it and the traditional Irish music community. In addition, a host of people involved in the media reconfigure both the music and the images associated with it in the creation and marketing of the products. These people stand outside the virtual Celtic community, but, like demigods who stand unseen outside but affect the lives of mortals, shape it, and give it substance. They and their products contribute to the construction of an *imaginal* Celtic music.

As we have seen, Irish music resides within a complex system of beliefs, including a strong sense of history, heritage, and authenticity, as well as in the social interactions that are based in large part on these beliefs. The beliefs that inform Irish traditional music are driven by a sense of place, described by flute-player Seamus Tansey in the following way: "The wind, the rain, the flowing river that shapes the minds and passions of our ancient forefathers inspiring them to harness together all the sounds of animals, minerals, birds and insects so as it molded itself into a melody of Ireland's soul" (Tansey 1996, 30). Irish traditional music communities maintain a strong reference to place. The place of Ireland is often credited with being the fountainhead of traditional music.[8]

Celtic music also resides within a set of beliefs about heritage and images of authenticity and history. But these beliefs are not grounded; they are imaginal. The virtual community of Celtic music differs from other musical communities in its lack of place. Or rather the place evoked in this community does not refer to an actual space, as it clearly does in the Irish sentiment expressed by Tansey. Stokes argues that "music is socially meaningful not entirely but largely because it provides means by which people recognize identities and places, and the boundaries which separate them" (Stokes 1994, 5). The Celtic virtual community does create a sense of place, but that place is located in the imagination. Its "place" invokes authenticity, heritage, and history, but it is neither derived from musical lineage nor rooted in any specific space.

Celtic music is situated in a postmodern landscape of images (both aural and visual), which has "no fixed roots but a flow, no simple exemplars, but an emerging aesthetic" (Veblen, unpublished). In a "world system of images [exists] a complex transnational construction of imaginary landscapes" (Appadurai 1990, 4). Celtic music is one of these imaginary landscapes. The exotic is portrayed by the drones of the pipes and their synthesized counterparts, and by the sound of Gaelic. Songs sung in Gaelic inhere a quality of alienness that is seldom modified by translation. This alien language is then used to construct imaginary time: a sense of ancientness or timelessness, from which the traditional tunes emanate.

> The image, the imagined, the imaginary—these are all terms which di-
> rect us to something critical and new in global cultural processes: the
> imagination as a social practice. . . . The imagination has become an or-
> ganized field of social practices, . . . and a form of negotiation between
> sites of agency ("individuals") and globally defined fields of possibil-
> ity. (Appadurai 1990, 5)

Image replaces identity, or rather manufactures identity in the postmodern global community. The Celtic imaginary is based upon "im-
age-centered, narrative-based accounts of strips of reality" (Appadurai 1990, 9). Individual artists negotiate their creative ideas and
their messages through globally mediated products.

The "imagination as a social practice" creates a paradox: a heritage
in which anyone can participate, simply through the imaginary. The
"mediascape" provides the means to journey to the Celtic of the
imagination. CDs provide three media with which to create the imaginal and open the door: the music sound, the cover art, and the liner
notes. The notes to *Celtic Odyssey*, a 1993 release on the Narada label,
describe Celtic music as "elemental, essential, inescapable . . . a love
of the sensual tempered by a profound respect for the spiritual," first
creating a world of mystery, and of a compelling exoticism—a ro-
manticization, an alternative world, an oppositional world both foreign and attractive. The *Celtic Odyssey* liner notes conclude: "Ancient,
ageless, Celtic music is, finally and indelibly, a journey of memory—
yours, whether conscious or unconscious, shared with the memory
of those who came before you. It is a memory as beautiful in its
starkness and complex simplicity as the massive stones at New
Grange" (Hitchner 1993). The owner of this CD is invited to participate in an imaginal Celtic heritage.

The image is amplified by the cover design, a field of standing
stones fading into a gray fog. The picture, entitled *Morning Mist at
Carnac*, and a quotation explaining its "Celtic mythology" are taken
from the book *Celtic Mysteries* by John Sharkey (1975). The discourses of both the image and the language of the text create a vivid
picture. The imaginal space, and the community that shares it, is
bounded by symbols of antiquity, timelessness, mystery, and the un-
knowables of paganism and mysticism. These descriptive terms, as
well as the ones from the liner notes—"elemental," "essential," "inescapable," "sensual," "spiritual," "ancient," "ageless"—are part of
a vocabulary that encodes the Celtic imaginary, makes it an almost
palpable reality.

The Celtic community is bounded by the commodity. As a symbol the commodity itself possesses the power to convey inclusion; to own it is to become a member of the group. Consumers, then, enjoy a privileged status in the virtual community. They complete the circuit left open with the loss of context. In a pub session musicians are sharing and communicating with each other within a social context that includes the patrons and staff of the pub, who share in the musical experience not through the process of consumption (except with a pint or two), but through a process of what one might call "active passivity"—being part of the scene, part of the context. In the virtual community the context is created by the producers of the CD, but it is activated by the consumer who projects himself or herself into the Celtic imaginary.

Notwithstanding its media-driven nature, Celtic music has always had at its heart traditional musicians making the music they learned in their musical communities. The popularity of traditional music following the folk revival of the 1960s encouraged musicians to exert their own agency to shape their musical worlds. The results were innovative performances on the concert stage, preserved and distributed on recordings. Planxty, whose first recording was released in 1972, included bouzouki and guitar player Andy Irvine, as well as Christy Moore, Donal Lunny, and Liam O'Flynn, all of whom figured largely in the innovative bands of the 1970s and 1980s. Irvine had traveled to Bulgaria; Eastern European music has continued to exert a great influence on him. The intriguing rhythms of this music formed the basis of a collaborative effort in 1992 between Irvine and Davy Spillane called *Eastwind*. Spillane, a superb player of pipes and low whistle, had been a member of Moving Hearts, formed in 1981 by Christy Moore and Donal Lunny. The groups begun in the mid-1970s, like De Dannan (with whom Andy Irvine performed for a while), The Bothy Band (with Donal Lunny), and Stockton's Wing, took Irish traditional music in the direction of hard-driving folk-rock. Moving Hearts took the driving energy of these groups and went wholeheartedly into the realm of rock, adding electric bass, synthesizer and drum kit, congas, bongos, and saxophone.

Davy Spillane, in addition to playing in Moving Hearts and his *Eastwind* collaboration with Andy Irvine, produced several solo CDs that took traditional music closer to the genres of New Age, pop, and world musics. On *Pipedreams*, released in 1991, Spillane includes a whole battery of keyboards that, along with the smooth layering of sounds and textures, create the "New Age Celtic Twilight" sound. He includes Simon O'Dwyer on *didjeridu* and *dord árd*,[9] Australian instruments, taking a turn toward world music. Keith Donald's sax playing gives some cuts a distinctly "modern jazz" feel. Sometimes Spillane's whistle and pipe playing are speaking the language of these musics, and other times they are playing a traditional reel surrounded by a pop band arrangement.

Perhaps any of these could be considered the beginnings of the virtual community; perhaps even the first recordings of the 1920s marked its inception. But these and other Irish traditional musicians who have participated in new and experimental forms also belong to communities of musicians who play together within the boundaries of their tradition. Former President of Ireland Mary Robinson observed of *A River of Sound*: "I see that with Irish musicians; that they're always going back; they always want to play with somebody; they always want to regroup with their own area even, and with musicians in their own area" (Ó Súilleabháin et al. 1995, episode 7). In a recent feature on Davy Spillane in *Irish Music* he describes "paying a price" for being the "rock piper" with Moving Hearts (Reich 1998–99, 12). Now he is returning to his roots, playing purely traditional concerts with fiddler Kevin Glackin.

What is happening to Irish traditional music within the global landscapes? Are we, as Mícheál Ó Súilleabháin has suggested, "experiencing a fragmenting of the structure into another form of Irish traditional music" (Ó Súilleabháin, quoted in O'Hara 1996, 6)? Or are the Afro-Celt Sound System and Kíla part of another community, one that includes Cappercaille and the Tartan Amoebas from Scotland, Gwerz from Brittany, and Loreena McKennitt from Canada? Perhaps this "fragmentation" is simply a feature of postcolonial reality, where individuals inhabit multiple communities and take on multiple identities. Through their own choice, and exerting their own agency in global markets, perhaps musicians can participate in both traditional and virtual communities.

ACKNOWLEDGMENT

Many thanks to Kari Veblen, who was initially to have coauthored this chapter. Much of the general conceptualization as well as some of the categories described in the last section, together with some specific interpretations in the second part of the chapter emerged from discussions we had prior to her leaving for a research trip in Ireland. In the end, time, distance, and schedule constraints prevented us from writing the chapter together. She was at the time, and remains, an inspiration.

NOTES

1. My use of the expression *traditional music*, which I nuance as I go on, broadly reflects usage among musicians in Ireland and elsewhere in North Western Europe to describe the predominantly instrumental common-practice dance music (jigs, slides, reels, polkas, hornpipes, highly ornamented free-rhythm slow airs and solo songs) performed in informal settings across the region.

2. Slides resemble jigs in their 6/8 meter, but have a predominant rhythm of quarter note-eighth note instead of the gig's predominant triplet; polkas are dances in 2/4 meter, slower than reels and generally less rhythmically complex than hornpipes.

3. Bunting's *A General Collection of the Ancient Irish Music* was first published in 1796 and George Petrie's *The Ancient Music of Ireland* in 1855.

4. See Turino (1993) and Noll (1993) for similar processes of standardization in early-twentieth-century nationalistic folkloric programs in Peru, and Poland and the Ukraine respectively.

5. Ó Riada thought the metal-strung harpsichord probably sounded more like the Bardic harp than the gut-strung Celtic harp, which had been introduced in about the turn of the century and was touted as "authentic" by folk revivalists.

6. Traditional music had come to be seen as "backward" and "rural" in light of the urban modernization of the 1950s (Hamilton 1994, 6).

7. It was edited down for a commercial video, but that was not widely distributed outside Ireland.

8. Note in particular episodes two and three of Ó Súilleabháin et al. 1995.

9. The *dord árd* is a Bronze Age horn; see Smith, this volume, for a fuller discussion of similar issues in an Australian context.

BIBLIOGRAPHY

Appadurai, Arjun. "Disjuncture and Difference in the Global Cultural Economy." *Public Culture* 2, no. 2 (1990): 1–24.

Blacking, John. "Some Problems of Theory and Method in the Study of Musical Change." *Yearbook of the International Folk Music Council* 9 (1977): 1–25.

Blacking, John. "Identifying Processes of Musical Change." *The World of Music: Journal of the International Institute for Comparative Music Studies* 28, no. 1 (1986): 3–12.

Breathnach, Breandán. *Folk Music and Dances of Ireland*. Cork: Mercier Press, 1971.

Carson, Ciaran. *Last Night's Fun: In and Out of Time with Irish Music*. New York: Farrar, Straus, and Giroux, 1996.

Cohen, Anthony. *The Symbolic Construction of Community*. New York: Tavistock Publications, 1985.

Crowley, Ethel. "Finding Myself at the Cultural Crossroads: An Interview with Mícheál Ó Súilleabháin." In *Under the Belly of the Tiger: Class, Race, Identity and Culture in the Global Ireland*, edited by Ethel Crowley and Jim MacLaughlin, 125–37. Dublin: Irish Reporter Publications, 1997.

Curtis, P. J. *Notes from the Heart: A Celebration of Traditional Irish Music*. Dublin: Torc, 1994.

Glassie, Henry. *Passing the Time in Balymenone*. Philadelphia: University of Pennsylvania Press, 1982.

Hamilton, S. Colin. "The Role of Commercial Recordings in the Development and Survival of Traditional Irish Music." Paper presented to the International Society for Music Education, Tampa, Florida, 1994.

Hitchner, Earle. "The Call of the Celts." Liner notes to *Celtic Odyssey*, Narada ND 63912, 1993.

Hobsbawm, Eric. "Introduction." In *The Invention of Tradition*, edited by Eric Hobsbawm and Terence Ranger. Cambridge: Cambridge University Press, 1983.

Melhuish, Martin. *Celtic Tides: Traditional Music in a New Age*. Kingston, Ont.: Quarry Press, 1998.

Meyer, Moe. "Dance and the Politics of Orality: A Study of the Irish Scoil Rince." *Dance Research Journal* 27, no. 1 (1995): 25–39.

Noll, William. "Music Institutions and National Consciousness among Polish and Ukrainian Peasants." In *Ethnomusicology and Modern Music History*, edited by Stephen Blum, Philip Bohlman, and Daniel Neuman, 139–58. Urbana: University of Illinois Press, 1993.

O'Connor, Roderick. "Still Rooted in the Tradition." *Irish Music* (March 1997): 6–8.

O'Hara, Aidan. "Fencing at the Crossroads." *Irish Music* 1, no. 9 (1996): 6–7.

Ó Súilleabháin, Mícheál. "'All Our Central Fire': Music, Mediation and the Irish Psyche." *The Irish Journal of Psychology* 15, nos. 2 and 3 (1994): 331–53.

Reich, Cindy. "The Price of Cool." *Irish Music* 4, no. 5 (1998–99): 12–13.

Sharkey, John. *Celtic Mysteries: The Ancient Religion (Art and Imagination)*. London: Thames and Hudson, 1975.

Stokes, Martin. "Introduction." In *Ethnicity, Identity and Music: The Musical Construction of Place*, edited by Martin Stokes, 1–27. Oxford: Berg, 1994.

Tansey, Seamus. "Music at the Crossroads." *Irish Music* 2, no. 3 (1996), 30–31.

Taylor, Timothy D. *Global Pop: World Music, World Markets*. New York: Routledge, 1997.

Turino, Thomas. *Moving Away from Silence*. Chicago: University of Chicago Press, 1993.

Vallely, Fintan, ed. *Clár*. Booklet for *Crosbhealach an Cheoil*: The Crossroads Conference. Dublin: Cian Park, 1996.

Vallely, Fintan. "Irish Music." In *Arguing at the Crossroads*, edited by Paul Brennan and Catherine de Saint Phalle, 143–61. Dublin: New Island Books, 1997.

Veblen, Kari, and Jackie Small. "Global Implications, Paradigms and Promises in Community Music." Paper presented to the ISME Community Music Activity Commission, South Africa, 1998.

Woods, Peter. *The Heartbeat of Irish Music*. Niwot, Colo.: Roberts Rinehart, 1997.

DISCOGRAPHY

Afro-Celt Sound System. *Sound Magic*. Real World 7243 8 41736 2 3, 1996.

Celtic Odyssey. Narada ND 63912, 1993.

Irvine, Andy, and Davy Spillane. *Eastwind*. Tara CD 3027, 1992.

Johnson, Jeff, and Brian Dunning. *Music of Celtic Legends: The Bard and The Warrior*. Windham Hill 01934 11181-2, 1997.

Kíla. *Tóg Go Bog*. Key KRCD 005, 1997.

Spillane, Davy. *Pipedreams*. Tara CD 3026, 1991.

FILMOGRAPHY

Celtic Tides. Putumayo World Music. Gregory Hall, producer, Mark Hall, director, written by Martin Melhuish and Mark Hall, 1998.

Ó Súilleabháin, Mícheál, Nuala O'Connor, and Philip King. ss (television production). Dublin: Hummingbird Productions, 1995.

6

"Home Is Living Like a Man on the Run": John Cale's Welsh Atlantic

Dai Griffiths

I've no business being in rock and roll. I've said it over and over again that I'm a classical composer, dishevelling my musical personality by dabbling in rock and roll.[1]

This line of John Cale's autobiography, *What's Welsh for Zen?*, suggests the confusion and ambiguity at the heart of his now-substantial output. There is, on the one hand, a profound sense of disdain for rock and roll, the art form that, after all, has sustained him for nearly forty years. But at the same time, on the other hand, there's a faith in individuality and self-expression that is either supremely confident—would you talk about your musical personality?—or, as "over and over again" suggests, the sense that no one is listening, an indication of someone who lives, as Cale's great obsessive song has it, "down at the end of Lonely Street."[2] Some of the sound bites Cale comes up with feel like the ones you'd get from some of rock's loners and blabbers: Zappa, Costello, Lennon, Morrison; Van Morrison is another Celt on record reminding everyone that pop music is just his way of slumming it: "I personally don't have anything to do with rock, in any shape or form. . . . I just find it hard to be a so-called pop star. It conflicts with creativity" (Flanagan 1990, 411).

Cale is bothered seemingly less by commerce per se—though he and Morrison are both well clear of hits, and have had to keep on producing—than by a more refined and reified idea of classical music. That Cale (or Victor Bockris, his editor) feels no need for inverted commas anywhere in the phrase "classical composer" in a book

171

published in 1999 just about says it all, and starts to point us away from the simple point about the difference between pop music as having to do with playing in bands and classical music as writing orchestral music, and toward the complex roots for this mix-up in South Wales, and perhaps by extension, in a certain moment of the Celtic mind-set.[3] This is a Celticism that festers underneath Victorian re-creations, a Wales that makes big money out of industry and is willing to lose its language accordingly. It is a scenario that finds the Celts and the Jews embarrassingly interrupting the speeches at a conference on the postcolonial; a crowd that refuses to leave a wake held for the modern, holding up the intended celebrations of the postmodern, till they are absolutely sure that the booze and drugs really have run out.[4] Another of the guiding theses here is that John Cale presents a worn, jaded, belated version of the adjective "Wagnerian," taking control of the whole caboodle from songwriting through singing and playing to production, with even some Svengali activity on the side, the story played to a bust of Beethoven on top of the piano, and enacted with staggering levels of drug taking and sexual adventure.

The keyword for Cale is flight. Born in Garnant near Ammanford in South Wales in 1940, he went to college in London and then took a chance and moved to New York City in 1963. After a period with La Monte Young's Dream Syndicate, he met Lou Reed and formed the Velvet Underground, at the time part of the group gathered around Andy Warhol. Cale left the Velvet Underground in 1968, after participating in only the first two albums. Although both were commercially unsuccessful, it is fair to suggest, and possible to demonstrate, that they are among the most influential of all pop albums, with legacies in glam rock, punk rock, and indie or alt-rock.[5] After one collaborative work with composer Terry Riley, he began in 1970 to record as John Cale, issuing a total of eleven solo albums mostly containing music recognizably in a rock genre relatively new at the time; as well as further collaborative albums with Brian Eno, Lou Reed (again), and Bob Neurith. Throughout this time Cale is back and forth between America and Europe, with particular success, it seems, in France. Latterly he has begun to issue nonvocal music more recognizably in a neoclassical or contemporary genre, largely soundtracks to French feature films, as well as one orchestral setting of poems by Dylan Thomas and, most recently, ballet music in Holland.

What I intend to do in this chapter is to read Cale's work against the westward movement of the Celtic Diaspora. I shall first rehearse an ever-current debate in theories of ethnicity that, thankfully for my purpose, looks to music for sustenance. I'll be suggesting not only that a Welsh perspective is important in understanding John Cale but that he, largely through the condition of exile, challenges any too-settled formation of what it was to be Welsh in the late twentieth century. I'll then mount a steady and straightforward review of Cale's work under three headings: voice, instrument, and production, the latter with particular attention to the cover version. The three headings are intended to be musical in a way that can culturally be read. A final section will return directly to the Welsh focus, suggesting effectively that Cale's exile has been, heroically enough to my mind, a necessary phase that has already enabled calmer but hopefully creative conditions to emerge in Wales itself.

HYBRIDITY

Including Cale, or anyone, under a banner of nation or ethnicity, is consciously to bring along considerable historical baggage. I approach this theme through an interesting spat in cultural studies, a moment where John Hutnyk presents a riposte to Paul Gilroy, whose formulation "anti-anti-essentialism" is an expressively inelegant way of articulating the problem under consideration (Gilroy 1993A, 102).

Anti-anti-essentialism captures, through its double negative, the condition of hybridity and Diaspora, which can be seen as a third stage in a progression that begins with "race" in the hell-holes of slavery and genocide, such residual, all-out racism representing a basic form of essentialism. In a second stage of reaction, there is possible, and now firmly established, a tolerant if potentially limp (or "tokenistic") multiculturalism, as anti-essentialism, which carries the danger of reinforcing categories it sets out to challenge. A more combative version of this second stage, antiracism, attempts to turn the tables back onto the oppressor. In the third stage, anti-anti-essentialism, there is an acceptance of and even a newfound celebration of difference and diversity and of the movements that underpin them, a hybrid identity that casts enforced Diaspora as the truest remnant of an invigorated modernity.[6] Gilroy, however, in an impressive concatenation that builds upon an earlier formulation of Stuart Hall, ties ethnicity to gender ("gender is the modality through which race is lived"[7]), and brings also an insistence on biopolitics alongside the markers of a rationalizing culture (Gilroy 1993A, 1994). In this passage, as is often the case, Gilroy has music in mind, and is pointing personally and positively toward listening as key to an essentialist understanding:

> Looking back on the adolescent hours I spent trying to master the technical intricacies of Albert King and Jimi Hendrix, fathom the subtleties of James Jamerson, Larry Graham, or Chuck Rainey, and comprehend how the screams of Sly, James, and Aretha could punctuate and extend their metaphysical modes of address to the black subject, I realize that the most important lesson music has to teach us is that its inner secrets and its ethnic rules can be taught and learned. (1993A, 109)

The passage can be reread with Irish substituted for black and, say, The Chieftains and Van Morrison as exemplars. The effect is too cozy; it's a seductive wonderland, the fairytale that finds Shane MacGowan and Kirsty MacColl able to carry on a seemingly and specifically Irish dialogue in New York City.[8]

Enter John Hutnyk. He notices that Gilroy is doing two things to which he, Hutnyk, is particularly sensitive. First, Gilroy appears to privilege forms of authentic music making, notably call and response, which for Hutnyk will require further categories to reflect Asian or, more specifically, a British Asian experience. Second, Gilroy's emphasis tends to underplay technological factors of production and dissemination (Hutnyk 1997; Sharma, Hutnyk, and Sharma 1996).[9] Hutnyk turns for case study to the band Asian Dub Foundation as being representative of what a "radical hybridity" might sound like. If Hutnyk's chosen example seems to me not quite to deliver his promise (this through of all things a lack of engagement with the sound of Asian Dub Foundation and an overemphasis on words) what interests me is, first, the whole premise of this collision and, second, what the debate says about the different forms of flight from which they arise. On the first point, there is something strangely comforting about Gilroy's prose style, which can lull at least this reader into a sense of too-easy assent[10]: The challenge to his position I'm sure would emanate either from the right wing or, as with Hutnyk, from another, different relation to the same problematic.

This second is a complex point, which, arguably, eventually surfaces in the legal distinction between Civil Rights legislation in the United States, and its eventual movement into affirmative action, and the Race Relations Acts in the UK. It turns on the relation between movement or flight and its direction, all of that on the one hand, and the other-directional knot of language and nation, all on the other. Across the black Atlantic that Gilroy describes, enforcement and oppression filters through slavery and English as language, albeit on the way to the New World; the British Asian arrives in the Old World with language intact. This may be why there will be echoes of Gilroy's position for a Welsh reader in that the British Asian experience, and the Asian experience beyond that is still one which can and does fall elsewhere, wherein lies the value of Gilroy's formulation for any overly optimistic celebration of Welshness even in exile.

The danger is the one that John Solomos and Les Back describe as summarizing racism and multiculturalism, their complex motions, into a crude opposition between a "repressive essentialism" and a "liberating hybridity" (1996, 150). If we set out through Cale to celebrate a Welsh Atlantic—modernity and double consciousness—in the service of which he stands musically as a solitary figure, we need to be clear, first, what takes the space that flight leaves behind—and it is worth pointing out that in Cale's case it is a relatively unenforced flight—and, second, whether the flight carries with it the baggage of its origin, bearing in mind the idea that one essentialism will be manifest in or deflected onto other forms. This double question concerns, effectively, Wales the place and the adjective Welsh, the nation and a state of mind, with language or accent their key markers in sound. "Welsh music" during Cale's lifetime was something that preserved its highs and lows through the thoroughly modern idea of state-subsidized art, an Arts Council for the nation that helped to mount performances of University-based composition, eventually, seemingly reduced to a dichotomy of Bangor in North Wales under Professor William Mathias and Cardiff in South Wales under Professor Alun Hoddinott.

Cale, a beneficiary of the same largesse through the National Youth Orchestra—how centrist these formations now seem!—knew his modernist music well enough, through performance and to an extent through the teacher's training he received at Goldsmith's College in the University of London. By crossing to New York City, he was entering a milieu, notably around LaMonte Young and at Warhol's Factory, which ran closer perhaps to an earlier "tradition" of the avant-garde (Bürger 1984). Cale carried with him on the plane to Idlewild a high disdain for pop music—folk music didn't enter the picture—which was to mean for him a great unlearning or deskilling, dumbing down even, when he was to find himself playing bass with what Sterling Morrison once called "a handful of artists, dancers, and musicians" (Bockris and Malanga 1983, 4).[11] While Cale came eventually to value the pop music of Wales, and even to see himself increasingly part of Welsh music, there were years and years of examples—Tom Jones, Shirley Bassey, Bonnie Tyler, Man the Alarm, as well as Welsh-language singers and bands Meic Stevens, Edward H. Dafis, Trwynau Coch—which passed him by. So while Cale the exile should not turn into a silencer of rooted activity there is in the 1990s a development, to which I shall return, for which Cale we can now see as having been the role model par excellence. Hutnyk's intervention, however, demands that we listen critically for an engagement with technology and for any trace of xenophobia across the global stage, and Cale's story is in this respect one characterized both by (his own romantic terminology) failure and heroism.[12]

VOICE

> There's only one good use for a small town—you hate it, and you know you'll have to leave.[13]

Perhaps Lou Reed's enduring contribution to the pop song, building on the lead suggested by Bob Dylan, is precisely his way of incorporating in preference to lyric's various fastidiousness the blunt prose statement, and this particular assertion describes a point where Reed, Cale, and Andy Warhol all find themselves deracinated in the 1960s. "He's completely mad," Reed once said of Cale, "but that's because he's Welsh" (Bockris and Malanga 1983, 100): Cale's rootlessness and what sounds like madness are most palpable in his voice.

Cale once described for a television program a scene from his childhood: "It would be very quiet on a Sunday. You could hear the people with pneumo walk up the street. I would be able to tell when somebody was going by the house 'cause I could hear the rasping."[14] From a novelist this would be striking enough. From a musician, and a musician who sings, somehow, it feels different. The awareness of a tiny code of sound to set alongside all of the other sounds and noises that go to make up recorded performances. The story about the miners struggling up the hill illustrates a moment in the history of South Wales that presumably happened again and again, as village upon village began to contain this trace, and is thus a reminder that while much of the discourse of race turns on visual appearance, social history can also be inscribed in voice, sound, and noise.

Pneumoconiosis, or "pneumo," the source of the "rasping wheeze that Cale would hear, is a chest condition that would afflict miners and a symbol of how South Wales transformed from its rural to its industrial base, in a complex movement alongside and contrary to a Celtic mythology preserved as a version of pastoral. Cale's voice is that of industrial South Wales, and from this point, two musicocultural points can be made. There is a Cale voice that is that of the lyric tenor (at its most charming on *Paris 1919*, Reprise 1972), a voice able to recite like Richard Burton. Cale's lyric voice would not of itself merit attention, plenty of equivalents found in any number of male voice choirs. In addition, however, there is also the Cale voice whose character is suggested even in song titles alone—"Fear," "Guts," "Sudden Death," "Taking Your Life in Your Hands"—once memorably described by Ian Penman as being "to normative pop lyricism what a Francis Bacon Pope is to a Page Seven Fella" (Penman 1994A, 73).

When recording his voices, Cale's production principles—"nothing counts unless the tape is running" (30)—tended to leave those features open like scars on the face, and that in their screams and noise and psychoses invite us to turn again to Roland Barthes. Barthes's essay on vocal grain, the lineage of which traces back through Julia Kristeva through Jacques Lacan to Sigmund Freud, his Oedipal scene and studies in hysteria, ends with the suggestion that "the simple consideration of 'grain' in music could lead to a different history of music from the one we now know," one in which less would be made of the technical idea of music without tonality (Barthes 1977, 189).[15] That history would also constitute a history of social sediment in the voice, of the landscape of noise: "it would be very quiet on a Sunday."

The voice's extremities in Cale will often accompany a consideration of the extremities of life. The Cale voice is most immediately
recognizable as that of the psychodrama, a scream or a strangulated
whine, a cry, or a shout. As lineage, Cale was as likely to have been
crossing genre from musical modernism: Berg's operas or Ligeti's
sets of *Aventures*, for example. In pop music's terms, there was the
voice of sanctifying gospel (Aretha Franklin, "Amazing Grace"),
burning soul (James Brown, "Cold Sweat"), and psychedelic fantasy
(Arthur Brown, "Fire"); it might be a precedent as simple as the
scream toward the end of The Beatles' "Hey Jude" that points further, since with Cale the thematic material spills into the sense of
ending, of how the three-minute record might stop in or fade into
some existential netherworld. The first example appears on Cale's
first album for Island records, *Fear* (Island 1974): there was preparation in "Ghost Story" on *Vintage Violence* (Columbia 1971), but *Paris
1919* (Reprise 1973) was notably and lyrically calm throughout.
Fear's title track announces some of the key slogans of the Cale psychodrama: "home is living like a man on the run," "life and death
are things that you do when you're bored," "say: fear is a man's best
friend." The track ends at a full stop, following a careful fragmentation: cymbals and jerky bass as creepy accompaniment to a voice finally left to expressionist ranting; the phrase "so say: fear is a man's
best friend" stretched and distorted, its rhythm elongated and compressed. Performed live in later years, Cale would take leave of the
song much faster. In *John Cale Comes Alive* (Ze), a recording made in
London in 1984, the line repeats twice only before "say" screams
away over dissonance; in *Fragments of a Rainy Season* (Hannibal),
recorded in Paris in 1992, the dissolve occurs on only the second repetition, the voice this time over piano clusters. It's as though Cale
builds a sudden brick wall to contain the earlier fade, with resultant
effect on song form.

The trick of "Fear Is a Man's Best Friend" was to serve Cale well.
Repeated over the years in examples such as "Guts" and "Rollaroll"
on *Slow Dazzle* (Island 1975; "Guts" recorded in France in 1992 receives an update very similar to "Fear"), "Engine" on *Helen of Troy*
(Island 1975), "Wilson Joilet" and "Russian Roulette" on *Honi Soit*
(A&M 1981). By the time of "Magazines," a track about military
hardware on *Caribbean Sunset* (Ze 1984), the Cale ending is sounding
like self-reference. In between the last two, however, is *Music for a
New Society* (Ze 1982), the *ne plus ultra* of Cale's binding of vocal deposit and thematic reference. *Music for a New Society* (Ze 1982) rep-

resents a genuine extremity, a point beyond which there was no point. The record contains three great moments of ending: the creepy laughter at the end of "Thoughtless Kind," the line and manner of delivery that ends "Sanities" ("a strong though loving world to die in"), and the all-out roar that ends "Damn Life."

As thematic marker, Cale's voice is something that binds together several of his "exile" features: mothers and wives, deracination, violence and madness, death. "Dirtyass Rock 'n' Roll" in the Cale song had made him "feel like an undercover Sigmund Freud," and the drama of family romance is here in pulp fatness. Cale found in the Presley hit "Heartbreak Hotel" a suitable map of this emotional landscape. On *Slow Dazzle*, his vocal performance is all horror-story hisses and screams, while the instrumental space of the band's crisp chords in Presley's original is filled with ominous, Munch-like swirls. By 1992, several versions later, performed live, "Heartbreak Hotel" has become a remarkable song almost in the manner of text setting, with florid piano embellishment.

Cale's voice is the marker of removal from origin, the mark of nature that emerges with Wales as accent, and with a number of early obsessions: on all thematic fronts, aging brings with it a playing-down, compression, and containment of earlier expression. There is a characteristic obsession with the figure of the mother, starting with "Half Past France" on *Paris 1919*, and prevalent on *Fear*: "Where To, My Son?" in the title track, and on "Gun," a link made between the mother and exile: "Mother of plenty, mother of none, you got me cornered, I'm still on the run." The theme is seemingly exorcised on *Music for a New Society*, with "Sanities" perhaps its endpoint. "Sanities" is the story of a woman whose mother, "white with time," bluntly calls her a failure; "choirs of angels" enable her to elude the charge. She enters a "friendship," which turns into a marriage; it is, however, a marriage "made in the grave." In a moment of deep, one might say Germanic expressionism, there is a "searchlight" that finds her "cockleshell and sure." A remarkable list of cities—to which I shall return—follows before the ending, "a strong though loving world to die in." This is a strange and harrowing track—it's hard not to elide Cale himself with the female protagonist—and the tying-together of motherhood and exile, rather understandably, appears to stop at that point.[16] An even more remarkable calming over time is found in Cale's reference to religion and the church. "Tell Me Why," on *Walking for Locusts* (Hannibal 1996), does something that the earlier records would hardly have dared: just before three minutes into the track, Cale goes gospel! There's a barrage of "world beat" percussion around here, which Cale had used on inordinate length in "Movement 6" of the Warhol score *Eat* (Hannibal 1997); but there's also the Lafayette Inspirational Choir, gospel-derived backing vocals having been since Madonna's 1989 single "Like a Prayer" one of pop music's most insidious reference points. The very end of "Tell Me Why" is characteristically questioning, but hearing Cale singing "There's a savior looking on" can't help but feel like Garnant's last laugh. "I'm the church and I've come to claim you with my iron drum," Cale was told on "Paris 1919." The pithy "Save Us" on *Helen of Troy* is perhaps the most subtle: "save us from the house of God" is the running theme, with Cale adding in some churchy organ as coding. By "The Sleeper" on *Artificial Intelligence*, Cale's agnosticism reaches an extreme point, with a weird but Welsh comparison of himself and his lover with Jesus and, yes, Satan. Cale's pact with the devil is tribute to the way that Wales' nonconformist chapel mentality (and nonconformist rather than modernist may be the most suitable epithet to describe Cale) pervaded even someone raised in the established Church.

If thematically there are gradual changes in the voice's role, vocal drama pervades the very form of the songs themselves. A Cale trait is for vocal intensity effectively to take the space of a song's melody and divide it through antilyrical words into much smaller diminutions (see Griffiths 2003). A simple example is found in "Mary Lou" on *Guts*, where the chorus hook (at 0.36) can be represented as follows:

```
X              X          X          X            (X
Ma-ry                     Ma-ry      Ma-ry        (Lou
```

is compressed (at 1.47) into:

```
X         X                        X              (X
Ma-ry     Watch out me Watch       out Watch out  Ma-ry (Lou
```

This is followed by a hearty scream over half of the next line. There's another fine example in "Leaving It Up to You" on *Helen of Troy* where the space formerly occupied by the desolate line "Looking for a friend, looking everywhere" is padded out to contain, first, "And if you gave me half a chance, I'd do it now, I'd do it now, right now, you fascist," and then, "I know we could all feel the same like

Sharon Tate, and we could give it all, we could give it, give it, give it all." The syllable count increases, and the whole nature and tenor of the words shift dramatically in the short but regularly divided time: Other examples are to be found on "Cable Hogue" and on "Wilson Joilet." I shall further consider other and similar aspects of Cale's songwriting when examining cover versions under a later heading.

To end this section, however, it is worth briefly mentioning Cale as spoken reciter. This has a subplot all its own, and again sees transformation across time. The earliest solo example links the story of "The Jeweller" on *Slow Dazzle* back to "The Gift" on the Velvet Underground's *White Light/White Heat*, where the voice is in both cases rather pinched and foppish, as though living up to some given idea of what English short-story recitation ought to sound like. In truth, several songs were blurring the distinction of speech and song: much of *Music for a New Society*—"Sanities," again—can stand as example. By the time of "A Dream" on the Warhol tribute *Songs for Drella*, Cale's spoken voice is far more engrossing: The Welsh deposit is still there, but the voice is calm and intimate. When Cale performs other texts—Kerouac, Swedenborg, Rimbaud, and Oscar Wilde[17]—it is often as reciter: the Dylan Thomas "settings" too are notably syllabic and flatly nonexpressive. With *Last Day on Earth*, the Neurith collaboration of 1994, an assured spoken voice is now doing something far less parochial, and that leads us on to the next section.

INSTRUMENTS

Doing evil is better than doing nothing.[18]

Because to be bad, Mother, that is the real struggle: to be bad— and to enjoy it! That's what makes men of us boys, Mother.[19]

There was much violence, usually caused by the import of black-leg labour, mostly in and around the small town of Ammanford.[20]

If the voice is always going to remain to an extent "natural," the authentic marker of biological inheritance, then instruments are learned markers of society and education. Cale tells how the absence of a viola at the grammar school he attended was the chance circumstance that gave rise to one of his most distinctive characteristics (and hard-to-elude descriptions): the viola player in the Velvet Underground. How the viola even figured in a rock band is a story that says much about the 1960s, representing a particular collision between the avant-garde and the garage rock band. It seems fairly clear that Cale was no pop fan, apart from an attachment to Presley as sonic symbol of escape from South Wales via the radio airwaves. It is possible to argue that without Cale the Velvets effectively ceased to matter—this is a view encapsulated for a listener by the first minute of "Venus in Furs" from the first album; but, who knows? Cale may have been as important to the band as the driving bass at the end of "I'm Waiting for the Man" and possibly as cosongwriter to songs described as being written by Lou Reed.

Cale became the viola. On "We Will Fall" from The Stooges, on Nico's *Marble Index*, on "Fly" from Nick Drake's *Bryter Later*, his and its presence are immediately recognizable. In a BBC television program interview, Cale describes the viola's melancholic effect, but it's worth returning to first base to remember that strings, classical not folk, are, more than any other instrumental family, learned through and through: Strings, everybody knows, have to be started young. The viola thus carries the weight, the presence, originating in South Wales, of an insistence on education as the gateway to liberation. The "peripatetic" system—orchestral instruments were taught by teachers of the instrument who would travel, "peripatetically," from school to school—was a genuine case of music as class liberation, and unlike in this respect piano lessons (which he also received), which were covered by private income, or singing lessons, a different and more complicated case. When you hear John Cale's viola, this background is partly what you're hearing. It is there, too, in Megan Childs's omnipresent violin in Gorky's Zygotic Mynci, or Sean Moore's trumpet solo in "Kevin Carter" on the Manic Street Preachers' *Everything Must Go*.[21]

Cale found himself in a New York City that had "stolen the idea of modern art" (Guilbault 1983), though he gravitated less toward the "uptown" modernism of total serialism and more toward the activity that eventually surfaces in minimalism.[22] It is worth noting the form of artwork in which Cale was participating, and from which the pop song was to emerge as commercially triumphant, mixed-media, art form. Arthur Marwick, who has earlier in his social history of the 1960s described rock music as "a kind of universal language" (1998, 19) and who also pointedly asserts that the following features "continued to dominate the arts for the rest of the century," (316) lists eight "absolutely distinctive and characteristic features" of the art of the period:

1. cross-over (high/low, popular/classical)
2. the blurring of boundaries (cross art form)
3. conceptualism (concept over representation, with key role for language)
4. indeterminacy or the aleatoric (chance, and range of possible meaning)
5. participation (inclusion of reader, viewer, listener, or audience)
6. technology (including electronic music)
7. radical criticism, revolutionary stances (social commentary/manifesto)
8. social and cultural practices (particularly "counter-cultural" ones) as "spectacle" (emphasis on novelty born of commercial and technological apparatus). (316–18)

It is clear from his autobiography's earlier chapters that Cale was well acquainted with musical modernism, both European contemporary music and the American avant-garde. But classical, I think, always continued to mean for Cale classical in the music-historical sense, and that amounts in all likelihood to Beethoven. Cale's viola curiously becomes a European presence reminding American art of the heritage it attempts to take on; note "European Son to Delmore Schwarz."[23] This line again culminates in *Music for a New Society* (Ze 1982), not known for its vocal and textural aspects, so much as those very traditional elements, the bass line and harmony. This line begins on "Child's Christmas in Wales," carries through "Sylvia Said," a B-side from the *Fear* session (Island 1974), and culminates in "Damn Life" on *Music for a New Society*, where the source in Beethoven's "Ode to Joy" is made spookily clear.

The more genuinely "modern" musical line emerges when Cale continues what the viola begins, especially in orchestration. While *The Academy in Peril* (Reprise 1972) contained orchestrated instrumental pieces, the integration into songs of an instrumental element from a high-technology form of scoring associated with musical modernism begins with the track "Paris 1919" itself, orchestral strings doubling piano, especially toward the very close of the track, as harpsichord pointedly doubles an inner line. Joe Boyd, in a radio program on Nick Drake, made clear that the sound world—arguably its single most striking element—in what is probably Drake's single most famous song owed much to Cale.[24] "Northern Sky," from *Bryter Later* of 1970, uses a Hammond organ for background "wash," closely bunched celeste clusters, and pointed piano lines, and Cale himself returned to something similar for his own song, "Ship of Fools" on *Fear*.

If earlier we saw voice as the residual marker of breaking away from Wales, Cale's instrumental internationalism points toward a readiness on his part to attempt to broaden pop music's sense of place. This again falls into several phases: a surreal and modernist Europe, America as Western frontier, and finally a genuine internationalism. The key indicator here is the actual naming of place: Cale has lists of place-names the like of which would be difficult to match in pop music.

On the early records, before *Island*, and notably *Paris 1919*, there is a gently surreal Europe of the mind: some places—Amsterdam, Andalucia, Antarctica, Charlemagne—seemingly chosen for their sound alone, as in "Antarctica Starts Here" and the first line of the song "Andalucia" ("Andalucia, when shall I see ya?"). The Paris of "Paris 1919" is the Moderns' haunt and forms a tie with Cale's production and rapid cover (on *Helen of Troy*, Island 1975) of Jonathan Richman's "Pablo Picasso." ("Pablo Picasso never got called an asshole: not like you.") "Half Past France" and "Graham Greene" on *Paris 1919* seem to me the most telling tracks: "Half Past France" manages to contain Dunkirk, Paris, Norway (a character called Old Helvig), Dundee, and Berlin. "Graham Greene" is very much of its time, with a touch of, yes, the Pythonesque humor of the vocal tracks on *The Academy in Peril* ("Legs Larry at Television Centre" and "King Harry"). As Cale pushes his Welsh accent a little further to mimic the Jamaican suggested by an underlying reggae beat, it's an early hint at a potential xenophobia—an important theme, to which I return. But this is Welsh as anti-English, with "umbrella," "Carruthers," and "Enoch Powell" all mentioned in jest. The chorus ("Welcome back to Chipping Sodbury") brings together a descending bass and eventual trumpet solo to which Cale was to return for "Dead or Alive" on *Honi Soit* (A&M 1981). It's an important track and one that looks ahead to the world of Gorky's Zygotic Mynci.

With "Ship of Fools" on Fear, Cale's place naming becomes fixed more on the handover from Wales to America: one moment Memphis and Tombstone, the next gradually approaching his home village Swansea, and its sonorous suburb Mumbles, Ammanford and, finally, Garnant.[25] On Cale's three records on the Island label there are several evocations of an American heartland, the "new place to dwell" of "Heartbreak Hotel": "Buffalo Ballet," "Darling I Need You," "Mary Lou," and "Cable Hogue" are examples, while "Leaving It Up to You" seems to engage with a Californian dystopia. These references seem very much of their time, a Wild West of the Welsh imagination, and it is to Cale's credit that he moves on, even though the songs on the Island label remain, as songs, among his most immediately recognizable.

Moving away from an American heartland, Cale's range takes on an interesting and international sweep, seemingly self-consciously so. By all accounts, he takes an interest in conspiracy theories in international affairs, and a friendship with the novelist Thomas Pynchon is apparently based on talking about "rocket systems" (Cale 1999, 238; Penman 1994A, 29). The album *Honi Soit* appears to be the instigator, in tracks such as the title track, "Wilson Joilet," "Strange Times in Casablanca," and, especially so, "Russian Roulette." The opening of the live album *Sabotage* (Spy 1979) is one of the most arresting and captures well Cale's confidence in dealing with broad issues (though sharpening the distinction between killing and dying is a pure remnant of psychodrama Cale). "Mercenaries are useless," he declares, "disunited, unfaithful. They have nothing more to keep them in a battle other than a meager wage which is just about enough to make them want to kill for you but not enough to make them want to die for you." Albums on the Ze and Beggars Banquet labels continue and extend the references, notable songs being "Praetorian Underground" on *Caribbean Sunset* (Ze 1984) and "Satellite Walk" on *Artificial Intelligence* (Beggars Banquet 1985). By now, too, the lists have become quite singular: "Forever Changed" on *Songs for Drella* (Warner 1990) pointedly lists "Burma, Thailand, and Hong Kong," "Entre Nous" on *Walking on Locusts* (Hannibal 1996) has the "Cote d'Azur," but also "Herefordshire," possibly a sign of returning to Wales.

This sets up *Last Day on Earth* (MCA 1994), Cale's collaboration with Bob Neurith, as a sustained examination of the theme of internationalism. "Maps of the World" is perhaps a culmination, with a huge list of place-names called beneath a song that makes strong statements about the status of place.[26] The traveler who has appeared throughout the album, and played by Cale, wants "the latest world atlas," but is told by Neurith that this may be precluded by the rapidity of change in world politics, "since the east has returned to the dance floor." Against repeated quaver-rhythm chords, Cale ponders this change and the idea that places have become valued only as metaphors and measures of people's lives. If earlier we saw that home for Cale was "living like a man on the run" then there is something poignant about the hook-line of "Maps of the World" repeating the line "I'm leaving for home tonight," except for the fact that place in the song has by now become a very fluid concept. In fact, in general, *Last Day on Earth* extends the verbal reference of pop song, mingling the terminologies of art history with that of international politics.

Cale's internationalism is a signal of a profound trust in modernity, albeit played through the pop song, an attitude that is in his most recent work, much of it instrumental, is extended or, possibly and paradoxically, undermined by an interest in "world music." Before ending this section, however, I'd like to consider a group of songs in which such a welcome readiness to engage in international affairs reveals a latent xenophobia: two of them, "Model Beirut Recital" and "Chinese Takeaway (Hong Kong 1997)," are on Cale's mid-1980s records *Caribbean Sunset* and *Artificial Intelligence*, respectively, while "Crazy Egypt," jointly written with David Byrne, is on the more recent *Walking on Locusts*. "Model Beirut Recital" is described in the autobiography as

> idiosyncratic, a rock song about Lebanon. I had a Lebanese guy with a very chequered background come into the studio. He was an arms dealer but I'd met him via an Israeli. He came in and recited the lines "Beirut, you're a whore and you've been raped. I spit on you." And the rest of it is just Israeli back-chatter. It was meant to deal with an obnoxious subject in a passionate, sympathetic way. (Cale 1999, 204)

While there can be little doubt that Cale will have direct knowledge and experience of the Middle East, there is nevertheless a case for seeing the track as too rapid an engagement with its subject matter. At the same time in England, Morrissey was also attempting at least to encompass, in songs like "Asian Rut" and "Bengali in Platforms," an Asian perspective at a time when an Asian presence hardly seems to have registered on the landscape of British pop.[27] Given the controversy that Morrissey stirred at the time, it must be admitted that Cale goes a lot further and actually imitates the voice of a Beirut resident, so engaging with all manner of murky matters about representation and expression. "Chinese Takeaway (Hong Kong 1997)" is, if anything, worse. Credited to Cale alongside Monnot Moustaki and Wood, this track takes the form of a drum beat and a simple guitar riff that is interrupted by a succession of "Western" music: Bach's D minor organ partita, Debussy's "Fille aux cheveux de lin," Elgar's "Nimrod," Beethoven's "Moonlight" Sonata juxtaposed with Morricone's theme to *The Good, the Bad, and the Ugly*, Bach's "Air on the G String," the theme from the British radio program "The Archers" (at which point there are laughs all round), Beethoven's "Für Elise," and Edith Piaf's "Milord." It's a throwaway and thoroughly execrable track already, an impression its title does little to offset. "Crazy Egypt" returns to David Byrne the compliment of sounding rather like Talking Heads, but again there seems to be little context for the assertion in their collaboration that "I think you're Crazy Egypt."

What's going on in these tracks? It's probably worth remembering that, despite enacting for liberals the air of revolution, the artistic modernists were by and large firmly right wing. Given Cale's credo, three times repeated in the autobiography, that doing evil is better than doing nothing, and his sustained position as rock star in exile, then he has probably developed a sense of self-certainty that can reach beyond a certain limit. It's probably true to say, too, that South Wales—a left stronghold in the UK and characterized by a tradition of working-class solidarity—nevertheless developed its own deep-seated conservatisms, and in which an inner certainty hardened in exile could be manifest as outward signs of xenophobia. We return to this topic further when considering Cale's songs and their resistance to cover; it may be that the pop song is at best a limited vehicle for the direct rehearsal of contentious political debate.

PRODUCTION AND COVER

Cale's record in and evident commitment to production confirms a "heroic" romanticism in being, as he would put it, a "composer's composer, a musician's musician, and a producer's producer" (Cale 1999, 145). He arrived in New York at a fecund time in the emergence of the hero-producer, with Phil Spector's work in Gold Star Studios in Los Angeles from 1963 to 1966 as inspiration, followed more immediately by Brian Wilson's work on the Beach Boys' *Pet*

Sounds of 1966. Wilson is in this respect Cale's eminence grise, *Slow Dazzle* (Island 1975) opening with "Mr. Wilson," an intended tribute. Reissued outtakes for and an early live performance of "Good Vibrations," Wilson's 1966 meisterwerk single, dramatizes for the listener the issues that Cale would have to grapple with.[28] The studio-bound, instrumental outtakes describe a space seemingly devoid of Beach Boys, with Wilson issuing commands from behind the glass; the live performance is all vocal charm built on notably unsteady instrumental support. As for Wilson, for Cale being in the studio meant the control of recording technology, but also the *un*-learning of the control of musical technique, and so it's arguably in the studio that Cale really does confront dislocation at firsthand. The result is again a very characteristic merging of talent and skill with a residual romanticism.

When Cale does get mentioned as producer, it's often in order to draw attention to the albums he produced for others: notably, and the guarantor of a place in the history of punk, debuts by The Stooges, The Modern Lovers, and Patti Smith. What has tended to be overlooked is Cale's own production of his own recordings, which take their bearings more from his production of Nico's *Marble Index*. This seems to have been a method that combined studio spontaneity with a kind of sustained attention to the consequences of multitracking. Cale has described the "technique" of producing *Music for a New Society* in helpfully precise terms:

> There was a certain style of arranging that happened on a Nico LP. I managed to separate the organ away from Nico's voice; then I would do a "pass" where I would choose an instrument and do something in another direction from the basic track; and then I would do another one that was entirely different from the one I just did; and I went on until I had about three or four parts that were totally disconnected. . . . Then I took out the middle part of it and just left the voice with all these parts floating around. (Penman 1994A, 73)

In a manner reminiscent of the recording principles of Brian Eno, Cale will emphasize the nature of recording as having to do with recording as something beyond performance itself: human expression captured on tape as something fragile in a soundworld not so far from a more modernist idea of electroacoustic music.[29] Yet again, *Music for a New Society* insists on consideration, this time as a profound examination of the human voice as ghost in a machine environment, an effect possibly captured in the weird photographs included on the cover of the original vinyl record. Where this edition ended with the track that has Cale's third wife, Risé, reciting over a record of Rimsky-Korsakov, the reissued CD includes a track even more radical, "Through the Library of Force," which plays out to a very strange amalgam of Debussy's "Clair de Lune," Wagnerian chord meanderings, using studio effects as cadence to the record.[30]

Although talking critically about production is still something new (Moore 1993, 105–10; see also Théberge 1997), a way into Cale's production work lies I think in the endings of songs, "song," for this purpose, itself a fairly unstable concept. Performed pieces of music end with cadences; records often end with fadeouts: Cale in the Island years, as we've seen, was trying to end performatively, to set a point of intensity further along the duration of a recorded song. With *Music for a New Society* and on the Neurith collaboration, *Last Day on Earth*, it is as though the idea of engaging with studio technology functions as a method of conclusion. Note the conclusions to tracks on *Last Day on Earth* (1994):

1. spoken word "I'm just an innocent here," fading, dissolving into noise and sound effects (rain);
2. spoken word "deserves everything," piano and noise, sound effect (airplane);
3. spoken word to banjo/viola "riff" to sound effects (gunshots and farmyard noises);
4. spoken (shouted) word with underlying marching steps to viola improvisation to keyboard fade;
5. studio effects and sound effects to viola to noise;
6. standard fade to cadential chords, slight studio effect, and drum beats;
7. cadential chords over standard fade to keyboard improvisation and chords, wind phrase;
8. standard fade of song to viola and studio effects;
9. standard fade of song to Eno/Lanois studio sound;
10. (Instrumental): fragmentation of sound—strings, drums—drum marchbeat to end;
11. cadential chords and viola—wind phrases to "imperfect" end;
12. fragmented material to standard fade;
13. song merges into keyboard chords and fragmentation to spoken word;

14. spoken word to fragmentation and lead to next song through piano and effects;
15. standard cadence through studio effect to held note;
16. studio effect with held note.

Consideration of Cale in the studio blurs any firm distinction between song, performance, and recording, a situation liable to challenge any fixed baggage that Cale in all likelihood carried about genius and originality. The cover version in pop music is always to my mind a fertile vantage point from which to view these issues, drawing attention not so much to a song's fixity as its recorded flexibility, its availability fixedly as song to remain still or flexibly as recording to adapt over time and place. Cale is interesting in this respect, on the one hand virtually defining himself through the cover of "Heartbreak Hotel," as a strong if selective appropriator of others' songs, but himself notably not covered by others.

This latter characteristic—of the 110 or so songs recorded I know of only the one Cale song covered[31]—puts Cale firmly with the writers of songs that set up resistance to appropriation. As a brief illustration, of The Beatles, McCartney songs are easily covered—"Yesterday" is one of the most covered songs of all—since they emphasize both in melody and words a sense of inclusiveness or community. The words basically don't say very much: "All the lonely people: where do they all come from?" Lennon songs are more resistant, since they rely more on the emotion and the voice of the recording itself; the words make strong statements and often say a lot about Lennon at the time: "A working-class hero is something to be." Or as Cale puts it in the autobiography: "I've always disliked songs that ask questions. Finding answers is more important" (Cale 1999, 265).[32] It feels as though Cale's songs are in this respect doomed to be filed in a pop category with some other songwriters passed over for the strength of statement: Kevin Rowland, Julian Cope, Robyn Hitchcock.

This all has to do with a strong sense of one's own character and personality. In singing a Cale song, what happens is that he occupies or takes over your own personality. In "Dying on the Vine," it's hard to work a way into the words. A line like "smelling like an old adobe woman, or a William Burroughs playing for lost time," and the song's scenario of military threat combined with "thinking about my mother." These things are wholly idiosyncratic.[33] Interestingly, the original recording of "Dying on the Vine," on *Artificial Intelligence,* was led, presumably by Cale's studio instinct, into an emphasis on Cale's voice, surrounded with doom-laden studio sound firmly of its time. It's only when the paraphernalia is stripped away, on the 1992 Paris concert, that the song emerges as a concise and encapsulated drama.[34]

When Cale chooses to cover a song, however, not surprisingly, it feels like a fight for control. Leonard Cohen's "Hallelujah" is again transformed by Cale, so that when Jeff Buckley came to record it, it felt as though he was performing the Cale cover rather than the Cohen original.[35] With "Heartbreak Hotel," to which I have already alluded, cover becomes obsession and form of self-definition. Rarely can a single song have been covered, performed, recorded so often; but also rarely does a cover version so "become" the appropriator.[36] That it is a song of Presley, font and origin of the musical myth of America and rock, which stands emblematically as Cale's vantage point is expressive enough; in the concluding section it remains only to suggest a way in which Cale's living as a "man on the run" and having to find "a new place to dwell," how all of this informs what eventually comes to pass, as his Aunt Mai would sing, "in the hillsides" and "in the vales."[37]

CONCLUSION

Libraries gave us power.[38]

People who don't change will find themselves like folk musicians, playing in museums and local as a motherfucker.[39]

Chwi a gewch wybod y gwirionedd, a'r gwirionedd a'ch rhyddhâ chwi.[40]

What's Welsh for Zen? ends as it begins, in Wales, and Cale struggles, especially toward the conclusion, to articulate the effect of the homeland and his deracination. Cale's descriptions of the homeland sometimes cross the line between nostalgia and sentiment; his relation to Wales, with so much spatial and temporal distance between them, seems primarily nostalgic and devoid of irony; bitterness, when it appears, is turned inward on the home rather than directed with any anger toward the social condition of South Wales. It's a far cry from the biggest Welsh band of the 1990s, Manic Street Preachers, who, especially on *The Holy Bible*, produced precisely such a sustained diatribe; that said, the band has always remained in the UK if not in Wales itself, and, unlike Cale, are all monoglot English speakers.[41] If earlier I suggested that Cale's exile left behind a certain state-sponsored version of Welsh music, then is it now possible to see Cale as the fulcrum, the Welsh Atlantic as a kind of necessary removal, which leads to the current condition of Welsh music?

Cale appears to have spotted his heirs in Gorky's Zygotic Mynci, of all the rush of bands to have appeared from Wales the one which most preserved a tension between the Welsh and English languages. Listening to Gorky's single releases, or an album like *Barafundle*, makes one wonder why Cale is so hung up on the idea that his work in pop music is some kind of delayed adolescence awaiting its proper elevation to the classical pantheon, even while he himself has to ascend to Parnassus through supplying music for mixed-media forms: settings of poetry, music for the dance or—for so many of its finest practitioners lowest of the low—film music.[42] To turn back to a fairly basic essentialism, it's a Welsh thing: Garnant has stood its ground, and is asking for more. The great irony is that Cale's carrying of the myth of modernity—genius, originality, Beethoven—has presaged a far more significant development: staying cool about the English language.[43] With this, several things follow.

First, the culture of South Wales has a model of how to proceed, since any specifically Welsh-language emphasis always tended to downplay it. Second, the idea of being innately bilingual becomes something confidently to be asserted rather than hidden away as an uncertain split of personality. Third and finally, the markers of Wales, listening to John Cale would suggest, are musical traces that sometimes can be heard and at other times need interpretation. The flag, the anthem, the rugby shirt, and dressing up as druids once every year, all of these may be one thing, but what one is really worth engaging with and defending in the idea of Wales is something far more complex and contradictory, and listening critically for its musical trace is a good place to start.

ACKNOWLEDGMENT

This article was published in an earlier incarnation in *Welsh Music History*, vol. 4, 2000.

NOTES

1. Cale and Bockris (1999, 218). Elsewhere, writing of his relation to orchestral musicians, he is keen not to appear as "some jerk who's using his name from rock and roll to come in and conduct a concert" (214).

2. "Heartbreak Hotel," studio version on *Helen of Troy*. Live recordings from London 1971 and 1984 and Paris 1992 are commercially available; the studio recording appears in all three compilations. A Cale discography can be found in *Record Collector* 159 (1992): 101.

3. Zappa and Costello, incidentally, both of whom have their own versions of the tension involved, would both articulate the point very differently from Cale. See Frank Zappa with Peter Occhiogrosso, *The Real Frank Zappa Book* (London: Picador, 1989), 139–97; Peter Doggett, "Elvis Costello: The Record Collector Interview," part 2, *Record Collector* 194 (October 1995), 92.

4. My key references for perspectives on Celticism include the following: Kiberd 1995; Smith 1993; Williams 1989; Smith 1989; Regan 1998.

5. "Possible to demonstrate": The first Velvet Underground features regularly in critics' polls, among which, *New Musical Express*, 2 October 1993 (6); *Mojo*, August 1995 (9); Palmer 1996, 296; Willis 1996. On the subgenres: Glam rock took bearings from Lou Reed; for punk, Cale produced the debut albums of The Stooges, Jonathan Richman, and Patti Smith; and alt-rock, see Schneider 1996, where the Velvet Undergound is found as, among other things, one of the "100 most influential alternative releases of all time" (4), and "the greatest garage recordings of the twentieth century," (14–15). See also Bockris and Malanga 1983.

6. This paragraph takes its orientations from Gilroy 1993A; I have also benefited from: Solomos and Back 1996; Malik 1996; Cashmore 1996; Goldberg 1994; Donald and Rattansi 1992; Hall 1997; Gilroy 1997; Gilroy 1993B; Baker, Diawara, and Lindeborg 1996; Morley and Chen 1996; and Bonnett 2000.

7. Gilroy, 1993A, 85. Gilroy adapts a statement at p. 55 of Stuart Hall in Baker, Diawara, and Lindeborg 1996. See also Hall 1996A, 411–40, 441–49, and 465–75.

8. The Pogues, "Fairytale of New York," *If I Should Fall from Grace with God* (WEA 1988).

9. A series of recent articles by Lawrence Grossberg would appear to support the view that different premises are now operating more generally in popular music and its reception. See Grossberg 1994, 1997, and 1999.

10. A good example is Gilroy's attack on Raymond Williams, in Gilroy 1987, 49–51.

11. It is worth noting again that Frank Zappa would better articulate his own relation to the tradition of garage bands such as The Kingsmen. See Zappa 1989, 39–50.

12. On failure, see Cale 1999, 268. On heroism, see Cale 1999, 209.

13. Lou Reed and John Cale, "Smalltown" on Songs for Drella.

14. BBC Wales television production, 1997.

15. Barthes 1977, 189. Barthes's distinction between pheno- and geno-text (182–83) is derived from Kristeva 1984. See also Lechte 1990; Rose 1988; Moi 1986.

16. Cale's agonizing over losing or leaving his mother reminds me of the Jewish mother in a novel such as Philip Roth's *Portnoy's Complaint* (1969): Another Jewish novelist mentions sexual endeavor "on a scale that no one who wasn't Jewish or Welsh could possibly understand the need for" (Jacobson 1984, 16). When stereotype mothers appear, however, it is worth remembering Kingsley Amis's searching critique: "If Jewish mothers are so unbearable, what makes them like that? Well: perhaps something to do with the position of mothers in Jewish society, in particular with how their men behave towards them. And if Portnoy Senior in earlier years was anything like Alex in rather later ones (and I suspect he was) then we can forgive Mrs. Portnoy a lot" (Amis 1970, 104–05).

17. These are found on, respectively, Kerouac—*Kicks Joy Darkness* (Rykodisc 1997), *Eat/Kiss* (Rykodisc 1997), *Sahara Blue* (Crammed Discs 1992), and *Chansons des Mers Froids* (Sony 1994), the two latter directed by Hector Zazou, and the last in collaboration with Suzanne Vega.

18. Cale 1999, 268. See also "Helmut Newton Told Me," "Wish You Were Here," "Oh! To Be Invited to the Venice Biennale," *Caged/Uncaged: A Rock/Experimental Homage to John Cage* (Cramps 1993), Cale's accompaniment to a recitation by Ann Magnuson.

19. Roth 1986, 268.

20. Morgan 1983, 284.

21. Gorky's Zygotic Mynci, (for example) *Barafundle* (Fontana 1997); Manic Street Preachers, *Everything Must Go* (Epic 1996).

22. There is a minimalist element in some of Cale's recent ballet music, possibly due to its being a technique that helps pad out stage time.

23. "European Son to Delmore Schwartz" was a track on the first Velvet Underground album.

24. Broadcast on BBC Radio 2, 20 June 1998.

25. "Garnant stood its ground and asked for more" I presume to be a reference to the pitched battles Cale describes at Cale 1999, 19. Cale's earliest recorded song, "The Soul of Patrick Lee" on *Church of Anthrax*, included reference to Bangor and Swansea Bay.

26. Among which: Zaire, Moscow, Rwanda, Zimbabwe, Botswana, Lesoto, Tanzania, Libya, Zambeze, Kalahari, Burundi, Mozambique, Namibia, Angola, Cuba, Somalia, Papua New Guinea, Cameroon, Sierra Leone, Senegal, Western Sahara, Morocco, Liberia, Estonia, Latvia, Nashville, Encino, Vancouver, Argentina, France, Syria, Catalonia, Oslo.

27. See *New Musical Express*, 22 August 1992.

28. Both included in *Good Vibrations: Thirty Years of the Beach Boys* (Capitol, 1993).

29. Anyone keen to hear wide open spaces in U2 would be wise to keep in mind the image of Brian Eno and Daniel Lanois boxed inside a studio: see Moore forthcoming. See also Tamm, 1989, 62–78.

30. The reader may now be tired of my constant reference to *Music for a New Society*, but see Penman 1994B. I do think the album defines a certain borderline of the possibilities of pop music, the one that touches on aspects of modernism and expressionism. A model for the kind of psychoanalytic reading that the album invites is found in Reynolds and Press 1995.

31. Billy Bragg, "Fear Is a Man's Best Friend," *The Peel Sessions* (Strange Fruit 1987), first broadcast 3 August 1983. Richard Thomas's sleeve note to the reissued *Animal Justice* EP (1999, originally 1976) mentions a cover by Bauhaus of "Rosegarden Full of Stones."

32. Mathias and Garlick mention a "strong awareness of form, technique, *wrought language*" (emphasis mine) as being characteristic of Welsh verse written in English (1984, 32).

33. See also, Garlick and Mathias (1984): "Certainly the presentness of the past broods over Anglo-Welsh poetry, often offering an obstacle to the outside reader—for whom the language is lucid accessible but, unless he has done his homework and can pick up the allusions, the poem remains opaque or yields only part of its meaning" (33).

34. A studio recording is also available, on *10% File under Burroughs* (Sub Rosa 1993).

35. Leonard Cohen, *Various Positions* (Columbia 1984), John Cale on compilation of Cohen cover versions, *I'm Your Fan* (East West 1991)—both these also found on John Cale single (Columbia 1991) along with Cale/Cohen collaboration, "The Queen and I"; Jeff Buckley, *Grace* (Columbia 1994).

36. Cale's cover of "Streets of Laredo" on *Honi Soit* sounds to me like an attempt to find another "Heartbreak Hotel."

37. "We'll Keep a Welcome" was known in the recorded version by Mai Jones; see Cale's affectionate memoir of his aunt at Cale 1999, 26.

38. Manic Street Preachers (Nicky Wire), "A Design for Life," on *Everything Must Go* (Epic 1996).

39. Davis 1990, 86.

40. John chapter 8, verse 32 ("And ye shall know the truth and the truth will make you free"). See also Paulin 1986, 29.

41. *The Holy Bible* (Epic 1994). See Price 1999.

42. In addition to several soundtrack albums, many of which are issued on the Crépuscule label between 1991 and 1995, see also John Cale, "Picture the Scene," *House of America* (EMI 1997), and "I Shot Andy Warhol Suite," *I Shot Andy Warhol* (Tag/Atlantic 1996). Cale's score to films by Andy Warhol have been issued as *Eat/Kiss* on Hannibal in 1997.

43. At the time of writing, devolution to Wales had occurred with Cale performing at its celebration concert in Cardiff in 1999. This seemed so much media hype compared to the enduring postcolonial saga of Ireland, on which see Eagleton 1999, 44–61.

BIBLIOGRAPHY

Amis, Kingsley. *What Became of Jane Austen? and Other Questions*. London: Jonathan Cape, 1970.

Baker, Houston A. Jr., Manthia Diawara, and Ruth H. Lindeborg, eds. *Black British Cultural Studies: A Reader*. Chicago: University of Chicago Press, 1996.

Barthes, Roland. "The Grain of the Voice." In *Image-Music-Text*, edited and translated by Stephen Heath, 179–89. London: Fontana, 1977.

Bockris, Victor, and Gerald Malanga. *Uptight: The Velvet Underground Story*. London: Omnibus, 1983.

Bonnett, Alastair. *Anti-Racism*. New York: Routledge, 2000.

Bürger, Peter. *Theory of the Avant-garde*. Translated by Michael Shaw with foreword by Jochen Schulte-Sasse. Minneapolis: University of Minnesota Press, 1984.

Cale, John, and Victor Bockris. *What's Welsh for Zen? The Autobiography of John Cale*. London: Bloomsbury, 1999.

Cashmore, Ellis. *Dictionary of Race and Ethnic Relations*, 4th ed. London: Routledge, 1996.

Davis, Miles (with Quincy Troupe). *The Autobiography*. London: Picador, 1990.

Doggett, Peter. "Elvis Costello: The Record Collector Interview," Part 2. *Record Collector* 194 (October 1995): 92.

Donald, James, and Ali Rattansi, eds. *"Race," Culture and Difference*. London: Sage/Open University, 1992.

Eagleton, Terry. "Nationalism and the Case of Ireland." *New Left Review* 234 (1999): 44–61.

Flanagan, William, ed. *Written in My Soul*. London: Omnibus, 1990.

Gilroy, Paul. *There Ain't No Black in the Union Jack: The Cultural Politics of Race and Nation*. London: Routledge, 1987.

Gilroy, Paul. *The Black Atlantic: Modernity and Double Consciousness*. London: Verso, 1993a.

Gilroy, Paul. *Small Acts: Thoughts on the Politics of Black Cultures*. London: Serpent's Tail, 1993b.

Gilroy, Paul. "'After the Love Has Gone': Bio-politics and Ethno-poetics in the Black Public Sphere." *Public Culture* 7 (1994): 49–76.

Gilroy, Paul. "Diaspora and the Detours of Identity." In *Identity and Difference,* edited by Kathryn Woodward, 299–346. London: Sage/Open University, 1997.

Goldberg, David Theo, ed. *Multiculturalism: A Critical Reader.* Oxford: Blackwell, 1994.

Griffiths, Dai. "From Lyric to Anti-Lyric: Analysing the Words in Pop Song." In *Analysing Popular Music,* edited by Allan F. Moore, 39–59. Cambridge: Cambridge University Press, 2003.

Grossberg, Lawrence. "Is Anybody Listening? Does Anybody Care? On Talking about 'The State of Rock.'" In *Microphone Fiends: Youth Music and Youth Culture,* edited by Andrew Ross and Tricia Rose, 41–58. London: Routledge, 1994.

Grossberg, Lawrence. "Introduction: Re-placing the Popular." In *Dancing in Spite of Myself: Essays on Popular Culture,* 1–26. Durham: Duke University Press, 1997.

Grossberg, Lawrence. "Same As It Ever Was? Rock Culture. Same As It Ever Was! Rock Theory." In *Stars Don't Stand Still in the Sky: Music and Myth,* edited by Karen Kelly and Evelyn McDonnel, 99–121. London: Routledge, 1999.

Guilbaut, Serge. *How New York Stole the Idea of Modern Art: Abstract Expressionism, Freedom, and the Cold War.* Translated by Arthur Goldhammer. Chicago: University of Chicago Press, 1983.

Hall, Stuart. "Gramsci's Relevance for the Study of Race and Ethnicity," "Two Ethnicities," and "What is this 'Black' in Black Popular Culture?" In *Stuart Hall: Critical Dialogues in Cultural Studies,* edited by David Morley and Kuan-Hsing Chen, 411–40, 441–49, and 465–75. New York: Routledge, 1996A.

Hall, Stuart. "Race, Articulation, and Societies Structured in Dominance." In *Black British Cultural Studies: A Reader,* edited by Houston A. Baker Jr., Manthia Diawara, and Ruth H. Lindeborg, 16–60. Chicago: University of Chicago Press, 1996B.

Hall, Stuart. "The Spectacle of the 'Other.'" In *Representation: Cultural Representation and Signifying Practices,* edited by Stuart Hall, 223–90. London: Sage/Open University, 1997.

Hutnyk, John. "Adorno at Womad: South Asian Crossovers and the Limits of Hybridity-Talk." In *Debating Cultural Hybridity: Multi-Cultural Identities and the Politics of Anti-Racism,* edited by Pnina Werbner and Tariq Modood, 106–36. London: Zed, 1997.

Jacobson, Howard. *Coming from Behind.* London: Black Swan, 1984.

John, Carey. *The Intellectuals and the Masses: Pride and Prejudice among the Literary Intelligentsia 1880-1939.* London: Faber, 1992.

Kiberd, Declan. *Inventing Ireland: The Literature of the Modern Nation.* London: Vintage, 1995.

Kristeva, Julia. *Revolution in Poetic Language.* Translated by Margaret Waller. New York: Columbia University Press, 1984.

Lechte, John. *Julia Kristeva.* London: Routledge, 1990.

Malik, Kenan. *The Meaning of Race: Race, History and Culture in Western Society.* London: Macmillan, 1996.

Marwick, Arthur. *The Sixties: Cultural Revolution in Britain, France, Italy, and the United States, c.1958–c.1974.* Oxford: Oxford University Press, 1998.

Mathias, Roland, and Raymond Garlick. "Introduction." In *Anglo-Welsh Poetry 1480–1980.* Bridgend: Poetry Wales Press, 1984.

Moi, Toril, ed. *The Kristeva Reader.* Oxford: Blackwell, 1986.

Moore, Allan F. *Rock: The Primary Text.* Buckingham: Open University, 1993.

Moore, Allan F. "U2 and the Myth of Authenticity in Rock." *Popular Musicology* 3, 1998, 5–34.

Morgan, Kenneth O. *Wales: Rebirth of a Nation 1880–1980.* Oxford: Oxford University Press, 1983.

Morley, David, and Kuan-Hsing Chen, eds. *Stuart Hall: Critical Dialogues in Cultural Studies.* London: Routledge, 1996.

Palmer, Robert. "Modern Rock Top Ten." In *Dancing in the Street: A Rock and Roll History.* London: BBC, 1996.

Paulin, Tom. "Introduction." In *The Faber Book of Political Verse.* London: Faber, 1986.

Penman, Ian. "European Son," *The Wire* 125 (1994A): 29–30, 73.

Penman, Ian. Review of the reissued *Music for a New Society. The Wire* 123 (May 1994B): 56.

Price, Simon. *Everything (A Book about Manic Street Preachers).* London: Virgin, 1999.

Regan, Stephen, ed. *The Eagleton Reader.* Oxford: Blackwell, 1998.

Rose, Jacqueline. "Julia Kristeva: Take Two." In *Sexuality in the Field of Vision.* London: Verso, 1988.

Roth, Philip. *Portnoy's Complaint.* Harmondsworth: Penguin, 1986.

Schneider, Scott, and the Editors of Rolling Stone Press. *Rolling Stone's Alt-Rock-a-Rama.* New York: Delta, 1996.

Sharma, Sanjay, John Hutnyk, and Ashwani Sharma, eds. *Dis-Orienting Rhythms: The Politics of the New Asian Dance Music.* London: Zed, 1996.

Smith, Dai. "Relating to Wales." In *Raymond Williams: Critical Perspectives,* edited by Terry Eagleton, 34–53. Cambridge: Polity, 1989.

Smith, Dai. *Aneurin Bevan and the World of South Wales.* Cardiff: University of Wales Press, 1993.

Solomos, John, and Les Back. *Racism and Society.* London: Macmillan, 1996.

Tamm, Eric. *Brian Eno: His Music and the Vertical Color of Sound.* Boston: Faber and Faber, 1989.

Théberge, Paul. *Any Sound You Can Imagine: Making Music/Consuming Technology.* Hanover: Wesleyan University Press, 1997.

Williams, Raymond. *Resources of Hope: Culture, Democracy, Socialism,* edited by Robin Gable. London: Verso, 1989.

Willis, Ellen. "Velvet Underground." In *Stranded: Rock and Roll for a Desert Island,* edited by Greil Marcus. New York: Da Capo Press, 1996.

Zappa, Frank with Peter Occhiogrosso. *The Real Frank Zappa Book.* London: Picador, 1989.

7

The Apollos of Shamrockery: Traditional Musics in the Modern Age

Fintan Vallely

Irish traditional music is becoming a victim of its own success. Its top artists live lives that two decades ago would be more associated with rock stars. The music supports hundreds of performers—hungry young Apollos of shamrockery blasting with guitars, ballads, and *bodhráns* through the thousands of "Irish" bars worldwide, local Irish pub-session musicians and major, popularly acclaimed and well-paid festival and concert-hall players. These feature currently in more than 2,000 CDs; the music is now taught theoretically in academic institutions, and with livings to be made, it is a viable career option. And so too an under life. For people with no grounding in its ethos are also attracted in, presenting themselves sometimes as pundits, producing cross-bred highs that are viewed from within Irish music as sometimes good, but more often naïve, arrogant, or just bewildering. Considered as the blossoming of a distinctly Irish music industry this is positive development—indeed adding up to a sophisticated classicization (Bohlman 1988, 134). But from within the genre of traditional music it can also be interpreted as destructive. This thinking draws on awareness of the dissolution of myths already achieved by those such as Georgina Boyes (1993), Dave Harker (1985), and, indeed by a large body of ethnomusicological scholarship.

But parallel with Bohlman (see in particular 1988) and others' patient logic, in the life of music in the real world there is also that other vital ingredient of ethnomusicology—the subscribing people. To them, myth bashing is not particularly important: They have merely to deal with the trees rather than the forest. It is largely ir-

relevant to them that the analyst catalogs the music as a forest containing an ecological balance of varied, indigenous base material,
classical influence, Baroque structure, and borrowed Scottish, English, and French artifacts that among potentially pathological urbanization and technology were given enough life support by Romantic politicization and Francis O'Neill[1] as to be able to survive
until rescue by the mass-recordability of the cassette, cozy resusci-
tation by large-scale production, and commodification. As Hobsbawm and Ranger (1983) so dazzlingly demonstrate, the seeming
absoluteness of tradition and nationality are easily demolished, but
one does also need human constructs to make sense of an otherwise
senseless existence. Few cultural inventions have greater appeal
than musics, and once adopted, these can progressively accrue ad-
ditional meaning, becoming vital to the plasma of identity.

At a *Cultures of Ireland* conference in Co. Cavan in 1991, I attended
a workshop participated in also by one David Blatherwick, the then
British Ambassador to Ireland. The session topic was "GAA[2] games
and Irish Culture," and all contributors constantly, confidently, and
casually referenced "Irish culture." Thrown off the British Council's
inclusion of science and technology in his own idea of "culture,"
eventually the imperial emissary asked in total confusion: "What IS
this 'Irish Culture'?" Everyone stared at him in scorn: They simply
KNEW what it was, even if they couldn't articulate it. For aside from
its huge, indescribably complex anti-Imperial political ethos, Irish
culture as experienced is wee girls in green dance costumes, the
harp, *ceili* dance, 1798, the famine, W. B. Yeats, and the Irish language. In Ireland the term *culture* is reserved for indigenous material
utilized in the construction of distinct identity, its conceptual notion
defined ideally a century ago.

An extension of this political/social/artistic vision is its use, with
other appropriate referents, to describe "Protestant culture," but still
the nineteenth-century model remains the meaningful standard.
Such a view is pragmatic. One knows who one is and that's that.
Anything else needed to be known in the twentieth century can be
accommodated, but under a different label. As, for example, the inevitable rejoinder to the "I'm an agnostic myself" cop-out on the vital question on religion: "Ah! But are you a Protestant agnostic or a
Catholic agnostic?" Culture is defined at birth, a handy working rule
that nobody in Ireland can escape from any more than could Eliza
Doolittle from hers. Even though one can be broadmindedly "plu-

ralist," one brings even to that notion one's birthmark—for "pluralism," particularly in Northern Ireland, means adding an "s" to the
established certainties of "culture," "identity," and "heritage."

But while cynical political manipulation is one thing, the birthmark itself is another—that is, not necessarily a bad thing. Over the
1990s we witnessed the disintegration of the previous half-century
of experimental European integration, people retreating to the cover
of ancient bards cloaked in modern flags, the heraldry of xenophobia retrospectively investing and reinvigorating itself with tradition.
There are few places in the world untouched by romanticism,
supreme among them Britain with the Cotswold cottage, flag-
waving, monarchy, beef, the Imperial mile, and "No! No Euros[3]
thank you!" Even so, Ireland is the favored fall-guy for accusation of
such comfortable, complacent, satisfying delusions, likely so because such were key to Ireland's pioneering physical rejection of
Empire and have been vital to survival without the colonial mantle.

Dating from the consolidation of separatist political feeling in the
wake of the Great Famine of the 1840s, Irish culture was gradually
assembled from selected artifacts, as "pure" as possible, clarified in
a way that the plain people could understand. In 1884 the GAA was
formed, and in 1892 the Gaelic League.[4] Definitions—the mapping
of cultural territory—were the order of the day, enabled by the
scholars and antiquarians of the Royal Irish Academy, and later by
such as Frank Kidson and Cecil Sharp in England. In the process, all
popular dance forms, including such as quadrilles (locally known as
"sets"), were frowned upon, and a clear definition of Irishness was
installed in people's heads in readiness for partition and independence in 1921. But the vision of "Irishness" in music was essentially
of the parlor. There was no notion of "authenticity" as we now apply the term, and the model was by today's standards nauseously
middle class. In the early years of the Irish state, however, the visi-
ble notions of identity so vital to a process of struggle against the
soldiers and civil service of a colonizing power became redundant.
One could simply be Irish by just being, this especially so for each
succeeding next generation.

So the language declined, and so too the music, and by the Second
World War, they were being undermined by Western popular culture in the urban centers. Postwar revival was set in motion, facilitated by great individual integrity from piper Leo Rowsome and
others, spearheaded by their organization CCÉ[5] largely favored

by—and often implying—a Republican political consciousness. The surviving indigenous music and playing styles of the major performers on all instruments became identified with what was "proper"; competitions used this as the yardstick for standards and acceptability. This was called "traditional" music, as distinct from "folk," the difference implying that here was a more than just a "popular" music form. For while it was practiced largely by the folk, in its finest moments it had been associated with traveling people and their myth of dispossessed grandeur, and with the gentry (*uilleann* pipers in particular, who contributed artistic focus and many tunes).

More importantly it also contained within it the suppressed indigenous classical music of the onetime court harpers who had become redundant due to Gaelic dispossession prior to the eighteenth century. Irish independence on its own had not proved capable of guaranteeing the survival of Irish music, for the new state viewed the ethos of European classical music as bona fide music expression. Rescue of Irish music could only be done by a substratum of society acting in a manner subversive of the prevailing dominant culture. Traditional—indigenous—music became a fifth column organizing an education system parallel to the official one of the Irish state, effectively a political model.

Hence music and ideology remained bound together, and so, embroiled in the internal class and other politics of the emerging state, an awareness heightened by the postwar emigration of many musicians, the notion of authentic Irish music—"the pure drop"—took three-dimensional form. This was not just a means to an end, but something that was already being done, with both folk memory and incunabula, an indigenous instrumentation, hugely varied repertoire and clear styles of performance. In the minds of many players the music was itself as challenging to Irish upper-class establishment values as the notion of Irish independence had earlier been to British supremacy. It was felt to represent a golden age of ruralness, the real people, a concept extended by ballad song to cover urban working-class identity, "the rare ould times." This was a vital revival and reconstruction tool.

In the midst of all of this, however, a young, rapidly urbanizing Irish population for whom (despite familiarity with Irish idiom in music and song) popular music aesthetics and values were more the norm. As interest developed in the traditional, they flocked to the new *fleadh cheoil* (plural *fleadhnna ceoil*) festivals, raising ructions and dispensing the menacing disposable income wildly, uncaring of the fragile understatement of the dialectics of rural fleadh host towns. In this period the term *purist* came to be used as critical of those who had invented the *fleadh cheoil* concept, who disliked urban-youth intervention into the new music scene, who only wished to play, or listen to, the music without the roaring, tearing, and drinking. Webster's dictionary describes a "purist" as someone who is "preoccupied with the purity of a language and its protection from the ingress of foreign or altered forms" (1971, 1846). With this consciousness, by June 1966 an *Irish Press* national editorial was naively suggesting a compromise between good times and "culture"— that *fleadhnna ceoil* should have marquee dormitories for the masses, "and for the purists perhaps special programs of traditional music could be arranged." (*Irish Press*, 2/6/66, 3)

Traditional music in their eyes was now officially the property of the people. It had passed beyond control of those who had rescued it, those for whom the word purist became established as a term of patronizing abuse. Gradually, however, in tandem with the repopularization of the music, and Ireland's adjustment to urbanization, over the years it lost relevance and fell into disuse until 1995, when, in the course of an RTE *Late, Late Show*[6] promotion of *River of Sound*,[7] audience hostility to guest Tony Mac Mahon[8] was expressed as "purism"—imputing something antisocial and unreasonable. Use of the term is of course not restricted to Ireland (or indeed just to Irish music). For instance, in an article endorsing West Cork, Irish *sean-nós*[9] singer Iarla Ó Lionáird's participation in the British techno dance-band Afro-Celt Sound System, *Folk Roots* magazine (October 1996) implied criticism of a certain strand of Irish Traditional musicians as "die-hard purist" (57).

GUCCI-PADDY: FASHION ACCESSORY
FOR THE LATE TWENTIETH CENTURY

The great problems for Irish music today come from a fashion-driven popularity outside the country: Irish music idiom is trendy— "Gucci-Paddy," so to speak. The music is central to the commercial invention known as "the Irish pub" where it becomes largely aural wallpaper (or "carpet," as Tony Mac Mahon more cuttingly sees it[10]); it has appeared in association with rock, and it can be heard all the time in advertising jingles for mostly food products (but recently for French *Citroen* cars). In commercial popular music it is perhaps represented best by the Afro-Celt Sound System, which kicked off by using Iarla Ó Lionáird's voice and Ronan Browne's uilleann pipes as its "Celtic" legitimation. Here too are other problems, for African black skin, lavish costume, *djembe* drum and *kora* harp are part of the equation. But the body of music they produce is generated neither by Celts nor Africans—it is produced electronically by two mere Englishmen (sic), and—as is its genre's demand—even when played live it relies heavily on dubbing. The *sean-nós* (if it can still can be called such) and the African material are designed as garments, add-ons adjusted to fit the synthesized master soundscape, an inversion of the prevailing notion of "accompaniment" in traditional music.

On stage the band is a visual reconstruction of the Victorian pyramid, the power balance of colonialism—squatting on the bottom in clouds of smoke the Africans (à la Bhopal?), the Celts on a level above, and dominating them all with the electronic control machines are the Englishmen. This music construction is described in their record label *Realworld*'s advertising blurb as "a meeting of African and Celtic tradition" (*Folk Roots*, 8/9/96, 68). The de facto experience is that Irish and continental-Africa cultures once indeed did meet—by casual trading in ancient historic time, much later as soldiers on colonizing ventures, then through "the missions," and often in prisons. They do still presently meet through famine and AIDS relief work today, sometimes in disco bars in Britain and the United States, and most recently via refugees in the Irish jobs and housing markets. But are the "African" and the "Celtic" compatible, and did they ever meaningfully—in the sense of culture exchange—meet? Is this music not just like simultaneously talking in two different languages in a room with a couple of jack-hammers? Continuing the marketing strategy, Afro-Celt's rationale is developed by leader Simon Emmerson's ignoring as irrelevant his own background in the British pop scene, in techno music. In the absence of any actual experience of Irish traditional music, he legitimates himself by trivializing the "Celtic" myth: "Celts is a very broad term. If you really want to get into it, no-one really knows who they were . . . no-one really knows where they came from" (*Folk Roots*, 8/9/96, 53)

So why does he bother with the term Celt at all? By implication, the mere Irish are now, in fact, "nobody." There is no "Irish" music; what we think of as Irish isn't really important. This is fine if one is rationally deconstructing, but this is not the case, for, as he explains further: "The Roman historian Tacitus remarked on a group of people with 'dark complexions and unusually curly hair.' This people's diaspora from the Middle East, through Africa to Europe, lies at the heart of the links between African and Celtic music and personality" (*Folk Roots*, 8/9/96, 52). Whatever one might think about the commonness or otherwise of curly hair, one can only speculate about which is his "Celtic" music—"National" (Breton, Irish, Southern Germanic, Galician, Welsh, Cornish, Scottish), stylistic (*sean-nós* or ballad), and so on. And which is his "Africa"? Is it south, central, or north (each implying different religions, cultures and musics), or perhaps Arabic? Bob Quinn's film *Atlantean*[11] at least was specific. The only conclusion to be drawn is that despite its intrinsic musical merits and independent following, the Afro-Celt Sound System is also a PR myth. It paints the synthesizers green to sell the product, and in step with the age of information, out of the disconnected, isolated, and innocent words of some of its artistes constructs a complementary ideology to tell us that Irish music, "African" music and Massive Attack[12] are really all the same thing. Music of course is all "just music," but what about the labels, those interesting separations and distillations that make it such a compelling, comforting aspect of human culture?

Of course the Afro-Celts are free to add what they like within the hagiography available to PR-speak, but the extension of such pick-and-mix to traditional Irish music from abroad is galling to many in Ireland. Particularly so because the pseudo-historical style of language is already familiar for its use by many of our own unconfident Irish innovators and "crossover" explorers who are dependant upon both the confidence and financial support of traditional music's considerable, present audience. As crossover people change over, to hold on to their audience they stretch and redeploy in new patterns of the already-existing traditional music vocabulary to support their fusions and interpretations. This is one of a series of contradiction-generated crises facing what we know as "Irish traditional" music the genre, as the end of the millennium that began with the harp was approached. It is a fallout from the means-to-an-end pragmatism that had initially drawn the stockades up around Irish and other traditional musics just a century before.

"TRADITION" AND "INNOVATION"
ARE NOT COMPATIBLE

The dictionary definition describes "tradition" as "the process of handing down information, opinions, beliefs and customs by word of mouth or by example. An inherited or established way of thinking, feeling or doing. A cultural feature preserved or evolved from the past. A doctrine or practice" (Webster 1971, 2422). "Innovation" is "something that deviates from established doctrine of practice; differs from existing forms. Innovate: to introduce as, or as if, new. To introduce novelties, make changes" (1166). Tradition is the word that has been at the heart of the vocabulary of the revival of Irish music; innovation is the qualifier used by the New Age interpretations of the music. But from their definitions it would seem that on some occasions at least they are doomed to contradict. "Black" and "white" can only be the same in greyness.

One could smile inwardly when Paddy Moloney of The Chieftains pulled pop-singer Sting out of the bag to sing the song "Mo Ghile Mear"[13] on their 1995 album *Long Black Veil*. To the outsider the performance was wonderful, and to some Irish-language promoters it was a coup. But to the mere Irish speakers it sounded perhaps as quaint as the Pope's attempt at English back in 1979—"Yang peephole off Ayerlant, aye laff ooo; aye veesh yoh a penis" ("Young people of Ireland, I love you; I wish you happiness"). Like language, and like any other music genre, traditional music in Ireland has its own internally regulated accent that is its sound. Any deviation is seen by those within it as different—maybe trying, often pleasant, sometimes hostile. Hanging onto a definite sound is a major hazard for any traditional music.

Music is part of everyday recreation. The traditional form in Ireland additionally has a modern invested, symbolic life as an indicator of Irishness, a birthmark of nationality. But no matter whether the performer is Séamus Ennis[14] or Michael Flatley, it also has another existence as a commodity. Performances are frozen in plastic, copied and multiplied; they can be rented, borrowed, given away and stolen; thousands or millions of listeners can witness the one event, over and over again, at any time in the foreseeable future, anywhere on the planet. With electronic sampling and synthesizing equipment, the personal sound of the player of a particular instrument can be passably reproduced. With the simplest of keyboards

and PA equipment, one person can fill the biggest stadium with organized sound. Rock bands pioneered all this: a four-piece could
produce the same volume that in a previous era would have de-
manded an orchestra.

Music like that demands talents other than mere musicianship. The
sound operator is artist, too, and the sound-manipulation equipment
is more important than the music instruments. Most importantly, any
performance can be dissected and reconstructed, combined with
other things and resold under different descriptions. Studio electron-
ics cost money, while marketing guarantees payment. Music is product, and the language of PR becomes the key to cultural success. Traditional musicians of course have been in the recording process for a
hundred years now. Patsy Touhey's[15] wax cylinders are still playable,
Michael Coleman and John McKenna[16] can still be heard and exercise
influence from CDs. But recording quality aside, the deeper we advance into the electronic existence the closer we come to worship of
the machinery as supreme, messenger more glamorous than the dis-
patch. The "technical" is another major hazard for traditional music as
an independent genre. As Marshall McLuhan said in the 1960s, the
electronic medium is becoming the message.

"WORLD" MUSIC

In September 1986 a group of ten International-Folk record-label
owners met in the *Empress of Prussia* bar in North London. They
were discussing artist promotion and the development of public interest in nonmainstream musics. This led to consider standardization of terminology. Joe Boyd (then of Hannibal records, now Ryko)
proposed pooling £100 each to promote one term by which they
could market all of their products. The term was *World Music*. As
Boyd said himself: "This was the most successful £ for £ promotion
ever done."[17] So successful, indeed, that some academics have
adopted it—for instance, Mícheál Ó Súilleabháin's postgraduate
music facility at the University of Limerick is known as The Irish
World Music Center. World music is a useful term in record shops,
particularly valuable where floor staff know nothing about music
and may have problems with where to shelve or find things.

But does it mean anything else? And, like electronic mediation of
music, does the concept influence worldview and taste in music? In

Japan, Irish music is to be found in the "world" category, along with various musics of the African continent and of Asia, and the non-classical musics of Americas and Europe. But other than being of the colonized, third, poor world, does anything actually unite these musics? Racially there is no unity—there could not be more variety; linguistically, hundreds of languages are represented. All of the individual national and regional genres use different singing styles, have fantastically differing instrumental musics played on an encyclopedic array of instruments. Some place song at the center, others are built around dance and sociability, while ritual and religion are foci for others. There are oral classical and folk systems, and most have a popular, modern end to their spectrum too. It is in their popular music that they all do share something—some kind of use of the standard Euro/American electric and classical instruments like violin, guitar, saxophone, keyboards, bass and drum kit. What unites them all, in fact, is their use (also) of exactly the same instruments that are used in western popular and classical musics. The Western musics are not, however, roped into the definition of the world, and so the term world music encourages thinking of everything non-Western as "the same." It does not provoke intellectual speculation about racial integrity, or about difference.

But it can be argued that musics of the world all overlap with each other anyway from region to region, that world wars, political annexations, colonization, the slave trade, exploring and missionary ventures have all already spread and shared music influences. Thus the harp in Ecuador is the legacy of Franciscan and Jesuit missionaries between the sixteenth and nineteenth centuries; Samba comes from West African slaves transplanted in Brazil; the use of the bow on fiddles comes from the spread of the Islamic empire; Irish *seannós* song may be related to either southern French medieval song or to Moroccan song via early sea travel in the North East Atlantic. Even so, the hybrid musics of any country or region at any point in time are what they are. They are of their place, as are languages, cuisines, and lifestyles. Irish music is Irish, Bulgarian music is Bulgarian, Senegalese music is Senegalese—their profound differences make a nonsense of the word *world* as a supposed genre. Even still, that is an intellectual argument, and there should be absolutely nothing wrong with having a category that can help locate comparatively minor-interest albums on shop shelves. In its practical meaning, world music is only a label, despite the racist implications. But if the label concept begins to dictate the content—as performance technology has done to performance content—then there may be serious concern for all Traditional musics that their integrity is threatened, their meanings suppressed.

THE RIVER OF SOUND

In 1991, *Bringing It All Back Home*[18] applied itself to establishing a relationship between emigration, the export of Irish tunes to the United States, their feeding into the creation of American Pop, its importation back into Ireland, and reexport to the world. In 1994 *River of Sound*[19] plotted development in Irish music, related its increase in popularity to a trend toward a fusion of similar folk musics of the world: It closed on a joint Dónal Lunny/Mícheál Ó Súilleabháin piece that involved kora harp played by an African woman. End of twentieth century Ireland produced many groups claiming or practicing fusions between differing kinds of musics. Often quite brilliant or challenging, these genetic engineerings were the offspring of Irish traditional with jazz, northern Indian, pop, rock, classical, baroque, Eurovision, Indonesian, bluegrass, American Old Time, Australian Aboriginal and "African." They were produced by many bands and individuals, among them Deiseal, Khanda, Kila, The Corrs, Dónal Lunny, Mícheál Ó Súilleabháin, Mel Mercier, Four Men and a Dog, Afro-Celt Sound System, and so on.

The questions raised are: Does the loss of pedigree create a tough, disease-resistant, grey, patch-eyed, sideways-trotting mongrel that can survive anywhere? Does it produce exotic breeds that need an incubator (or a high wage) to independently survive? Or does it bring out new, hidden, and useful things that have otherwise been unknown to the present generation of musicians? The answer is probably "yes" to all. But it can also be said for certain that when the typical German or French band plays Irish music, it sounds like a German or French band playing Irish music. An Irish traditional musician listening to one of their own groups playing the German or French mightn't reveal much, but someone from within "the other's" parent culture will be more critical. Even so, if Japan has credible pipe bands and Western-style, classical orchestras and, notably, Irish traditional players, then with practice, other nationalities probably could get Irish traditional music "right." And the actual crossovers in style are all perfectly "legitimate" and natural things to happen anyway.

But still, Mícheál Ó Súilleabháin's compositions do seem distinctively of the chamber orchestra, Sean Davey's of the symphony orchestra, Bill Whelan's the popular big stage; Dónal Lunny has the captivating, circular, short motif of rock music, the Afro-Celt Sound System is dominated by a techno ethos, Deiseal by jazz. But despite being more like "other" things, these musics are claimed as syntheses, fusions, crossovers—innovations. But are they not just manifestations of people based in Irish traditional music who are extending the gamut of their playing to be something else? And aren't classical, blues, jazz, and rock music already the products of logical evolutionary movement out of literal, melodic traditional musics? Is not the idea of "fusing" current traditional music with current classical, blues, jazz, and rock an anachronism? Can it be anything other than something that is not only neither one nor the other—but nothing in particular at all? A series of pleasantly organized sounds, but, like simultaneously spoken different languages, culturally meaningless except to its practitioners? We all are capable of broad taste, but it becomes a challenge to put faith in, meaning on, or feel for music "(A+B)" if one already actually has intelligible separate contexts for musics "A" and "B."

This of course is the conservative argument. Against it is the truth that since the world is simultaneously an irrational mosaic, marl and purée of separateness and blending of cultural, social, economic, and political artifacts and circumstances, then it makes perfect sense to have mixed-up musics. And the evidence of the past hundred or so years suggests that the center cores of older music genres will most likely survive independently despite the deviations. In the sense that music is organized sound, all of these modern traditional-idiom composers and bands are of course producing music—with differing degrees of aesthetic and commercial success, and often with wonderful imagination. There cannot be any question that they shouldn't be doing it, for music is about doing what you do and that is that; fashions come and go, some things last, some don't, the most powerful may come to dominate, as always. Those composers and bands are doing what is perfectly natural to do as thinking and explorative musicians: Obsession is always obsession; a challenge is a challenge.

Problems arise, however, when the structures and tactics that are used to sell music in the modern world are applied to an artist's work. As an irate (traditional) singer Dick Hogan put it after Mícheál Ó Súilleabháin's contribution to the Crossroads Conference in 1996,[20] "These people can do what they want, but let them not call it 'Traditional' music." It could be argued that Dick himself has no room to talk—his typical repertoire is Percy French,[21] hardly the stuff of anything other than the world music principle: the Parlor annexing the haggard.[22] But nevertheless this is the nub of the problem with *Bringing It All Back Home, River of Sound*, and lately with The Afro-Celt Sound System. In lavish, studied PR they see and sell their work as part of "the tradition."

In April 1997 the University of Limerick's Niall Keegan played flute in Trinity College Dublin to illustrate a music-education lecture by David Elliot of University of Toronto.[23] The audience remained silent when the speaker voiced his vital assumption that what everybody had heard was "traditional Irish music." He did not realize that their absence of comment indicated in fact that they hadn't heard the player do traditional, they heard him play his improvisations out of traditional. Not being particularly familiar with Irish music, the lecturer of course had no way of knowing otherwise, but to the musically aware audience, however, once the player had altered the ground rules, his music was different.

From within the (necessarily) conservative core of what is traditional Irish music, the self-styled innovators are often not viewed as being part of the genre; they are seen as having moved outside it into a limbo—crossed over to another form of music. Admission of, or identification of the location of, an actual "crossover" point is as hazardous to establish, as prone to fabrication and sensitive to accusation as a 1970s British Army border incursion from Northern Ireland into the Republic of Ireland. But there is, definitely, a threshold, even if mobile or fluid, governed by a consensus. The reluctance to acknowledge a foot in one or more music camps—the insecurity that will not let go of the traditional apron strings—leads to the most annoying aspect of crossover music. This is its hanging onto, and use for validation of, the carefully evolved language that belongs to, and is only of any real meaning to, traditional music as such. Loss of a language of self-description, evolved for the specific purpose of revival and elucidation within that music, therefore becomes another hazard for the traditional.

THE TRADITIONAL THRESHOLD

Yet even so, all of this—inaccurate reproduction, loss of personality to technology, suppression of meaning, loss of a self-descriptive language—represents no more of a worry than many other challenges facing all aspects of Irish cultural identity at the new century's beginning. The export of the music, the recording industry, the branching into other fields, the keeping up of connections—all are parts of a jostling that in the long run keeps minds alive and the body of the music healthy. Commerce is of course ruthless, and maybe the end (i.e., work for traditional musicians) justifies the process. And indeed there is nothing wrong with people saying what they like as long as it is what they believe—the world is full of conflicting interpretations of the same information.

But the experience of the traditional music revival has been that such a professional hard-sell is also the hallmark of pop music marketing, the selling of the very music genre that has been historically numbingly pathogenic to, and ideologically devaluing of, the whole concept of traditional. In the Irish experience, parlor-pop, come-all-ye-pop, showband-pop, Eurovision-pop, and international-pop are already this century's ever-changing, universal-access, tabloid musics. They can be pleasant, sentimental, valuable, and socially expressive; interest in them may persist or fade, they may well establish their own independent nostalgias and traditions, and even slide seamlessly into what is seen as traditional. While that is a different argument, nevertheless, objectively, pop pillages and both it and the concept of world music in intellectual terms trawl the music cultures of the planet for catchiness, if not mediocrity.

Ultimately this is an economic struggle; the borrowing of traditional music's language of self-description is not just a battle of words for minds, but for credibility, power, audiences, and performance space. If there is any such thing as traditional music, one is foolish not to be defensive and should be cautious about blanket absolutions in one "big happy family" of musicians.

PURISM ONCE AGAIN

In all of this there is too a debilitating challenge to literal, craft musicians and the patient process of handing on music skills, their history, and their interpretation. The debate has revived the old myth

of "purism" from the darkness of closet ignorance—this despite its
having been debunked twenty years ago, mostly through patient
persistence by a small number of broadcasters. For gradually it came
to be realized that without the collective efforts of purists there just
would not be any commercially viable traditional music. In 1966 it
was ignorant media and local authority officials who so derided the
convictions of musicians and music lovers.

Today, however, purist is not only being used as a dirty word by
the businessmen, but (increasingly often) by the fair-weather pundits
of crossover music. And sadly (for genre integrity) it is now heard on
the lips of some reputed traditional performers as well. The postmodern music world is brashly commercial and—compared to the
society and pace of traditional music this last century—it has an un-
nerving absence of principles. As entertainment, traditional music is
obliged to be in there, but it has to fight its corner using the realworld machinery and keep its powder dry. What unites the big
names in Irish music—Bono, Christy Moore, Sinéad O'Connor, the
Clancys, The Dubliners, and The Chieftains—is not tradition (as
Bringing It All Back Home implied), but money and success.

Music is not "all just music"; each genre has standards. Fusion
and crossover are battles over important things—influence, power,
wealth, and the timetable and logistics of cultural change. H. W.
Fowler quipped that those who find themselves stigmatized as
purist have a right to know the stigmatizer's own place in the purist
scale. Taking this into the arena of the traditional, those who are stigmatized have not only a sensible right, but also an aesthetic obligation, to search among qualifications, financial interest, and political
maneuvering for the motivation for their detractors' demeaning de-
rision.

ACKNOWLEDGMENT

This chapter develops one originally published in *Graph*, 9 (1998).

NOTES

1. "Captain" Francis O'Neill, his Chicago collections of the early twentieth century had a profound influence on repertoire, as much for the fact of
their existence as their resource content.

2. Gaelic Athletic Association, formed in 1884 to promote indigenous Irish games, these identified as hurling (similar to the Scottish shinty) and Gaelic football (rather like the present Australian Rules game).

3. Britain, a European community member, took a decision not to utilize the common European currency, which was introduced in 2002.

4. The promotion body for the Irish language, and, as a consequence, music, song, and dance also.

5. Comhaltas Ceoltóirí Éireann, literally the Society of Irish Musicians, formed in 1951 to reverse the decline of the indigenous music, song, and dance. It eventually spread all over Ireland and into Irish Diaspora areas abroad, and remains today the organizer of the *fleadh cheoil* network of music festivals.

6. *The Late, Late Show* was a long-running, hugely popular, and influential weekly magazine program that often presented specials on traditional music.

7. A major 1994 television series jointly sponsored by BBC (national British television) and RTÉ (national Irish television), which interpreted the historical practice of, and development of, Irish traditional music, the latter illustrated in part by the composition works of the series presenter, Prof. Mícheál Ó Súilleabháin.

8. A traditional music producer for many years with RTÉ, a highly acclaimed musician himself, a staunch proponent of "authenticity." His flagship TV program was titled *The Pure Drop*.

9. *Sean-nós*—lit. "old style" song—it is sung in the Irish language, is associated with Irish-speaking areas, and employs a high degree of melismatic ornament.

10. He sees pub locations as merely permitting wholesale "trampling" of the aesthetic of the music.

11. A film by Bob Quinn, 1986, which argued that Irish music owes something to Islamic culture, that the "Dark Ages" of the European mainstream coincided with the "Golden Ages" of Arabic Spain and Ireland, and that via sea travel there was a period in which Irish song (*sean-nós*) was so influenced. See also Vallely 1999.

12. The English group that arguably originated the techno/jungle "sound system" clubbing genre of modern electronic music.

13. An Irish-language song dating to the Jacobite period, of anthemic status in Munster.

14. An iconic uilleann pipes stylist in the latter half of the 1900s.

15. An uilleann piper in Chicago who recorded, advertised, and sold his playing on wax cylinders from 1901 on.

16. Mid-twentieth-century Irish traditional recording artistes who exercised considerable stylistic authority on account of their discs being sent back to Ireland.

17. Boyd's words, in a paper given to the 1994 Womex (World Music Expo) presentation in Berlin.

18. 1991, five-part television series for BBC/RTE; originator Philip King, Hummingbird Productions, Dublin.

19. See note 7.

20. *Crosbhealach An Cheoil*, The Crossroads Conference—concerning tradition and change in Irish traditional music—held in Temple Bar, Dublin, organized by an independent group of traditional musicians and teachers, 17–19 April 1996; the bulk of its papers were published in 1999 (for résumé see <www.theflute.com>).

21. Percy French of Roscommon, 1854–1920. A prolific satirical songster who utilized a music hall-cum-classical style to comment on life as it was. His works stand as a genre on their own.

22. The farmyard at the back of rural homes, typically an environment deficient in beauty.

23. Boydell Room, Trinity College Dublin, 4 April 1997, part of a five-lecture tour circuit that took in universities in Dublin, Cork, Galway, Limerick, and Belfast.

BIBLIOGRAPHY

Bohlman, Philip V. *Folk Music in the Modern World*. Bloomington: University of Indiana Press, 1988.

Boyes, Georgina. *The Imagined Village: Culture, Ideology and the English Folk Revival*. Manchester: Manchester University Press, 1993.

Harker, Dave. *Fakelore: The Manufacture of British 'Folksong', 1700 to the Present Day*. Manchester: Manchester University Press, 1985.

Hobsbawm, Eric, and Terence Ranger, eds. *The Invention of Tradition*. Cambridge: Cambridge University Press, 1983.

Vallely, Fintan, ed. *The Companion to Irish Traditional Music.* Cork: Cork University Press, 1999.

Vallely, Fintan, Hammy Hamilton, Liz Doherty, and E. Vallely, eds. *Crosbhealach An Cheoil—the Crossroads Conference*. Dublin: Whinstone, 1999.

8

"Celtitude," Professionalism, and the *Fest Noz* in Traditional Music in Brittany

Desi Wilkinson

At the time of writing—the turn of the twentieth and twenty-first centuries—Brittany is an area of intense activity in the realm of traditional dance music and other folk music genres. This chapter begins by taking stock of the principal cultural conditions that have led to such a profusion of activity. It then goes on to show how the confluence of these cultural factors, together with French socioeconomic legislation, have created a climate in which many are able to make a viable living from playing varieties of traditional music. A look at the organizational structure of the *fest noz* ("night festival" or "night dance," plural *festoù noz*) and its relation to the world of professionalism in traditional music is followed by a discussion of the practical workings of the *système d'intermittent du spectacle* (a system of socioeconomic legislation).

Recent surveys indicate that positive attitudes to the preservation and promotion of Breton language and culture are the norm in Brittany (Favereau 1993, 34–35). There can be no doubt that these attitudes have their roots in the initiatives began by cultural activists in the 1950s and pursued enthusiastically by like-minded people during the 1970s and 1980s (see Wilkinson 1999, 50–64). The majority of the Breton population today are not political separatists—in this respect they are no different than their forebears throughout the nineteenth and early twentieth centuries—but substantial numbers of them are cultural regionalists. As a consequence of the cultural and socioeconomic climate issuing from this reality, traditional dance music and the round dance have come to represent the most accessible and inclusive expression of *bretonnitude* (local Pan-Breton identity) and by extension *celtitude* (global pan-Breton identity or Celtic identity) in Brittany today. Celtitude is the French word for ways of expressing or experiencing "Celticness." For me the twin concepts of bretonnitude and celtitude imply a psychosocial construct, a set of assumed—though constantly debated—attitudes and attributes. I suggest that precisely because these terms are imprecise and abstract, they constitute a useful and nonexclusive way of describing the cultural reality under discussion here. Bretonnitude and celtitude, then, imply less a statement of ethnic belonging and more to ways of experiencing or participating in a cultural world shaped in Brittany and the occidental francophone world in recent years by a pan-Celtic "imagescape" (Slobin 1992).

Some commentators have argued that the 1970s generation of Breton cultural activists have received too much credit for the healthy state of Breton music today and that the efforts of their predecessors—whose contribution was both significant and necessary—have been in some way forgotten. They point out that traditional music was in a continual state of adaptation to new situations with each passing decade and that there was no need to juxtapose the extreme standpoints of "death" and "rebirth" current in the 1970s (see Becker and Le Gurun 1994 and articles in *Musique Bretonne* concerning this period). It was during the 1970s, however, fortified by a reinvented popular celtitude promoted largely by the activities of musician Alan Stivell and his like, that there was a dramatic increase in the amount of people participating in traditional music and dance. Significant numbers also began to take an active part in the collection of local music and dance forms for the first time. Dastum (meaning "to gather") is currently the principal organization concerned exclusively with the collection, archiving, and dissemination of Breton traditional music. It was founded in 1972 by a handful of young musicians. Dastum has accumulated a vast archive of field recordings that it puts at the disposal of all interested parties. Its aims and objectives are described as: "The collection, conservation, diffusion and development of Brittany's ethnological heritage with particular emphasis on oral traditions and traditional music (*Musique Bretonne* 1994 December, 2).[1] According to Pierre Crépillon, who is both a *sonneur* (traditional instrumentalist) and a founding member of Dastrum, the organization is essentially apolitical. Its members may hold widely divergent political viewpoints, but this has not interfered with its work.[2]

The main geocultural demarcation line in Brittany is based on research carried out by Paul Sébillot in 1886. It is often referred to as
the "Sébillot line" (Favereau 1993, 40). This line indicates the limit of
spoken Breton and it remains relatively accurate today. Effectively it
divides Brittany into western Brittany (Basse Bretagne—the area
where Breton is still spoken) and eastern Brittany (Haute Bretagne
where French and Gallo—a nonliterary form of Langue d'Oïl—are
spoken).[3] Although some dance forms are common to both parts,
most genres are likewise classified as either *"haut-breton"* or *"bas-
breton,"* since their most antique expression, the practice of singing
for the dance, is language based.

Because of the pivotal symbolic importance of the Breton language to bretonnitude one could speculate that the non-Breton-
speaking population—the majority—are viewed by cultural activists as "less Breton" than Breton speakers.[4] Among the many
activists that I have spoken to, however, I have found this attitude to
be quite rare. It is true that haut-breton musical forms have received
less attention in the promotion of pan-bretonnitude—and this is
commented upon by some haut-Breton musicians—but it is reason-
able to suggest that because of the ubiquity of the French language,
these forms were deemed intrinsically more secure, hence the
greater level of activity in the bas-Breton region. The crucial importance of the Breton language to Breton identity is concisely summed
up in the words of Gilles Servat one of Brittany's most popular balladeers—who sings in French for the most part. He says that "The
Breton language is not the sum total of Brittany, but without it Brittany ceases to exist. Or perhaps just a one-legged Brittany" (*Le Peuple Breton* 1996, 15). Ultimately, however, it is at the level of the local—dancing the round dance at a *fest noz*—where pan-bretonnitude
in the cultural sense begins. To "feel Breton," therefore, is to experience a sense of belonging to a locality that has its own emblematic
particularities and through this "belonging" to relate to the general
geocultural area that is Brittany.

LOCAL IDENTITY, "PAYS," AND THE FEST NOZ

The word *pays* is habitually used on wine bottles from various parts
of France, as in *vin du pays de Gard* ("wine from the 'Gard' country"), for example. In relation to food and drink use of the term is

commonplace. *Pays* can also be an important word in the vocabulary of the understanding of a local cultural matrix and this is particularly significant in the case of Brittany. The word can refer to a
large area (as in the case of the bas-Breton bishoprics linked to the
four dialects of the Breton language) or it can be a small rural village or town-land. Often it can be quite an arbitrary reference dependant on where groups or individuals place it in relation to
themselves. Both linguistic and folklore research have identified areas by distinctiveness in costume, language, or dialect. Interestingly
the work of the nineteenth-century French geographers Elisée
Reclus and Paul Vidal de la Blache (see, for example, De la Blache
1979) sets a strong precedent for this type of thinking, pioneering
the study of the relationship between natural elements and hu-
mans. Reclus, a figure of boundless energy, was an anarchist and an
outspoken antiracist and anti-imperialist sociopolitical commenta-
tor. The early-twentieth-century French academic establishment
was not as reverential in its attitude toward him as they were to the
aristocratic La Blache who steered clear of politics. It is only in the
last few years that Reclus's passionate magnum opus *L'Homme et la
Terre* (1906–1908) has been revisited and recognized for its comprehensive erudition.[5]

In the Breton context, the Pays Gallo for example, is a linguistically designated *pays*. It refers to the area where Gallo is spoken.
In terms of traditional costume, the delineation of *pays* may come
directly from the type of lace headgear worn by women (see Creston 1995). The most striking *coiffe* (lace head adornment) is that
of the Pays Bigouden an area southwest of Quimper. The *coiffe
bigoudène* is an intricate, tall, funnel-like structure. Because of its
impressive proportions, it is perhaps the most photographed and
tourist-friendly of all the traditional Breton coiffes. The names of
some *pays* may go back many centuries and have associations that
have become obscure over the passage of time. In this way some
of the more popular round dances have become the most important association with regard to *pays*. A prime example of this is the
"Pays Plinn"; the *plinn* is a dance form found in the Pays Fañch.
The word *fañch* is seldom used now and the entire area is now
simply called the "Pays Plinn." *Pays*, in association with music
and dance, may be a relatively new delineation derived from folklore research in the late 1960s, but in this way some old spaces
have been reenergized, thus reestablishing them as important lo-

cal cultural signifiers of community (see Guilcher 1963; *Musique Bretonne* 1996, 142–43).

The idea that the basic political and social units of Western life are becoming more and more amorphous has been with us since the beginning of the twentieth century. In the type of scenario that Alan Lomax has called "cultural grey out" (see Lomax 1968), Western anglopop commodity culture, to cite one example, is deemed to lead the legions of the culturally passive into an abyss of eternal blandness and predictability. However one might understand this phenomenon, and the cultural forms it suppresses or supplants, many alternative forms of music continue to catch people's imagination. In the case of Brittany and other parts of Europe, traditional music still occupies an important niche, charged with cultural significance. A downside of this of course is that the music and songs can easily be attached to interethnic struggles. The perceived symbolic authenticity and "rootedness" of such music has meant that it can be unscrupulously manipulated more easily than perceived "international" genres.[6] In the normal course of events, however, traditional music fulfils a more everyday yet ultimately more profound role—that of a broad and transethnic communal and aesthetic rallying point. This means that through the act of participation in the social life attached to traditional music—attending a *fest noz*, for example, or playing a tune—people who are not "ethnically" Breton are included without question. This way of expressing ethnicity, or, more accurately, "belonging," regularly overrides ideas of the patriotic or nationalistic. The latter is something that is only invoked periodically or in politically charged situations.

The *fest noz* does two important things vis-à-vis identity. First, it celebrates local identity expressed in the *danse du pays*, the most meaningful and accessible way of "being Breton" for many. Second, it further activates an inclusive pan-Breton identity in both a cultural and a social sense. The *fest noz* is both a vehicle where localized dances and music can be celebrated—thus maintaining local social cohesion—and a melting pot where choices are made and a symbolic pan-Breton repertory in dance and music emerges. In this way, the modern *fest noz* event, where the round dance[7] is performed, is the most important public expression of contemporary bretonnitude. *Festoù noz* are attended on a weekly basis throughout the year by large cross-sections of the community. They operate, both symbolically and practically, in the everyday social production of bretonnitude.

When people refer to an area of Basse Bretagne known as *les montagnes*—the mountains—(specifically *Les Monts d'Arrée/Montagnes Noires*) as "the center of Brittany," the implication is more spiritual than geographic. *Les montagnes* are viewed as the heartland of the Breton language and by extension accepted by many as a symbolic Breton cultural locus. Importantly it was in the Monts d'Arrée that the by now "traditional" *fest noz* was reinvented. The core dance genre of this region is the *gavotte montagne* and this dance has become a mainstay at all dance events throughout Brittany (see Gavotte 1998). The first *fest noz* as we now know it was organized near the village of Poullaouen in 1955. Effectively its promoters sought to encourage the creation of a new social context for the performance of the purely vocal form of *kan ha diskan* (singing for dancing in the Breton language), and in addition to promote afresh the art of the traditional *bombarde* (pastoral oboe) and *biniou* (bagpipe) duet. *Kan ha diskan* means call and response. It is an overlapping vocal performance technique particular to *les montagnes*. It may only be the specific hallmark of the montagnes region, but *kan ha diskan* has a symbolic importance to Breton identity that far outweighs the actual number of its performers, resonating throughout Brittany and beyond it into the Breton Diaspora. As a direct result of this important initiative, many older performers started to sing and play again, reliving the songs, music, and ambience of their youth.[8]

The *fest noz* is currently by far the most popular cultural event concerning the performance of traditional music in Brittany. The generic Breton term *fest noz* is now habitually used in non-Breton speaking areas to describe a major social event, authenticated by its association with *kan ha diskan* and *les montagnes*. In general, as stated above, the *fest noz* does not convey the heavy burden or exclusivity of heritage sometimes associated with the celebration of a cultural identity; it is a socially inclusive event. *Festoù noz* are therefore of the utmost importance to the performance of traditional music in Brittany and, as we shall see, professionalism in music. It is the act of clasping hands or linking arms with the small finger and dancing in a circle—symbolic of community—which is central to the *fest noz*. Various forms of round dance dominate the contemporary event and as such they are also the tangible expression of pan-bretonnitude.

Festoù noz received another major boost during the 1970s Celtic folk-renaissance period, yet outside of major festivals they remain essentially community events. The round dance is not the sole preserve of *les montagnes*, but it was at this particular location and involving a particular dance genre—the *gavotte montagne*—that the event as we now know it was first constructed.[9] Many people have told me that they cannot envisage living without this event; they feel the need to participate in round dancing regularly. Others say that attendance at the *fest noz*, even without dancing, is central to their sense of self and belonging. The following quotation, taken from a handout given to participants during a Breton and Irish dance workshop at Confort-Berhet near Lannion in August 1996, accurately describes the nature of the event.

> Since the beginning of the 1970s, the *fest noz* has adapted itself to modern life. Along with the language it has become the principal expression of Breton identity. It has an important social, cultural and bonding role; it doesn't have a lot to do with staged performance—such as concerts (from time to time of excellent quality) or costume parades which evoke a bygone age for a passive public. The *fest noz* is an inclusive celebration in which everyone participates, from the singer, musician or dancer to the server or client at the bar. (Untitled document, author unknown)

The use of the term to describe any kind of large social gathering has been debated, particularly in the 1970s. However, in terms of both the cultural significance and the financial turnover generated by these highly popular events, the *fest noz* has become vitally important as the symbolic focus of a whole range of activities.

Above, I have tried to describe the fundamental cultural dimensions of the localized and pan-Breton world of traditional music in Brittany, and particularly the way in which the pan-Breton and the local constantly bleed into each other. This social world of Breton traditional music, based primarily on the *fest noz*, can and does function distinctly from the world of what has become known as "Celtic" music, but it is also a key factor in the maintenance of a Celtic music scene per se. The popularity of the Breton *fest noz* combined with innovatory French social legislation, to which I turn later in the chapter, has created the unique situation of a large body of professional traditional players, largely united by a set of shared values and motivations. In order to enlarge the scope of how we conceive of sociomusical life in Brittany, however, it would be useful first to consider the way Breton musicians understand Breton music's "Celtic" dimensions.

CELTITUDE AND *MUSIQUE CELTIQUE*

It must be said that not all of the musicians who play Celtic music
are traditional dance musicians. Dan Ar Bras, the well-known
folk/rock guitarist who represented France in the Eurovision song
contest of 1996, is a case in point. But it is traditional dance musicians and singers who embody the link between the local and global
in the Breton context. When musicians active in the world of pan-
bretonnitude as expressed in the *fest noz* move outside of this arena,
performing on the concert stage and doing foreign tours, the majority do so as Celtic musicians. They play at Celtic music festivals or
in the *café cabaret* circuit. In pursuing this career path—or falling into
this category—they do two things. First they enter the global domain as part of the "world music" phenomenon and second they become part of a predominantly professional performance scenario.

   The Celtic world is, with varying degrees of magnitude and significance, a prime imaginary location for many postmodern New
Age mystics. Northwestern Europe is perceived as the original
homeland of the Celts and North America has implicit Celtic connections. For many who live in these areas, celtitude represents
something positive. If there is something one does not like about being one of a horde of French, Germans, Spanish, Italians, or Anglo-
Saxons, one can be a Celt. There are historical reasons why many Europeans (and Americans) make this choice if they feel the need to.
There is an industry around the Celts that provides all the material
and spiritual wherewithal for adherence. As McDonald has pointed
out, "the Celtic area now extends far beyond philology, into politics,
race, economics, culture, and morality" (McDonald 1989, 116).

   Celtitude can thus encompass a whole range of cultural expressions ranging from obscure Druidic rituals to business strategies
(and I have been part of both).[10] During the last three decades of the
twentieth century, there has been a new fusion of the building blocks
of music, mythology, history, and politics in Brittany to give contemporary meaning and form to celtitude.[11] Though one might continue to view them through the lens of some well-known critiques
that point to the constructed and by implication artificial nature of
the Celtic imaginary (see Kiberd 1996, 3–4; Trevor-Roper 1983;
Chapman 1978 and 1992), they give shape to a definable and tangible social reality, which demands to be treated as such, whether one
accepts the given logic of its pedigree or not.

Music is central to contemporary celtitude. The notion of a pan-Celtic music is spoken of, relatively unself-consciously, as a simple and an established fact, in relation to which category Breton music might be, in complex ways, elided or distinguished. Musician, researcher, and enthusiastic pan-Celticist Polig Montjarret, a key figure in the town twinning schemes between Ireland and Brittany that have flourished over the last twenty years, is relatively unequivocal. In the foreword to his large collection of Breton tunes (1984), he wrote: "Concerning the question 'is Breton music Celtic?' I have no hesitation in answering that it is not, and that does not harm in any way its values, its qualities and merits" (xv). Montjarret cites Irish and Scots Gaelic music as central to his understanding of the category of Celtic music. In this he shares the attitude of most people in the contemporary anglophone world remotely concerned with such issues. He suggests that Breton music and dance are, by contrast, more closely allied to Gregorian chant and the mid-European troubadour tradition. It is quite different in character to both the Scottish and Irish dance music traditions and their north American cousins, all of which are generically related and considerably "more modern" (Montjarret 1984, xiv).

One might contrast this scholarly viewpoint with the less-discriminating, though popularly held, approach to the category of Celtic music expressed below. Raymond Travers, in *Rough Guide to World Music*, assumes a unified field, of which Breton music is undoubtedly a part:

> Breton music, which draws richly in its themes, style and instrumentation on the common Celtic heritage of the Atlantic seaboard, has been for centuries a unifying and inspiring part of the culture of the province. Despite the intermittent efforts of a reactionary clergy to stifle its popularity, it survived the union with France and the general suppression of indigenous art and language. (1994, 28)

Certainly the first point the writer makes is valid. Overall, however, it is vague and leaves three important issues unresolved. These are the origins—Celtic or otherwise—of Breton music, the description of Brittany as a province, and the role of the clergy vis-à-vis the music. These issues are infinitely more complex than the above implies.

Nonetheless the description given is typical of a popular perception of Celtic music today. Celtitude is a notion that possesses ever changing and constantly reauthenticated meanings. An ever-expanding zone of Celtic interconnectedness is there to be claimed by large numbers of Europeans and Americans. Many in France have told me that they love Celtic music. People travel to Brittany from many parts of the country to experience the *ambiance celtique*, a synonym for many for the simple notion of having a good time.[12] For the tourist from other parts of France, however, it matters little whether the music they hear is Irish, Breton, a Scots pipe band, or a Welsh choir; its all *musique celtique*.

THE FESTIVAL INTERCELTIQUE DE LORIENT

The Lorient festival is the flagship of francophone celtitude. Held in mid-August every year since 1970, it is also the biggest Celtic festival in the world. The Interceltique, and others like it (notably the Fête de Cornouaille in Quimper), are extravagant public displays of contemporary Brittany's concern with a pan-Celtic identity. The directors of the Lorient festival continually work on worldwide promotion in which music plays the most prominent part. Recent publicity for the festival states that: "The international ensemble of the FESTIVAL INTERCELTIQUE was created in order to present a panorama of Celtic music to the world, they are all top class musicians. . . . The ensembles of the Festival Interceltique have a vast repertoire of ancient and contemporary music drawn from all the Celtic lands" (*L'Interceltique* 1996). The musicians in this case are all Bretons playing what is deemed to be Celtic music. Aside from the economic benefits of the festival, its promoters are engaged in what could conceivably be referred to as what Mark Slobin describes as "visibility shifting through self-conscious creation and promotion" (1992, 10). That is, one might understand the festival organizers as trying to create a francophone center for the Celtic Diaspora, with ready acknowledgment of Parisian support.[13]

It is, without doubt, a notion of *la musique celtique* that attracts people there year after year in the tens of thousands. Many artists from the folk and rock music scenes in Ireland, Scotland, Brittany, and Wales, together with Galicia, the United States, and Canada, both well-known professionals and hosts of amateurs, have played at Lorient at one time or another. For the week-long duration of the festival, the town is transformed into a Celtic capital. Traditional fare of crêpes, cider, and assorted fast foods are consumed throughout the day, and conveniently placed book and record stalls reflect the literary and artistic output of the Celtic world.[14] Keynote *grands spectacles* (big shows) symbolically comprised of artists from all over the notional Celtic world have been both initiated and financed through the auspices of the festival throughout its existence. These concerts and parades seek to portray unity in diversity. Treasa Ní Earcáin (1995) well captures the ways in which celtitude is presented for popular consumption in Lorient. She cites the following speech by the master of ceremonies for one of these events, made in front of a capacity crowd. "Ladies and Gentlemen, welcome to tonight's Nuit Magique. The Celtic people have suffered long and hard. They have resisted military occupation and the ravages of emigration and have come through it all with their culture intact" (Ní Earcáin 1995, 21, her translation).

On this occasion, in 1995, which included pipe bands from both Unionist and Nationalist political traditions in Ireland, one can but wonder at the complex implications of this announcement. Just like *kan ha diskan* and the round dance, the show was continuous, with each act bleeding into the other: an imaginary blending of all into a colorful metaphor for Celtic continuity. Together with the ongoing *fest noz*, this type of event provides the central focus of the festival.

Lorient has become an example to emulate for many other organizations all over Brittany and France. The musical globalization of bretonnitude in this context has valorized both a social process and a perceived reality that eclipses local and global, a process aptly characterized as "glocal." In drawing an analogy between *les montagnes*/Lorient, *gavotte montagne*/*musique celtique*, and *fest noz*/interceltic music festival—in the Breton context—I suggest that the concept of place, genre, and event can be viewed as an encapsulation of the parallel ideas of local and global identity as expressed through music. It reflects, perhaps, part of the new "relationship between cultural space and physical place in our time," opening up ever-widening vistas of diasporic experimentation (see Lipsitz 1994).

It is the "unofficial" side of the Lorient festival that catches the imagination of many, however. In this context the words *festival interceltique* take on a new meaning in the popular imagination and are often jovially substituted by the words *festival interceltcuite*, which means literally, "the inter-Celtic completely-plastered festival."[15] People from all over Europe meet in bars throughout the town, carousing in Celtic Mardi Gras mode until the small hours. Irish traditional dance music sessions form the mainstay of common ground at these informal gatherings.[16] The festival is very important to the local economy, and although some complaints may be voiced concerning the late-night antics and drinking habits of some of the more boisterous Celts, they are usually followed by a comment supporting the idea of the festival. Lorient is at once a celebration of efficient postmodern myth building, cultural expression, and a highly successful economic strategy. It is of considerable importance to the symbolic production of celtitude in Brittany, as well as the local economy and tourism in western France more generally.

BRETON CELTITUDE AND ALAN STIVELL

In general, the notion of Celtic identity prevalent in the British Isles and the anglophone world is still largely synonymous with Gaeldom, and the local attachments such a concept implies. Musicians, even in Ireland—the engine-room of a perceived Celtic Diaspora elsewhere—have usually not engaged explicitly with a broader Celtic musical imaginary. In Brittany, by contrast, many musicians have been traveling a pan-Celtic musical pathway since at least the early 1970s. The fashions have varied. Celtic Ireland and Irish music are now being appropriated by many musicians in the world of Breton celtitude (see Wilkinson 1999, 277–319). Some folk musicians there (and in France) describe themselves quite unself-consciously as Celtic musicians and their repertory usually reflects the vicissitudes of such fashion.

La Tène–inspired trinkets and jewelry, spiral necklaces and earrings, plastic *triskel* (Celtic spiral) and *hermine* car stickers, in short "low level cultural paraphernalia" (Vallely 1995), have been present in abundance throughout Brittany for at least thirty years. It coexists with wholly pan-Breton paraphernalia like pancakes (*crêpes*) and cider. Much in the same way as the charismatic and entrepreneurial Sobieski Stuarts (the Allen brothers) invented Clan tartans in early-nineteenth-century Scotland (Trevor-Roper 1983, 37), a reinvention of small symbols unifying the concepts of Breton national/cultural identity and ancient Celtic heritage has been underway for some time. Alan Stivell and Lorient have been trendsetters in this regard.

Breton-Celtic imagery is used in everything from the literature of environmentalist groupings to product lines.

In the field of professional musical celtitude, Alan Stivell is undoubtedly a pivotal figure. Stivell has been described as "the godfather of the modern Breton music scene" (Broughton et al. 1991, 28). He is one of Brittany's most influential musical figures and arguably the first international star of Celtic music. He could be said to have invented himself during the late 1960s from his Parisian base as the quintessential modern Celtic musical mystic. At that time, he was a regular performer at "the hootenannies at the Centre Américain on the Boulevard Raspail" (Brekilien 1973). He was born in Paris to Breton parents as Alain Cochevelou; many prominent Breton cultural activists share this type of background. A multi-instrumentalist he went on to play in *bagadoù* (bagpipe and *bombarde* bands) and at *festoù noz* covering the whole spectrum of Celtic music and adopting the Celtic harp as his main instrument.

His early career has been the subject of a considerable body of biographical writing.[17] Stivell—which is his adopted name—means "source" in the Breton language. He has had a prolific professional career to date. In what could only be described as an affectionate though markedly tongue-in-cheek manner, he is often alluded to in the Breton musical milieu by his underground pseudonym, "Raymond la Source." In popular Glasgow parlance, any male person can be referred to as "Jimmy"; if we apply this precedent, the expression "Raymond la Source" translates something like "Jimmy the Wellspring." It is a humorous, leveling marriage of the familiar and the epic. Many professional Celts in Brittany and elsewhere have since followed Stivell's lead. Brekilien (1973), which documents Stivell's early career, is an unabashed act of hero-worship. Here Stivell is credited with being the progenitor of Celtic music. Brekilien states (with considerable justification) that Stivell invented Celtic folk music and became a sort of messianic figure for young Bretons. "He has been approved of (*il est plébiscité*) by the mass of the youth, he has brought something to them. Something that they were waiting for" (1973, 61).

On the sleeve notes to the English-language edition of his best-known recording, *Live at the Olympia Theatre in Paris* (Fontana 1972), he sets out his stall quite clearly, invoking a unified Celtic tradition in the space of a couple of succinct phrases—the stuff of which history, legend and, as has been shown, commercial success is made.

So his originality springs from traditional Celtic music, which he considers to be at the origin of white-American folk music and of many
groups' inspiration (some of the Beatles' songs are true Celtic themes).
Neither recognized nor exploited yet, Celtic music is now given a
chance according to Alan Stivell.

Historian Jacques Vassal describes Stivell's concert at the Olympia
Paris in 1972 as "the revenge of young Brittany in the heart of
Sodom" (1973, 114). Vassal also strongly criticized Stivell's detractors who accused him of being involved in Breton activism and
Celticism only for the money. Many musicians, some of whom
could not necessarily be described as fans of Stivell's music today,
are nonetheless quick to acknowledge the energizing effect that
this concert had on the many who heard extracts from it on their
radios at home in Brittany. It was a very public valorization of bretonnitude and Breton music, and an important and cathartic moment in the birth of a new Breton consciousness. On this live
recording, Stivell also makes the potent symbolic gesture of
singing a song about the Irish revolution. A plaintive prelude in
Breton entitled *"Telenn gwad war ar garreg"* ("Bloostained harp on
the rock") follows. It is sung to the air of the famous Irish song
from the penal times *"An raibh tú ag an charraig?"* ("Were you at the
[mass] rock?")

Stivell follows this with a version of "The Foggy Dew."[18] With this
song, and a rousing electrified version of the set dance, "The King of
the Fairies," he could be said to have unleashed Irish music on the
francophone world as part of a general Celtic inheritance. He most
certainly did make Irish music more accessible to a larger public and
at the same time he opened a window into Irish history and politics
for a new generation of young people throughout Brittany and
France. Similarly he introduced the music of Scotland, Wales, and
other Celtic zones. The fact that he sang in English but not in French
on this particular album was also significant. French was a threat to
Celtic Brittany but English was evidently considered a valid Celtic
tongue. On this level his musical strategy mirrors a definition of
French culture as the "other" by which Breton Celts identified themselves. Presumably he also had his eye on the anglophone popular
music market, although at that time English still had a certain exoticism in France. English was—and has so far remained—the language of global "first world" success in popular music. Stivell has

been known to sing in French, however; the francophone market is important to professional success in Breton music.

Viewed against the sociopolitical turmoil and the profound hopes of the 1960s, both in America and Europe, one can appreciate more realistically where Stivell drew his inspiration. Aside from the freshness and attractiveness of his music at that time, he was articulating the spirit of a generation in a particularly Breton way. And, one might suggest, a particularly French way. Stivell's appeal was strong throughout the length and breadth of France. The old France, epitomized by Charles de Gaulle, was singularly unattractive to the youth. The Paris riots of 1968 were to signify yet another cathartic moment in the history of France and indeed Europe in general. New identities were actively being sought by a new generation and students who made common cause with workers. For some it was sociopolitical revolution, for others an opportunistic bandwagon, for others still it was the hippie nirvana of "tune in and drop out."

For the majority it was probably a combination of all these elements. Stivell's emblematic musical search for "roots," which would symbolically offer something fresh and new, yet of ancient lineage, was in tune with the idealism of the time and fitted the mood in Brittany. Although reputedly unhappy with the hippie image he felt record companies wished to foist upon him in his early career, Stivell did offer a composite image of flower power, lyrical mystery, sociopolitical concern and rootedness—a new cool Bretagne. During this period, such a powerful urbane and youthful image was at once a break with the tarnished prewar image of political bretonnitude (see McDonald 1989) and an accessible statement of Brittany's global celtitude. This view of Brittany stood in sharp contrast to previously received ideas of provincial backwardness (see Vassal 1977, 40). Stivell represented an image that married youthful exuberance, new idealism, and rock-star gloss with older traditions.

Stivell and his generation, it can be argued, first established the linkage that currently exists between bretonnitude and contemporary celtitude. It is now a conspicuous part of youth culture. During the late 1990s a young Breton friend of the family, my son, and I spent some time discussing the youth culture scene in Brittany. Among the usual "techno-heads" and "grunge rockers" that make up part of the perceived alternative (to pop) music scene, another group emerged, known as the *baba breizoù*. This translates roughly as "cool Breton heads"[19] and it refers to the youthful partisans of

Breton/Celtic culture who regularly frequent *festoù noz* and demonstrate their cultural choices in obvious ways. They might wear Triskel earrings or features from the *Gwen ha du* ("white and black"—a reference to the Breton flag) such as a necklace with a heraldic hermine suspended from it. In speaking of this group in the third person our young friend looked at his own attire and, moderately surprised, exclaimed, "In fact I'm a baba breizoù!" Following traditional music and its attendant generic developments is popular among a large section of the younger population all over Brittany and beyond. While this has been the case for many decades, the naming of the group, so to speak, is a new development. The *baba breizoù* or simply *breiz* (meaning "Brittany") are recognized as a distinct youth grouping by their peers.

I have looked briefly at the nature of bretonnitude and celtitude earlier and shown how they have been implicated in the growth of the *fest noz* and the festival event respectively. For the majority of the professionals who play Breton traditional dance music, the *fest noz* is their bread and butter work. In the concluding part of this chapter, I would like to explain how bretonnitude and celtitude operate as exactly this "bread and butter work." This work takes place in a complex interlocking structure of local initiative and public funding, regional arts grants, and the like, though in many, local initiative has predominated. It would be useful, then, to consider ethnographically the organizational structure of the event and the Système d'Intermittent du Spectacle, a French government-sponsored scheme designed to encourage the orderly professionalization of musicians and connect musicians with events.

This is a world in which I have been personally involved as a musician, and something should perhaps be said about this, and the area in which I worked, first. My experience of regular *festoù noz* relates for the most part to time spent in the rural environs of the village *communes* (communities) of Cavan, Prat, Confort-Berhet, and Pluzunet throughout the 1990s. These communes lie roughly between the towns of Lannion and Guingamp in the bas-Breton area known as the Trégor. The Trégor is a prerevolutionary bishopric in origin. It gives its name to one of the dialects of the Breton language, Trégorois. *Festoù noz* were held in or around these locations throughout the year. Many people traveled from other regions to attend them and many locals in turn traveled to events in neighboring districts. These communes are not situated along the coast and as such are not major tourist destinations during the summer. Regular cultural activities have played an important part in attracting people to them.

The Trégor is famed for its coastline, the celebrated *côtes de granit rose* ("pink granite coast"). As one approaches it from any direction this feature is displayed prominently on all tourist road signs. In this instance it is used to define the Trégor in terms of its geographic features. The département of the Côtes d'Armor, in which most of the Trégor lies, was called the Côtes du Nord up until 1990. This change of name has, according to many, served to make it sound more Breton, more maritime than cold, more celtique. The Conseil Général first put up bilingual road signs in the *Trégor bretonnant* (Breton-speaking Trégor) during 1990. The fact that such a development took place at all is testament to the lobbying carried out by local activists during the 1970s and 1980s. During my stay in the Trégor the area had already become noted for its vibrant community of cultural activists.

Given these relatively recent public affirmations it remains a recognizable space with a past, a present, and a future. Lannion is the region's capital. All types of Western music are part of the scene. Pop music, rock music, and its multitude of subgenres, *varieté française* (popular French songs), together with brass bands and Western art music. There are many performance spaces in the area; bars, nightclubs, theatres, halls, and churches. Practically every small commune in the region has its own fully equipped *salle des fêtes* (village/community hall). *Festoù noz*, however, were conspicuously popular. "Who are this band *fest noz*?" commented a member of a visiting band of rock musicians from northern France who I spoke to briefly in 1994. "Their posters are everywhere, the papers are full of them . . . they must be making a fortune."

ASSOCIATIONS AND THE PROFESSIONAL MUSICIAN

The *association* provides the means by which everybody, even the most recalcitrant, can be drawn into community life. All members of an association work in a voluntary capacity. They can however employ people to work on their behalf, as in the case of a large charity, for example. The *Quid* (encyclopedia) provides detailed information on the nature and obligations of associations. According to this important source there were 730,000 registered associations in France in 1994, 611,300 with paid employees, 118,700 without. Of these 21 percent are involved with sport, health, and social action; 13.6 percent with leisure, commerce, employment, and consumer affairs; 12.3 percent with education and vocational training and 8.2 percent social life; 7.9 percent are concerned with housing and the environment. A further 6.8 percent are dedicated to hunting and fishing while 2.8 percent are described as involved with culture and tourism. These figures are followed by a 0.02 percent whose activities can't apparently be classified (*Quid* 1996, 1444).

Associations reflect all elements of society ranging from the purely social to business and politics. Most people in the area where I lived were involved with several associations. To form an association there must be at least two people; afterward there is no upward limit on numbers. They have to have legal status in the locality especially if they are seeking public money for sponsorship of events. To do this they must register at the center of local government nearest to them (the *préfecture* or *sous-préfecture*). If they do not do this, they cannot sign checks or have a bank account. As the treasurer for the Confort-Brehet–based association Kanfarded ar Vilin Goz once remarked, "Life in France is based on associations. You have to create an association if you want to do anything at all."[20] In addition to the associations that hold *réunions* (meetings) at weekly or monthly intervals, single-event or single-issue bodies such as *comités d'action* ("forums for action") come and go regularly. Going to a *réunion* anywhere in France, outside of the workplace, serves a social as well as a practical purpose. The local press usually mentions all of the *réunions des associations* held in the area. A common feature of local news coverage is numerous photos of businesslike-looking people siting around tables with notepads in front of them.

The most proactive of the local associations concerned with musical activity between 1992 and 1994 in the area where I lived were Modall, Kanfarded ar Vilin Gozh, Awel Dro, and Youankiz Plunet. Between these associations and a few others (either alone or acting in collaboration with other bodies such as Dastum), a year-long program of dance classes, music classes, concerts, and *festoù noz* was assured. They attracted a wide cross-section of people, ranging from the local youth in the case of Youankiz Plunet ("The youth of Pluzunet") to specialist musicians and artists in the case of Modall.

The organization of a *fest noz*, from idea to event, involves large numbers of people, usually acting in a voluntary capacity it must be added. It is a significant example of local community enterprise, often undertaken without financial help from any type of sponsoring body.[21]

At least half of the performers at contemporary public access *festoù noz* are, however, full-time professional musicians, while others, though described as amateurs also receive a fee for their work. The terms *amateur* and *professional* in this sense do not reflect the relative abilities of the musicians or singers. Some amateurs are highly skilled and may be regarded as masters within the tradition, whereas some professionals may have little or no status as traditional musicians. Nor do these terms imply a distinction between those who play for money and those who don't.

What, then, is a professional? The professional has posters, CDs, and a publicity campaign; possibly management. These attributes are as much defined by a *kind* of payment, though in Brittany this involves a complex set of relationships within the predominantly amateur organizational structure of the event. The professional's fee includes the social insurance contributions that he or she is obliged to make. Payment in this context involves a protracted filling in of forms at the end of the night. Many *fest noz* organizers find this procedure stressful but the professional musician will insist upon it. For professional musicians it is of great importance that their performance is registered as every engagement they undertake contributes toward their eligibility for pay-related unemployment benefit. Amateurs, too are paid, but paid in such a way that their fee can be read as expenses. Their payment is usually less than the fee allocated to professional musicians, because, in the case of the professional, the fee must take account of the various contributions and deductions the artist and indeed the organizing association itself is obliged to pay. The issue of amateurism and professionalism in traditional music is one of considerable controversy, but for the moment it has not sown the seeds of a general division among performers.

Written contracts between organizers and performers are a matter of course, even when the parties are well-known to each other. All the above tasks are apportioned during the various *réunions* (meetings) held in the period leading up to the event. When one considers that over a thousand people may attend a large *fest noz*, a significant amount of money is transacted. If the night has been a success,

Wilkinson

the event generates enough social and economic capital to launch itself the following year. If not, it may simply disappear. As pointed out above, many *festoù noz* are not subsidized by public funds and therefore they must be independently viable. Organizational structures are very much dependent upon energetic local initiative. This is of crucial importance. *Festoù noz* now currently support a lifestyle for a large number of professional traditional musicians—particularly groups—in Brittany.

That is not to say that there was no historical precedent for professionalism in traditional music in Brittany. The skill of the *sonneur* was highly prized, but effectively he could not really accumulate wealth or property.[22] He was confined to an economically low status by the rural society in which he worked. By the advent of the twentieth century, however, payment for the services of sonneurs became standard; most traditional musicians, it must be said, also worked as small farmers. Full-time professional traveling musicians had become rare. Now, however, new social legislation is in place, legislation that is inextricably linked to the popularity of *festoù noz* over the last twenty years. Taken together with this legislation, the popularity and frequency of *festoù noz* have made the possibility of becoming professional, in the modern sense, a reality for traditional musicians. That means inclusion in mainstream socioeconomic life for the first time ever.

Flute player Jean-Michel Veillon draws attention to both the relative fragility of the *festoù noz* and the tenuous nature of the lifestyle dependent upon them.

> It's all due to the existence of the fest noz, without the fest noz it would be impossible. Even if there are lots of festoù noz, I believe they are still a fragile type of event and it's best to be vigilant. Because all it takes is a government taking restrictive measures concerning such things as late closure, drink sales outlets (*buvettes*) and the like and that could completely destroy (*laminer*) the fest noz in a year. Where would that leave the groups who play practically full time at festoù noz? For them it's all over. They'll have to play another type of music. (Interview, Cavan, November 1994)

Given their ubiquity at present and the nature of the social legislation supporting professionalism, *festoù noz* may appear to be partly institutionalized, but they clearly have an inherent fragility, which has the potential to affect professionalism should circumstances

change in the future. However it must be said that many of the politically aware professionals that have been working within the *système d'intermittent du spectacle* will jealously guard their status,
which has no counterpart in any other European country. It is to that
that we now turn.

THE SYSTÈME D'INTERMITTENT DU SPECTACLE

The history and development of the *système d'intermittent du spectacle*, which roughly translated means "unemployment benefit scheme
for irregulars of the entertainment industry," but is linked to the
overall social contract in French society, is an interesting and highly
important issue. It was initiated by government in 1974 but its successful operation since that date has depended on the cooperation of
employers, management, and workers rather than governmental
vigilance. However, I do not intend to examine this history and its
implications in detail, nor to examine how exactly the system
amasses and distributes funds as a part of the French social security
network. The experience of technicians, impresarios, and actors—
who are also its beneficiaries—is of great importance, too, but not
my primary concern here. What I am more concerned with is the
emergence of a particular kind of musical professional in the *fest noz*
system, ultimately with a view to considering the ways in which
change in the social organization of the system accompanies or generates change in the cultural values that are also part of it.[23]

With regard to the issue of professionalism in traditional music,
Brittany offers an example without parallel in other parts of France
or elsewhere in Europe. According to professional sonneur Youenn
le Bihan, speaking of the situation vis-à-vis traditional music in the
early 1990s, "there are over a thousand intermittents du spectacle in
Brittany, therefore many live from Breton culture. Brittany has the
highest numbers of professionals" (*Le Peuple Breton* 1992, 1). At the
moment, the number of *intermittents du spectacle* in Brittany is second only to that of the Paris region.

Most of these musicians perform in groups, but the *fest noz* star
system is also linked to competition structures that were put in place
in the past. This too has had its effect on professional careers. Competition success ensures that good young performers of *kan ha diskan*
and promising *sonneurs de tradition* will quickly rise to the top of the

pile should they so wish. A win at the yearly *kan ar bobl* ("songs of the people") competition could in this respect launch a professional career. The *bouc d'or* ("golden goat") is its Gallo/French equivalent. Engagements to sing at *festoù noz* are usually the direct result of such successes. Winning competitions therefore represents a "head start" or "symbolic capital" (after Bourdieu 1977) that can be turned to economic advantage by a skilled professional.

The first step in understanding how the *système d'intermittent du spectacle* works is to define it. The shortened term *intermittent* is used to describe someone who is a beneficiary. For better or worse, this word is now practically synonymous with "professional musician." It is at this point important to state, however, that not all professional musicians, actors, or technicians are intermittents. The organization that represents intermittents—the *FN SAC-CGT*—estimates that the status is held by only half of all professionals in France.[24] There are a variety of reasons for this, ranging from stardom on the one hand to perhaps simply an anarchic disposition on the other. The star, for example, especially if he or she is earning over a certain sum per year, is automatically excluded (though this has not always been the case). Those performers who happen to be earning considerable sums from royalties may also be much better off opting to be self-employed. On the other end of the scale, however, there are minimum requirements concerning the conditions to be fulfilled in order to benefit from the scheme. These requirements prove so elusive as to make the task of qualifying impossible for many.

Intermittent du spectacle, therefore, is not simply a job description. Rather, it is a status under which professionals in the entertainment industry can receive payment (unemployment benefit) for periods of inactivity. What this means in practice is that France operates a specially tailored system that guarantees a minimum monthly income for people engaged professionally in the world of entertainment. This world includes actors, agents, and technicians as well as musicians. The working musician or actor, not the superstar, is the one who stands to gain most by becoming eligible for this status. The system recognizes the irregular pattern of the musical profession and legislates accordingly. As a result, many professional musicians in France are either actively seeking to become intermittents or have already acquired the status. Musicians are employed by a wide variety of different employers, ranging from the patron (owner) of a modest café cabaret, a recording studio, or a local community association, to a large theatre complex or national television. The most common contract is called a *contrat de durée déterminée de travail*, that is, a short-term contract, where the beginning and end are clearly defined. The processing of the sporadic work patterns of the musician is the cornerstone of this system. It is both complicated and cumbersome, but most professional musicians feel that the security it offers is worth the effort involved.

The first step in becoming an intermittent is to register for work at the local office of the national employment agency, the ANPE (*Agence Nationale Pour l'Emploi*). After stating that one is a professional musician looking for work, one inquires about the possibility of becoming an intermittent. The ANPE seldom if ever actually finds work for musicians but this process is standard procedure for everyone registering for employment. The *déclaration mensuelle* ("monthly statement") made to this agency outlines the artist's periods of work and inactivity. It is obligatory. It provides the ANPE with a ready-made check list of engagements. This list is then set against the list of performance fees that the musician eventually brings into the local office of the ASSEDIC (*Association pour l'Emploi Dans l'Industrie et le Commerce*) when registering a claim for pay related benefit. The ASSEDIC is the benefit claims office. The individual cannot become an intermittent unless he or she has been making this monthly statement to the ANPE. It is from the ASSEDIC that benefit eventually comes. The *carnet d'intermittent* ("intermittents log book") is obtained from the ASSEDIC. It is a booklet of forms in triplicate. A separate form must, in theory, be filled in by each employer (and the employee) at the end of each contract and an up-to-date pay slip provided. One set of forms represents a concert or a consecutive series of concerts for the same employer. One form is for the employee's records, one for the employers, and one for the ASSEDIC. It serves as a record of all the short-term contracts the musician undertakes; it also shows the tax, social security contributions, and various other sums that have been paid by the employee and the employer. Every aspirant must carry their *carnet d'intermittent* to all their engagements.

Any artist habitually employed on a series of short-term contracts is eligible to register as an intermittent. Anyone with *un contrat de durée indéterminée de travail* ("a long-term or open contract") is not eligible to become a beneficiary of the system, even though their work may be identical to that of the intermittent. A permanent salaried member of a state body like the national symphony orchestra, for instance, would not qualify as a potential intermittent. The criterion for participation in this system is relatively exclusive and strictly applied. It functions for most musicians this way; one performance fee is the equivalent of twelve hours' work. The time factor here takes into account preparation and travel to and from the performance. According to the *Guide Pratique des Intermittents:* "The employee . . . can claim the first payment of benefit when he can prove he has worked 507 hours (or its equivalent in cachets) . . . in the twelve month period prior to his last contract" (*FN SAC-CGT* 1993, 10).

In terms of single cachets (short-term contracts/a single fee), therefore, the minimum number necessary to enter into the system is forty-three in any calendar year. In my experience, finding this number of decently paid engagements is difficult. In addition when the musician works for more than five or more continuous days with the same employer, his day's work or cachet counts for eight hours instead of twelve. There is also a limit of two to the number of individual cachets a person is eligible to declare for one day. Many musicians of course exceed these guidelines for minimum benefit. In this case they ultimately receive their monthly allocation *à taux plein* ("at the top rate") for a longer period than those who satisfy the minimum conditions. Benefit is pay related. That is, the more one earns in a period of high activity, the more benefit one receives during periods of inactivity. If the individual is working for an entire month, no payment is made in respect to that month. Only days of inactivity are covered.

As I have indicated, there are different rates and these rates relate to two factors. First, the number of hours worked in the calendar year preceding the claim of benefit and second the calculated average fee earned by the musician during that period. According to these criteria, the musician is placed on a sliding scale of payment each month. Basically this sliding scale of payment operates in a downward direction until *la date anniversaire* ("the anniversary date") is reached (*Guide Pratique* 1993, 13). This date is exactly a year to the day when the musician logged his or her last cachet in the initial application for the status. At this point, the musician's file will be reexamined to establish if he or she has fulfilled the conditions required to remain as an *intermittent du spectacle*. These conditions as I have said are strict, and if as little as one contract is missing, a new date must be chosen to enable the exact same conditions—507 hours work minimum in a calendar year—to be met. Most musicians are agreed that the first year spent attempting to qualify for entry into the system is without doubt the most difficult. The material benefits of belonging to it are such that the motivation to actively seek declared work is high.

When one becomes an intermittent, the monthly return changes to a more detailed document, requiring specific information on all one's engagements. Payment of monthly benefit in respect of days of inactivity commences when all the conditions have been fulfilled, that is, one month after the musician has logged his or her year's store of fees at the local branch of the ASSEDIC. Providing that the musician continues to fulfil these conditions every consecutive calendar year thereafter, he or she has a secure minimum income every month. He or she also has all the normal services available to any employee in sectors. This includes health coverage and a pension on reaching retirement age.[25] Becoming an intermittent also opens up a range of possible services to the individual. These include instrument insurance and car insurance. The system as a whole considers careers in the long term. After five years one can take a year off work in order to pursue a career-related educational or vocational course. Payment continues at a fixed rate. These courses are advertised regularly and are often reserved for *intermittents du spectacle* only. Account is taken of periods of inactivity due to illness but the same conditions as before must be fulfilled if one is to remain a beneficiary of the system. The system allows those who are working according to its conditions to have a lifestyle that is fully integrated into the socioeconomic fabric of French society.

In addition to the benefits mentioned above, intermittents receive two weeks' holiday pay and a return train ticket per year to any destination in France. This contribution, also taken at source, is referred to as *les congés spectacles* (CS). It translates roughly as "artists holiday pay." Like the benefit payment itself, the CS allowance is pay related so the more one earns the more holiday money one receives. In my experience, because of the various deductions, the first year is particularly difficult. The initial agreed *salaire brut* ("gross fee") reduces significantly after the various contributions have been made. For example, in pre-Euro days, from a modest fee of 500frs one could expect to get around 270frs net. Rebates, if appropriate, are calculated at the end of the tax year. In keeping with the norm for the self-employed, most professionals assiduously hold on to petrol receipts, restaurant bills, and a variety of other bills that can be associated with their professional duties. While it must be said that participation in the system seems logical, a concentrated effort is required if one is to qualify as a beneficiary. One is also required to put up with a formidable amount of paperwork.

This, in principle, is how the system works. How, though, is it perceived by its intended beneficiaries, and how are these perceptions involved in the ways in which musicians manage their working lives? First, musicians are concerned with its political frailty. When Jacques Chirac and his center-right coalition came to power in 1994, some artists expressed concern that the *système d'intermittent du spectacle* may be undermined. This type of unease among the artistic community is more or less constant. Interestingly, the system was first introduced during the early 1970s by another center-right government headed by Valéry Giscard d'Estaing. On closer analysis the type of strategy employed by Giscard was perfectly in tune with the sociopolitical climate of the post-1968 period. This was a period when capitalist development, after the unrestrained American model, had to be tempered by the social reforms necessary for political stability in France. According to John Ardagh, Giscard (then French president) saw that "if capitalism went ahead with little regard to any social philosophy, then the barricades and the red flags might come out again one day" (1977, 668).

The status of *intermittent du spectacle* evolved to its present form during the tenure of the socialist administration led by François Mitterand, from the early 1980s into the mid-1990s. Ironically it was during the Mitterand years, when attempts to introduce more socialist policies became frustrated by a flood of capital from the country, that the scheme came nearest to being revoked. This was seen by many intermittents as portentous of a climb down before reactionary elements. I spoke to some intermittents in the early 1990s who felt that a move to make the system more exclusive was inevitable. They further suggested that if the seeds of division were sown among their ranks, everybody would suffer. This suspicion was given official expression by comments in the April 1993 edition of the *Guide Pratique*. In this issue the writer exhorted all professionals in the entertainment business (both intermittents and full-time employees) to be ever vigilant and to show solidarity:

> If we do not remain proactive, the employers with the complicity of certain confederations, would not hesitate to undermine our inter-

professional solidarity. In these circumstances, we have no other choice but to pull together in order to prevent any potential new set back, in the knowledge that this struggle cannot be separated from that of employment in general, the defence of artistic creation and production. (*FN SAC-CGT* 1993, 7)

While there are anomalies concerning the practical day-to-day workings of this system, professionals who have been intermittents for many years are convinced of its comparative efficiency and fairness. They are protective of their hard-earned status and object to anything that threatens to undermine it. This applies equally to playing *au noir* (undeclared) or any perceived government/ employer-orchestrated strategy. Some unscrupulous people known among intermittents as *faux amateurs* ("false amateurs") have been known to undercut professionals deliberately. Most people are anxious to find a way of allowing the tradition to embrace both amateurism and professionalism in the local context and there is—as pointed out above—a general understanding concerning this issue in the *fest noz* circuit. One wonders, however, what will transpire when circumstances change, notably when the older performers are no longer active and the intermittents and amateurs are all in the same age group. Some cultural activists fear a situation where professionalism encroaches too much on the domain of traditional music and smaller public local events become impossible to run. The overheads involved and the bureaucratic hassle of paying and declaring professionals can serve to demoralize local organizations. There is an ever-increasing number of intermittents and the demands of the performing rights organization, the SACEM (*Société des Auteurs Compositeurs et Editeurs de Musique*), further complicate the affair.[26] All this amounts to ever more stress on the musical ecosystem represented by the *fest noz*. This scenario is not without a touch of irony. A system that was created by a government exercising social conscience is, in some situations, at odds with the maintenance of a popularly generated traditional genre in its local context.

The arbitrary conditions faced by professional musicians in many other European countries are regarded by some of their counterparts in France as *la galère*, literally "the galley." From their perspective, the everyday work situation faced by professional traditional musicians in Ireland, for example—the paid pub session—are decidedly unenviable. Some artists in France fear any future pan-European legislation on music professionalism in the belief that this would automatically mean a devaluation of the status they enjoy. In principle, however, the spokespersons of the musician's union are in favor of the introduction of similar legislation throughout the European community. In the particular case of the Celtic countries and their geographic location on the edge of Europe, some in Brittany have suggested the principle of an *arc atlantique* (see Favereau 1993, 14), serving to unite music professionals in these areas, both in a symbolic sense and economically.

Because professional status is a proven pathway for traditional and folk musicians in Brittany, many young musicians from other parts of France, particularly those involved in Celtic music, see moving to Brittany as a logical professional strategy. I met three such people in Quimper in the summer of 1997. They told me they intended to remain in Brittany and try to become intermittents. They suggested that elsewhere in France such a strategy is practically impossible with traditional music. All three of these musicians played Irish music. Their objective in coming to Brittany was to have the opportunity to play Irish music more regularly. This move, although logical from their perspective, is seen by some musicians in Brittany as more competition for work in an already-saturated market. Furthermore it is also perceived as having the potential to undermine standards of musicianship, particularly in Breton music. Inevitably many of these players, having little or no experience of Breton music, find places for themselves in the ever-increasing number of *fest noz* groups. Pierre Crépillon has suggested that to reduce one's definition of music professionalism to "forty-three fees"—the way some people describe their strategy these days—is a lamentable state of affairs (personal communication, July 1997). In his view, this narrow definition of professionalism had the potential to undermine both the sprit of music making and good musical standards. There is also a fear that the system will break down should too many try to become intermittents. It is also true to say that too many intermittents on the scene makes music professionalism itself less mysterious.

The exclusivity of music professionalism, accompanied by a certain reticence concerning "the tricks of the trade," is a common tactic of survival in most cultures and societies (note, for example, Langlois 1998). Many Breton traditional musicians who have been intermittents since 1984 say that they did not become aware of the existence of the system until that year, though it had been on the statute books since 1974. They imply that Paris-based musicians had been trying to keep it a secret. Operation of this—in principle, public—system is clearly regarded as a professional mystery, open only to initiates. The information concerning the *intermittent* system is not on public display at the offices of the ANPE in the same way as other career information, though it is, of course, made available on request. I came to understand the system through constant quizzing of my musician friends and direct experience. The whole process, aided by my own ingrained suspicion—as a musician—had the curious feel of a ritualized rite of passage. It is by no means easy to qualify for receipt of the benefit, so in this sense alone it is a rite of passage. The individual's capacity to negotiate this rite of passage and become an *intermittent* also serves as confirmation of their professional status and to some extent, business acumen, organizational capabilities, and singleness of purposes.

The system is tailored to the needs of those wanting to work exclusively as music professionals. Musicians who have other jobs lose money every time they are declared as an intermittent. This happens automatically when one works for large public bodies like state television or theatre companies for example. The musicians in question pay the same rate of contributions as other full-time professionals, but they do not gain anything from doing this. Although generally accepted in good faith by those in this position, some have been prompted either to leave their other occupations and become full-time professionals or to stop playing with declared professionals, thus undermining the system in the eyes of some. Combining the status of intermittent with other professional activities, matching up different social security funds, is problematic.

Another perceived disadvantage of this system is the sheer weight of paperwork (often contemptuously referred to as *paperrasse*) required after each single transaction of money between the employer and the employee. At the end of an event, the musicians and organizers have to sit down and sort out what certainly appears as a complicated array of paperwork. There is an obligation on the part of the employer to engage the system when they employ an intermittent. The process starts with a visit to the local URSSAF (*Union de Recouvrement des Cotisations de Sécurité Sociale et d'Allocations Familial*, or "Center for the Collection of Social Security Taxes and Family Allowance")—sometimes in advance of the concert—to purchase a *vignette* ("special tax label"). This vignette proves that they, as an occasional employer, and the artist have paid the relevant social welfare contributions. The onus is on the employer to fill in the relevant papers and to calculate the relevant financial allocations. If one is engaged by a theater or a large cabaret, the system normally runs smoothly. However, many employers are justifiably put off by the intimidating paperwork, in particular the proprietors of a small café cabaret or local associations who may have come together in a small village to organize a once-off event. As far as they are concerned, this bureaucratic scenario is increasingly replacing the hitherto simple "wad of notes in the back pocket."

It is often claimed that because of the paperwork and the extra expense involved in hiring declared professionals, that intermittents have lost work to people who are working "on the black." One way to avoid this perceived disadvantage is to make use of an intermediary organization like Allo Jazz. Allo Jazz offers its services to both musicians and employers for a fee. In this way, all the paperwork is taken over by Allo Jazz and a lot of stress and confusion avoided. What happens is that the employer makes out a check to the Allo Jazz organization instead of paying the musician directly. In effect Allo Jazz then becomes the employer. What Allo Jazz does (for a small fee on each transaction) is to route funds to the appropriate sectors of the social security system in respect of the employer and the employee. To avail of their services one must first register with them.[27] The musician then posts his or her cachet (gross fee/pay) check to them together with the contract between himself or herself and the organizer. After a few days he or she receives all the necessary paperwork and a smaller pay check (the net fee) made out to him or her by Allo Jazz. This process, although a little costly, I found to be worthwhile as it maintained good relations with patrons and thereby increased the chance of playing at the same venue again. Many feel that the service provided by Allo Jazz should be part of the overall system and not a service offered by state-sanctioned private concerns. Some musicians, armed with calculators, their *carnet d'intermittent*, and books of pay slips, do it all themselves—with the employer gazing on in wonderment. I have seen this type of situation become fraught with tension as musicians attempt to explain the intricacies of the system, at around 3 o'clock in the morning, to a tired and emotional organizer.

Some self-employed people in other sectors view the status of intermittent as privileged. I have heard the phrase *"Monsieur l' inter-*

mittent, tranquille Emile" used to refer to its beneficiaries. This can be translated roughly as "Mr. Intermittent, I'm all right Jack." Many for whom irregular employment is also a reality would prefer a status similar to it. In this sense, its exclusivity can be viewed as a form of artistic privilege. Some also suggest that the operational bureaucracy arising from the system has succeeded in turning the assumed "free-spirited" musician into a businessman to the extent that many now consider the portable computer and the mobile phone more essential tools of the trade than musical instruments. For the moment these modern accessories have prestige value beyond their utilitarian value. Implicit in this type of observation, however, is the suggestion that the system has demystified the bardic element of being a musician. Because of its status as an ethnic sound icon—the property of all—some believe that traditional music in particular should never have a commercial value. A spurious conclusion that too much wealth or organization is in some way bad for creativity can be the outcome of such deliberations. This type of speculation serves to perpetuate the insidious mythology that would justify not giving the creative artist—if a traditional musician—his or her due. This is a public attitude that condemned many traditional musicians to alcoholism and penury in the past (see O'Neill 1913).

Many professionals cite the existence of the intermittent system as having provided an impetus for creative activity in Breton traditional music throughout the 1980s and 1990s. They say that once an intermittent, one can set aside time for rehearsal and thereby develop musical ideas and repertoire. Room to maneuver and consolidate one's position becomes more possible. Many have also suggested that the conditions created by their situation as intermittents has also allowed them to exercise greater control over their performance situations. The system gives them time to organize work in advance and to decide what engagements they would or would not do. In this way musical strategies can also be adapted to enable movement between different performance contexts. All this can be done without the pressure of having to hustle continually for cash in an unreliable market place. It is as intermittents that many enterprising Breton dance musicians who have regular cachets from their performance at *festoù noz* reemerge as Celtic cabaret artists. They work from a strong supportive base—the regular *fest noz* circuit. Clearly aside from the aesthetic desire to play another style of music or to perform in another context, the ability to be constantly adaptive in terms of professional strategy is essential. I have spoken to many musicians whom have tried and failed to become an *intermittent du spectacle*. The frustration of someone who manages to accumulate, say, 450 hours' work for several calendar years, but who cannot make up the short fall, is obvious. As I have suggested, however, a certain diplomatic ambivalence to this reality thankfully prevents constant acrimony at social events.

CONCLUSION

I have tried to show in this chapter how musicians in Brittany have managed their professional lives over the last thirty years, developing identities in relation to the Celtic music phenomenon and exploiting a niche created by the interaction of state cultural legislation (the *système d'intermittent du spectacle*) and a local tradition of public festivity (the *fest noz*). The issue bears on some pervasive issues in ethnomusicology concerning the perceived tension between professionalism (together with forms of musical education designed to produce professionals) and the communal maintenance of tradition (see, for instance, Cooke 1986 and Debord 1988). It also bears on the process of postmodern enculturation described as "glocalization," concerning the ways in which transnational cultural flows produce intensely experienced senses of local identity. My main concern in describing the working of the *système d'intermittent du spectacle* in such detail has mainly been to insist on the importance of understanding patterns of labor and payment when trying to understand a local "scene," one that has produced a rich form of pan-Celtic musical imagination. The ongoing production of a Celtic imaginary by professional musicians, by those who employ them, and by those who listen to them at *festoù noz* and concerts will continue to owe much to the evolution of this particular, and, in my view, highly effective, form of state patronage.

ACKNOWLEGMENT

The author would like to thank the IRCHSS (the Irish Research Council for the Humanities and Social Sciences) for their support.

NOTES

1. All translations are the author's own; the French is only rendered where important interpretative issues hinge on translation.

2. Personal communication, Quimper, July 1997.

3. For details on language issues in Brittany and France, and relevant maps, see Wilkinson 1999, 32; Ó hIfearnáin 1995; Favereau 1993, 28–29; Abalain 1989, 208–10; Kuter 1981.

4. See Bithell's comparative comments on language and ethnicity in Wales and Corsica, in her chapter in this volume.

5. For an overview of his work, see Elisée Reclus' *L'homme et la Terre*, edited by Béatrice Giblin (1982 and 1998). La Blache is the author of the *Tableau de la géographie de la France* (1903). His maps graced most French classrooms throughout the first half of the twentieth century.

6. We had a radical example of this phenomenon, related to the Bosnian war, in the early 1990s. As is well known, Bosnian Serb leader and indicted war criminal Radovan Karadzic, himself a traditional singer, made extensive use of traditional Serbian melodies to stir up emotions and incite ethnic hatred.

7. In French, the *danse en rond* or in Breton, *dañs tro*.

8. *Kan ha diskan* and the *binioù/bombarde* duo are now recharged with symbolic significance for Breton identity. During the late nineteenth and early twentieth centuries, the image of the *biniou* was often denigrated by the Parisian and provincial "politicocultural élite" (implicitly their own impression of themselves) who used the term *biniouserrie* to imply rustic triviality or nonsense. By the 1950s these more ancient traditional outdoor instruments had already been losing some ground to more recent imports, such as the clarinet (introduced in the last decades of the nineteenth century) and the Highland bagpipes. The accordion in all its manifestations had also been present from the turn of the century.

9. Other people have informed me that similar local initiatives were taking place in Haute Bretagne as well at this time, but the event in les Monts d'Arrée remains the most widely documented.

10. Kiberd engagingly explores the links between the two:

The fact that many of the most successful business 'achievers' in society have been enthusiastic *Gaeilgeoirí* (Irish language activists) has strengthened arguments for a connection between cultural self-confidence and economic success. . . . The major moral—it is not too strong a word—is this: that, if the native culture of a people is devalued and destroyed for the sake of material progress, what follows may not be material progress of the kind hoped for, but cultural confusion and a diminished sense of enterprise. (1996, 652)

11. Parts of the Iberian peninsula such as Galicia and Asturias and northern Italy are now included in Euro-Keltia, principally through connections

reconfigured from ancient history and expressed through folk music. In these areas, Celtic music—or in some cases local traditional music reinvented as Celtic—is popular. In Spain this trend began (significantly) after the collapse of General Franco's repressive regime. I remember this period well. Many of my Breton musician friends traveled there throughout the 1980s to play at large festivals. They returned with descriptions of a social catharsis taking place among many young Spaniards, reminiscent of the era of "flower power" and the hippie movement of two decades earlier in most other western countries. Both Lisbon and Oporto have been hosting large Celtic music festivals since 1983, under the auspices of an entrepreneurial association called Mundo Da Cançao. Irish, Scottish, and Breton groups are regular guests and, in some cases, have provided models for newly reconstituted folk groups in these regions. While on a visit to Spain in 1993 at a festival in Segovia, I saw an Asturian group using a wooden concert flute, bodhran, and highland pipes. These instruments, in this particular form, are all recent additions to the musical landscape there. The Celtic music group, particularly after the Scottish model, is the popular symbol of a perceived celtitude to many Iberians.

12. The organizers of *Le Festival Celtique de Savoie* describe their attraction for celtitude in the following way: "to choose the Celtic world is like digging up one of the roots of the tree of life and exposing its hot entrails of miseries and joys in order to find therein the simple comfort and fortification of having a good time (*le simple reconfort de la fete*)" (*Planète Celte* 1996, 15, author's translation). Celtitude here approximates to one of the myriad interpretations of what the Irish refer to as having "the crack"—an expression that currently suffers from tedious overuse.

13. Note, for example, director Jean Pierre Pichard's comments in *Le Peuple Breton* 1994, 26. Parisian support for the Celtic, as opposed to Breton nationalist dimensions of the festival, are readily understandable. Euro-Celts are less of a threat to the European political establishment than a disgruntled Breton nationalist minority in France (to cite but one example). This may be one reason (aside from genuine attempts at inclusiveness) why all things pertaining to the cultural diversity of France have been promoted throughout the 1990s and early 2000s. The last two songs to represent France in the Eurovision song contest have been inspired by North African *rai* and Celtic music respectively. Dan Ar Bras sang the 1996 entry in the Breton language notwithstanding the fact that France is the only country in the EC that has not signed the Charter in relation to the protection of minority languages. Jacques Chirac has recently proclaimed his willingness to sign, but stressed that this will take time as it involves changing the French constitution. The constitution states that French is the only language of the Republic.

14. During the week immediately preceding the festival the recently established (2001) and excellent *Université d'été* ("summer university"), run by

the Université de Bretagne-Sud and loosely allied to the festival, runs seminars, lectures, and music master-classes) chiefly concerning historical and cultural aspects of life in the Celtic idioscape.

15. I first heard this expression for inter-Celtic drunkenness used by a presenter on *Cheri FM*, a local pop radio station in the Trégor. *Prendre une cuite*, literally "to take a cooking," is a standard way for people throughout France to describe getting drunk.

16. Reiss and Vallely's chapters in this volume present differing interpretations of the phenomenon.

17. For detailed accounts see *Racines interdites* ("forbidden roots") in *Musiciens et musiques* (1979). A comprehensive overview of his recordings can be obtained from ceolas on the Internet, http://celtic.stanford.edu/artists/Stivell.html 1996.

18. I remember listening to this recording with great pleasure in Belfast in 1975. It also valorized the Irishness that had no public value in Northern Ireland at that time. The *Foggy Dew* is perhaps *the* best-known Irish rebel song concerning the 1916 rising. An instrumental version of the song first appears in Bunting's collection of 1840; the author of the twentieth-century verses is unknown. There is, incidentally, a group of French musicians currently performing Irish folk music and song who go by the name of *The Froggy Stew*.

19. Perhaps partly drawn from the expression *les babas cool*—French hippies in the 1970s.

20. Personal communication, J. P. Le Toquer, August 1993.

21. Volunteers are required to prepare and serve food, to organize a bar, to work as bar staff, and to collect money at the entrance. Others are involved in organizing and contracting the artists, an activity that includes the sometimes stressful task of negotiating *cachets* (fees) with the musicians and practicalities like hiring equipment and sound-checks. Together with publicity in the local press, posters have to be made and paid for. Scaffolding, lighting, and the podium must be obtained and erected. In this matter, material and labor are often donated freely by local tradespeople willing to help out. In some cases accommodation may also be necessary.

22. Many nineteenth-century sonneurs made a living from their music, playing at weddings, pardons, and other local events. The method of payment at that time, however, conformed more to the idea of "spheres of exchange" (Douglas 1967, 119–47) than a cash payment. The musician was usually paid in food, drink, and lodging, or with material goods considered appropriate to his itinerant lifestyle. In the nineteenth century, money changed hands only in the context of a wedding or some exceptional circumstance. *Musique Bretonne* cites the appearance of Breton sonneurs at the World Fair in Paris at the turn of the nineteenth century, an appearance for which the sonneurs received a fee. See Merriam 1964, 123–43; and for an

Irish perspective, Wilkinson 1991, 37–41, on musical status and professionalism.
    23. I should, again, establish a personal context for this section. When I
moved to Brittany in 1992, it was essentially to work on a project initiated
by the group Bleizi Ruz and their association—Association Pellgomz. The
nature of the work was the creation of a musical drama evoking the story of
the pilgrim route to Santiago de Compostela in Galicia. This ambitious project involved musicians from different European countries. I began my professional career in Brittany as an *intermittent du spectacle* from the outset
without fully comprehending the system.
    24. Fédération Nationale des Syndicats du Spectacle, de l'Audiovisuel et
de l'Action Culturelle CGT, 1993.
    25. The first intermittents in the Breton music scene began to qualify for
retirement in 1998.
    26. There has been a similar controversy in rural Ireland over the last few
years over the question of small rural pubs who run traditional music sessions, paying a licensing fee to the IMRO (Irish Performing Rights Organization).
    27. The registration fee was 150frs in 1994.

BIBLIOGRAPHY

Abalain, Hervé. *Destin des langues celtiques*. Paris: Editions Ophrys, 1989.
Ardagh, John. *The New France: A Society in Transition, 1945–1977*. London:
    Pelican, 1977.
Becker, Roland, and Laure Le Gurun. *La Musique Bretonne*. Spézet: Coop
    Breizh, 1994.
Bourdieu, Pierre. *Outline of a Theory of Practice*. London: Cambridge Univer-
    sity Press, 1977.
Brekilien, Yann. *Le "Fait Stivell" ou Le Folk-celtique*. Rennes: Nature et Bre-
    tagne, 1973.
Broughton, Simon et al., eds. *Rough Guide to World Music*. Penguin: Har-
    mondsworth, 1991.
Chapman, Malcolm. *The Gaelic Vision in Scottish Culture*. London: Croom
    Helm, 1978.
Chapman, Malcolm. *The Celts: The Construction of a Myth*. London: St. Mar-
    tin's Press, 1992.
Cooke, Peter. *The Fiddle Tradition of the Shetland Isles*. London: Cambridge
    University Press, 1986.
Creston, René-Yves. *Le Costume Breton*. Spézet: Champion-Coop Breizh, 1995.
Debord, Guy. *Commentaires sur la Société du Spectacle*. Paris: Éditions Gérard
    Lébovici, 1988.

De La Blache, Paul Vidal. *Tableau de la Géographie de la France*. Paris: Librairie Jules Tallandrier, 1979.

Douglas, Mary. "Primitive Rationing: A Study of Controlled Exchange in Economic Anthropology." In *Economic Anthropology*, edited by Raymond Firth, 119–47. London, Tavistock Press, 1967.

Favereau, Francis. *Bretagne Contemporaine: Langue, Culture, Identité*. Spézet: Skol Vreizh, 1993.

Guilcher, Jean-Michel. *La Tradition Populaire de Danse en Basse-Bretagne*. Paris: Mouton, 1963.

Kiberd, Declan. *Inventing Ireland*. London: Vintage, 1996.

Kuter, Lois. "Breton Identity: Musical and Linguistic Expression in Brittany." Unpublished Ph.D. thesis, Indiana University, 1981.

Langlois, Tony. "The Gnawa of Oudja: Music at the Margins in Morocco." *World of Music* 10 (1998): 135–56.

Lipsitz, George. *Dangerous Crossroads: Popular Music, Postmodernism and the Poetics of Place*. London: Verso, 1997.

Lomax, Alan. *Folk Song Style and Culture*. Washington, D.C.: AAAS, 1968.

McDonald, Maryon. *We Are Not French: Language Culture and Identity in Brittany*. London: Routledge, 1989.

Merriam, Alan. *The Anthropology of Music*. Evanston, Ill.: Northwestern University Press, 1964.

Montjarret, Polig. *Toniou Breizh Izel*. Brittany: Bodadeg Ar Sonerion, 1984.

Ní Earcáin, Treasa. "Issues of Celtic Identity: A Study of the Festival Interceltique de Lorient." Unpublished M.A. diss., Belfast, Queens University Belfast, 1995.

Ó hIfearnáin, Tadhg. *Summary of Report on Breton language in Euromosaic: The Production and Reproduction of the Minority Language Groups of the EU DG XXII*. European Commission, Brussels, 1995.

O'Neill, Francis. *Irish Minstrels and Musicians*. Chicago: EP, 1913.

Quid (encyclopedia), edited by Dominique et Michèle Frémy. Malesherbes: Editions Robert Laffont, 1996.

Racines interdites (interview with Alan Stivell, M. Legras, and J. Erwan). In *Musiciens et Musiques*. Paris, Editions Jean-Claude Lattes, 1979.

Reclus, Elisée. *l'Homme et la Terre*, edited by Béatrice Giblin. Paris: Editions La Decouverte, 1998.

Ritchie, W. F., and J. N. G. *Celtic Warriors*. Aylesbury: Shire Archaeology, 1985.

Slobin, Mark. *Micromusics of the West*. Chicago: University of Illinois Press, 1992.

Travers, Raymond. "The Breton Accent." In *Rough Guide to World Music*, edited by Simon Broughton et al., 28–31. London: Penguin, 1994.

Trevor-Roper, Hugh. "The Highland Tradition of Scotland." In *The Reinvention of Tradition*, edited by E. Hobsbawn and T. Ranger, 15–41. Cambridge: Cambridge University Press, 1983.

Vallely, Fintan. "The Knights Templar's Dream: Politics in the World of Traditional Music in Northern Ireland." Unpublished M.A. diss., Queens University Belfast, 1995.

Vassal, Jacques. *La Nouvelle Chanson Bretonne*. Paris: Éditions Albin Michelm, 1977.

Wilkinson, Desmond. "Play Me a Lonesome Reel." Unpublished M.A. diss., Queens University Belfast, 1991.

Wilkinson, Desmond. "The World of Traditional Dance Music in Brittany." Unpublished Ph.D. thesis, University of Limerick, 1999.

PERIODICALS AND PAMPHLETS

FN SAC-CGT (Fédération Nationale des Syndicats du Spectacle, de l'Audiovisuel et de l'Action Culturelle CGT) booklet 10 (1993).

Guide pratique Des Intermittents Du Spectacle (1993).

L'Interceltique Lorient (Autumn 1996 edition; magazine of the festival).

Le Peuple Breton (January 1992).

Le Peuple Breton (1996).

Musique Bretonne (December 1994).

Musique Bretonne (1996).

Planète Celte (1996; bimonthly magazine of the Lorient festival).

OTHER SOURCES CITED

Alan Stivell. http://celtic.stanford.edu/artists/Stivell.html 1996.

Danse Bretonne/Irlandaise à Confort-Berhet (Author unknown) 1996.

Gavotte. http://www.bmol.imfini.fr/culture/danses/gavotte 1998.

9

"You Cannae Take Your Music Stand into a Pub": A Conversation with Stan Reeves about Traditional Music Education in Scotland

Peter Symon

Edinburgh is the center of popular and commercial activity in traditional and folk music in Scotland. Like Dublin in Ireland, Scotland's
capital city has become the hub of the country's varied traditional
and folk music scenes (rivaled only in some activities by the Shetland Islands). Fittingly, given the city's status since 1999 as the seat
of the devolved Parliament and Executive (following the implemen-
tation of the UK government's 1998 Scotland Act, which provided
the country with a measure of political autonomy in key areas of
policy, including health, education, local government, housing,
transport, economic development, culture, and the arts), Edinburgh
is an urban arena in which the cultural politics of music resound
throughout an eclectic range of spaces, both physical—pubs, church
halls, streets and public spaces, schools, theaters, community centers, and university students' unions—and imaginary.

In the late 1980s a new phase of heightened national self-
consciousness emerged in Scotland. During the decade that followed,
the cultural politics of national identity were played out with renewed
conviction. Traditional musical forms—always closely associated in
the popular imagination with notions of "cultural heritage"—were
linked in popular discourse to the nationalist project more strongly
than were other popular musical forms. It is undoubtedly true that
some musicians liked to present themselves as bearers of a more "anthemic" strand of national tradition. Yet when the actual practices of
traditional and folk music in Edinburgh during the 1980s and 1990s
are considered, along with their representation in nationalist discourse, the more problematic and complex—ambiguous, even—the

articulation between music, "cultural heritage," and national identity appears to be.

Three related sets of issues emerged. First, during the late 1980s, the concern with establishing a "national identity" for Scotland co-incided with the emergence in America of the category of "Celtic music." At first, for many people, Celtic simply meant "Irish" (as, arguably, it still does). But with the globalization of the genre during the 1990s, more and more of what was previously termed "Scottish" traditional or folk music began to be encompassed and "Celticized." When the latest Celtic revival began, in the 1960s, many Scots were, to paraphrase Tom Nairn, "amazed" to find they were considered by other nationalities to be Celtic; but, by the 1990s, numerous aspects of Scottish culture had, to a greater or lesser extent, embraced Celti-cism in its different forms: including music. A radio program called *Celtic Connections* (designed carefully to blend Irish, Scottish, and other music, and modeled in part on Fiona Ritchie's *The Thistle and Shamrock®* American NPR program) was put on air by national net-worked BBC Radio Scotland in the early 1990s. Shortly afterward, an eponymous music festival was launched on a grand scale by the newly opened Glasgow Royal Concert Hall. Two bands—Capercail-lie and Runrig—emerged as standard bearers of Gaelic language folky pop and rock, respectively.[1]

By the mid-1990s, the more commercial end of Celtic music had had sufficient airplay, marketing, and live gigs to have impinged upon the consciousness of a youthful, overwhelmingly urban, chart-listening Scottish audience that had previously been largely un-aware of it—but that, like all youthful consumers of popular music, was highly sensitive to genre labels. Part of the cultural politics of Celtic music, in this context, was the renegotiation of the relation-ship between Celtic and other genres of commercial popular music. Additionally, the national began to become displaced by the transnational as a point of reference in the reception of Celtic music, adding another set of tensions—and scope for further fracture—to those already existing between Irish and Scottish sources and id-ioms, between Gaelic- and English-language users, and between the different worlds of music and dance encompassed by the label "Scottish."

A second way in which the relationship between traditional mu-sic, "heritage," and identity is articulated involves the process of learning to sing and to play a musical instrument. In Edinburgh, as in many other places, learning Scottish music takes place in a wide range of settings, both formal and informal. Participants in the world of folk and traditional music like to emphasize the importance of certain preferred modes of learning, usually those involving the oral transmission of tunes, songs, and techniques through informal interaction between musicians. Yet in the Edinburgh of today, the situation is becoming more and more formalized, with tutors being employed to teach groups of adult learners Scottish music. This method of musical learning is well illustrated by an adult education project that has been running in Edinburgh since the 1980s. I first learned about the "alpies"—participants in the Edinburgh Adult Learning Project (ALP) Scots Music Group, the subject of this chapter—from Derek Hoy, a fiddler in the Edinburgh-based group Jock Tamson's Bairns, when I was doing fieldwork in Edinburgh in 1995. This was, I was told, a phenomenon worth examining. Here were cohorts of adult learners moving through a more or less formally organized educational program. In this program the students were exposed to a model of learning that reconstructed the idealized tutor-learner relationship in a group setting; often, in fact, in pub sessions, that had become in the 1960s and 1970s a popular locus of musical activity in the city.

The third issue that is often asserted is the sense of community that those engaged in the celebration of traditional musical heritage are said to share. The question is, as Gillian Rose has identified, what sort of arguments about "community" (in this case, particularly, "national" communities) are being put forward in relation to Scots music? In research into community arts interventions in two of the city's peripheral housing estates of Wester Hailes and Craigmillar, Rose had found that the people involved in the arts projects in these spatially marginalized communities, while describing their areas as coherent communities on the basis of shared poverty and marginalization had, nevertheless, refused "to construct their sense of community in a manner which would create a uniform group of insiders and, by implication, an excluded group of outsiders" (Rose 1996, 95).

Edinburgh is a highly divided city, both socially and geographically. The experience of the city for the poor, many of whom are living in the peripheral housing areas such as those discussed by Rose, contrasts starkly with that of its many affluent residents, including those who work in the professional, financial, government, and education sectors. These relatively privileged groups occupy a different space, socially and physically, in the city from the marginalized groups. There are a higher proportion of incomers to the city, including many English people, among them. To what extent does the delivery of traditional music tuition within an adult education setting provide opportunities for the mixing of Edinburgh's social groups—"people from all walks of life"—and to what extent might the national identity be negotiated within this setting as a web of interconnections rather than as an "us and them" policing of imagined ethnic boundaries?

The following conversation explores some of these issues. It took place on 8 September 1998 when I met Stan Reeves, supervisor of the Edinburgh Adult Learning Project Association at the Association's office on Dalry Road, in Gorgie, Edinburgh. The project's institutional origins lay in the program of night classes provided by the (now abolished) Lothian Regional Council's Community Education Department during the 1980s; and before that as an urban aid program, managed by the local authority with central government funding. The City of Edinburgh Council now funds the jobs of two education workers and an administrative worker. The funding is provided with the aim of developing adult education in the community in partnership with the ALP Association. The ALP Association itself is a self-governing association of students.[2] Gorgie-Dalry is neither a peripheral housing estate nor the historic core of the city occupied by the wealthy. It is in the inner west of the city, its housing typified by blocks of small, nineteenth-century tenements. These formerly housed families of workers, many of whom had jobs at the nearby breweries; but now the area has undergone social recomposition, with the loss of older jobs locally and a modest amount of gentrification.

As well as being a community educator, Reeves is also a musician, playing Scottish music on the "button box" (button accordion) with the Robert Fish Band, one of Edinburgh's most well-known *ceilidh* dance bands. He grew up in the "staunchly Protestant" mining village of Stonehouse in Lanarkshire, along with fellow Scots musician Norman Chalmers (of Jock Tamson's Bairns); both also qualified as photographers. I first met him a few days before our appointment at an informal session at the home of Derek Hoy. He had spoken then of some of the philosophy of the project, some elements of which are fairly frequently encountered in community cultural development theory (e.g., drawing on the work of Paulo Freire), but containing others that harked back more to the notions of colonialism and its cultural counterpart, "internal colonialism," which were debated with commitment in the 1960s and 1970s.[3] It made sense, then, to begin our conversation by asking about the political origins of the project.

POLITICS AND COMMUNITY EDUCATION

SYMON: In *Fiddles and Folk* Wallace Lockhart[4] mentions the ideology of the project. . . . What was the thinking behind this project and how did it develop?

REEVES: Well, as it says in there, he refers to the 1988 launch of "a new program of classes and events under the title of Scotland and its People." But, as he says, "there was a considerable gestation period to the setting up of the Scots Music Group" (Lockhart 1998, 120). So I'll talk about that gestation period. It was actually in two phases. The first phase was in 1988. That was an investigation by this organization into Scots culture in general. We looked at education, politics, the law, community life—a number of different topics. We got all the people that were currently involved in the Adult Learning Projects to meet in focus groups—that would be the best way to describe them—over a period of six months. . . . We decided to draw breath and, instead of looking at local issues, to look at national issues (because people not only exist locally, they also exist nationally). 1988/1989 was a very significant period in the growth of identity and cultural renaissance in Scotland at the time.

SYMON: Why was that? In the wake of the election in '87?

REEVES: Yes. The people of Scotland felt as if they lost that election, in general terms, because the majority of people did not vote for the Tory party.

SYMON: There was also the Poll Tax,[5] I suppose?

REEVES: The Poll Tax was around at that time. Also, there was the Constitutional Convention.[6] There were James Kelman's novels, which were giving a voice to what in fact had been a community development project: writers' workshops throughout Scotland. . . . Every modern [Scottish] novelist you could think of was in a writers' workshop: Janice Galloway, James Kelman, Irvine Welsh, Delys Rose, Brian McCabe, Alan Warner . . . all of them have been in a writers' workshop. We set up the second writers' workshop in Edinburgh, I think the third in Scotland and—this is an aside—after that (which would be 1981), in 1983, two years later, there were twenty-six writers' workshops in Edinburgh. We held a conference for writers' workshops at which we reckoned there were between 200 and 300 writers' workshops in Scotland at that time. That was going from the late 1970s, when there was one—in Glasgow University, which is the one that James Kelman went to. It went from one to 300 in a period of about four years. . . . Nobody has ever done any research into that phenomenon. . . . It's died away now, it's probably down to about 150 writers' workshops, or maybe less, but there are some very long running writers' workshops now. Ours has been going for about fourteen or fifteen years—ALP Writers' Workshop.

So it's within the context of that general cultural questioning, that's probably the best word for it, a kind of cultural exploration that was going on in the media and, politically, the rise of the SNP and the drive for devolution, and this notion that really we should think about it more carefully than we had in the 1970s [the last referendum on devolution for Scotland was in 1979] and come up with a plan. . . . Everybody was talking about it so we thought, "Let's give ordinary people a chance to do that." So we got them to meet in groups and talk about all these kind of issues.

SYMON: Who were these people?

REEVES: They would be students . . . we had a parents' center, a photography center, some media studies courses . . . a variety of different courses, local issues courses, people involved in community development groups as part of the Adult Learning Project. . . . So you've got these people all sitting thinking about what are the key issues facing Scotland today. We would come up with statements like "People in Scotland are forever singing about their history, seem to be almost obsessed by it, but in fact know nothing about it, because they actually get very little historical education." At that time, for instance, there wasn't a Chair of Scots History at Edinburgh University. That was put in some time later and then they tried to do away with that Chair and there was a public outcry and it was reinstated. There are very, very few courses in Scots History and very, very few graduates in it. Consequently, most of the history teaching profession know very little Scots history. The curriculum wasn't there. It's changing now, but people who're in their thirties, forties and fifties had been taught very little history, certainly almost none at secondary level. So history would seem to be an important thing for a citizenry to know, something about its past. So we decided to do popular education and history.

Alone among most European education systems, we don't have as a requirement to teach what you might call "civics." . . . There's no requirement to find out how your parliament works, how you vote, all that kind of stuff. So we wanted to have a branch of the organization which we would call "The Democracy Group" and that would look at democracy, because we were all saying we want to change how our democracy runs. So we thought, "Well, we could just study what democracy is, and find out."

Land was another key issue. It is said that people in Scotland are forever singing songs about being exiled from their land while they still live in it. It's ironic, the songs of emigration and exile that people sing. Eighty-six percent of the people live on two percent of the land and we had that terrible period of the Clearances in the latter part of the eighteenth century but in the nineteenth century as well. Our relationship to the land is very strange. So we wanted to investigate that and see what that might be and see if there was any community action we could take.

But then we started to talk about Scots' reputation for being aggressive and not assertive—very authority-ridden—and reasons for that. People often talk about these things. We talked about the fact that something about that feeling might be reflected in our relationship to the arts; in that, in fact, we don't involve ourselves very much in the arts. A branch of that was really getting people to find a voice. That's where the music idea came out. We said, "Well . . . [sighs] how would a mature Scots democracy express itself musically?" We said, "Well, let's look at traditional music first." That was when we had "Phase Two"—which was the consultation specifically on music, a year later—it would be '89. I just scooped up everybody I knew in the community who had anything to do with traditional music and asked them to come in and just simply talk about what the issues and problems were for them.

TRADITIONAL MUSIC AND MUSICIANS

SYMON: Why did you focus on traditional music rather than other musical forms?

REEVES: Because of the historic connection. It's connected to the place. It's connected to the history. It's connected to the whole broad identity. . . . So we thought traditional music would be really important, and also that traditional music held within itself a painful contradiction, which seems to be at the heart of Scottish identity, which is this: on the one hand, we seem to value our past and traditions; and on the other hand, we're very, very embarrassed by them. It's to do with our sense of inferiority. [Coughs] It seems to be very problematic. Our traditional music seemed to have been more trivialized than any other European traditional music, and that seems to be a problem. The contradiction is really continually denied by a lot of people in the Scots music establishment. They really don't want to look at the problems. They want to get on with their music. They like their music the way it is and they just want to get on with it and they don't want to ask any questions about it. If you start asking questions they get very, very annoyed at you. So we thought, there's no point in trying to convert people or hector people. What we should do is something positive: teach people about traditional music, so that they knew something of the background. We thought the best vehicle for that would be to teach them the actual instruments and the songs.

That's why we started it, and it just kind of blew up in our face, really, in a positive way. We thought it would be one of ten subjects that we would put on in this program called *Scotland and Its People—What's Happening to Us?* (The name of the program was based on a radio series made in Northern Ireland, about five years previously, called *Northern Ireland—What's Happening to Us?*, that was looking at sectarianism in Northern Ireland. . . . We just stole the title, because we liked it. We didn't consult them about it or anything!) People flooded in the doors and I had to keep booking rooms and booking tutors. It got bigger and bigger. We started making a profit and we couldn't handle it. . . . We paid the tutors, then you start feeling responsible for the tutors. They are getting a substantial bit of their income off it. So you think, "We had better get a class going next year." And so it grows. The Scots Music Group now has a turnover of about £60,000 a year. We'll enroll 500 students this autumn.

We now have branches of it. "Fiddle '98" is the biggest national fiddle festival. That's run by volunteers. We also have the Youth Gaitherin', which is a week-long festival of traditional music for young people in Edinburgh.[7] That's now branching out and is starting to have weekly classes. It's in two primary schools as well. Then we've got autonomous groups who have met through ALP. We have eleven ceilidh bands associated with the project.

SYMON: Where do the sessions happen?

REEVES: When we first started, we approached publicans and said, "Would it be alright if musicians came in here and played tunes?" and they said, "Aye, OK." We started in the Ardmillan Hotel. . . . They actually came back to us—we'd stopped going there—it came under new management and the management approached us and said, "Please could you come back and have your session?" We now have a number of sites that have sessions: The West End Hotel has a Monday and Thursday session; and then on a Wednesday night there's the Diggers [The Athletic Arms]; Thursday night, there's the Antiquary; Monday night there's the Fiddlers Arms. You'll find people from ALP at all those sessions. You'll also find people from ALP at the Sandy Bells [Forrest Hill Bar] sessions as well and the Tron and the Tass. So, there are about ten pub sessions a week that I know about. People keep telling me about ones I don't know about. About four or five of them we've actually set up, and the rest have just happened or had been happening. People are meeting in each others' houses. They are also hiring rooms and forming more autonomous groups. So we have got a women's group called the Baguettes [laughs], a twenty-five-piece orchestra called the Skerwud Band . . . it's a [lowland] Scots word. . . . *Skerwud*—"pure mad." . . . We've got another autonomous group called Auld Spice. A whole lot of retired people came to a day-time mixed instrument class. About twenty-six people enrolled in that, and they've gone on, and all the unemployed people have left and got jobs. They were left with the retired people who are much more dependable in their lifestyles. So they formed the backbone of this eleven-piece band called Auld Spice. There's usually about six or seven of them: three or four fiddles, a couple of accordions, drums, flute and whistle. They go out and gig a lot. They go to old folks' homes. They started off doing all these hot reels that are really popular with young people today, and then they have drifted more and more towards the Scottish country dance band repertoire and the more "Old Timey" kind of music. They're playing sing-along stuff as well, that old people really like.

SYMON: What are the backgrounds of the people who participate in the Group?

REEVES: The vast majority would be white, lower-middle class, Scots Protestants, I would imagine. They would be predominantly people in their late twenties or early thirties upward. They would be "lower-middle class," generally . . . a lot of people whose class of origin would be "respectable working class." We have to remember that the social class profile in the 1950s was very different from what it is now. For a lot of people now in their forties, their parents would have been probably classed as working class. They would be people who had been the first in their family to get higher education—a lot of people in that category; a lot of people who've benefited from the education system, particularly in the 1960s and 1970s.

A lot of folk who are "immigrants," in that they are not Edinburgh folk. Quite a lot from Edinburgh, but there would be a higher proportion of incomers than you would expect in the normal make up. I think we probably get more Edinburgh folk in now.

SYMON: Is there a parallel with the Welsh language learner phenomenon? Fiona Bowie[8] wrote about the stereotype learner: the English, middle-aged, middle-class woman with a couple of young kids who moves to Wales and then wants to learn about Welsh culture. There's some antagonism toward them among indigenous, rank-and-file Welsh people. That way into Welsh culture is the language. In Scotland it's a different story, but does that parallel exist here or not?

REEVES: Not to any significant event. There are people who would fit that profile, obviously, and probably more in the music section than, say, in the politics section or the women's studies section. I personally think it's fair enough. I think if you move to a country and don't have any curiosity about its language and history and culture, you are a pretty sad person, you know? I mean, when you go to Barcelona, you buy the Rough Guide to Barcelona and read it from cover to cover—I bet you do!—on the plane. You'll be telling people from Barcelona things they never knew about their own city because they've never read the bloody book, you know? So there is that element in it, that kind of inquisitive thing where you really want to apprehend the culture. I think that's good. But it's not very significant. . . . It is mostly Scots—about 80 percent, I would think. With a lot of them, there's some kind of connection with traditional culture, maybe one or two generations back. We've probed that and found it to be the case. . . . We have people right up to their eighties. You get a lot of people whose families have grown up, so they might be in their forties or fifties and they're wanting to do something in their spare time. . . .

Then you get a lot of people, in their late twenties, early thirties, who are enthusiasts, who are right into Celtic music and have heard music and have bought albums of The Battlefield Band or whatever. They go to folk clubs, they go to folk festivals, that kind of thing, and they've decided they want to learn a traditional instrument.

Then there's another category which I would call the "translators": the people who have had a significant amount of musical education—formally, as part of their schooling—who find that they have no social outlet for their musical skills. So they want to come and learn traditional music because they think it'll be much more sociable—as it is. So you get this huge bloc of people who benefited from the upsurge in musical education in schools—in the sixties and seventies—who can knock out a tune on a fiddle, but they generally can't do it without music. They can't play by ear. They've got no performance skills at all. All they can do is read music and translate it onto their instrument and they want to do something more useful with it. I would think that almost 50 percent of people would fall into that category. But if you think of the number of people that must have gone through that sausage machine in the 1950s and 1960s in Edinburgh. . . .

You've got to think about the end product. What is the end product? It is that people would be able to exist in their communities as artists, as more musical people. They would be able to practice traditional music. They would be able to play at family weddings. Or they might form a band or whatever. They might help their kids. Performance is the end point.

I would imagine probably between 80 and 90 percent of people who studied an instrument at school never pick it up once they have left school. You would look at that and say, well, in my view, they haven't had their eye on the end product. They haven't made those youngsters capable of playing a musical instrument on their own. They can only play a part in an orchestra. We don't want to reproduce that. We don't want to produce 80 percent of people who can sit in front of a music stand with twenty other people and play a reel and then the rest of the time they are just not capable of doing it.

So that affects how you teach, quite dramatically. The first thing is, you have got to get people to develop their ear. The ear thing is very,

very important to me. I mean, if they can already read music, that's a good thing. It's a good skill that you can use. I read music. How I learn most of my music, is actually through the written page. But they must play from memory. They must go through a memorization process (a) so that they can carry their music with them and (b) because it fundamentally alters the way you perform music. . . . It's very difficult to teach someone an idiom. If I learn a tune and then memorize it, I will inevitably play it with a Scots accent because that's what I have been listening to all my life. I have been listening to Scots music, so I won't do it consciously. It'll just come out like that, but only if I memorize it. . . .

It's a very difficult hurdle to get over. We get people who say [in a whining, "greetin" voice], "Aw, naw, I can't learn by ear. I can't do it." They've been in the classical music mode and they actually don't want to do it. You just have to say to them, "Well, you'll never be a performer. You'll never be able to perform in the community, because you cannae take your music stand into a pub!" Because, you set up a music stand and it's saying something [in a "posh," prim voice], "I am going to give you A Performance now." It's just, like, you can't connect. I could go on and on. . . . My own view is that every traditional musician should be able to perform solo. I can't do that with all of my music but with some of it I can. That would be my aim.

SYMON: There are quite a few women who get involved in ALP. That is almost a reversal of the situation in the folk revival in the 1960s and 1970s, when the instrumental scene was predominantly male. . . .

REEVES: The instrumental side in the 1970s was almost completely dominated by men. In the folk song revival, earlier, there were a lot of very, very significant women—Jeannie Robertson and Belle Stewart and all those people. So there are a lot of women who are now in their fifties who are excellent traditional singers.

The gender balance shifted in the 1970s when instrumental music got more popular. It was a kind of macho thing—the four instrumentalists who would get drunk and go to France and get a few gigs; form a band and "put it on the road, man!"; be a bit wild, and all that. Most of them would not have had much formal musical education. They'll have learned it either in their families or, predominantly, off records. Basically what was happening was that Irish music was coming out on records—on Topic, Gael Linn, Green Linnet, all these labels were very significant. People went and bought the records, learned the tunes, formed a band, put it on the road, got pished! That was basically what happened.

A lot of the young women that have come forward have had more formal education. They are half a generation behind. Catriona Mac-Donald is a really good example.[9] She is from the Shetland Islands, so she came through that system of education there. By the time she was a youngster there were peripatetic music teachers in Shetland Islands Council schools, with [the late] Tom Anderson, so they were being taught traditional music. Shetland is the only part of Scotland where traditional music is taught to any significant amount in the schools. Because of that, there are hundreds of people in the Shetland Islands playing the fiddle; and lots and lots of girls—lots of them. The Young Heritage group was nearly all girls. In fact, it's almost getting that boys won't play the fiddle because it's a girls' thing.

MAKING AND SUSTAINING A LIVING:
BANDS AND PROFESSIONALS

SYMON: Have any of the groups that have been formed gone on and made a career out of it?

REEVES: Very few. A lot of them won't ever be good enough to become a professional musician because they've started too late in life when their life is already too busy. I mean, you know yourself, if you want to become a professional musician, you really need four hours a day. There isn't actually any shortcut to that. You need four hours a day for at least four years to get to that level. You find that in traditional music there are people doing that, people who are signing on the dole and just spending every night of the week down playing sessions. Or when they have been at college, when they've been young, they've had this period of intense concentration on the music, so they can get to a standard where they could actually make a living at it. But our guys, in the main, won't do that. Some of them are playing in dance bands, where they can hide a little bit; but, in terms of a concert band, you have to have something a bit special to make a living at that.

The ability to make a living in traditional music has only come about in the past ten years. I mean, Jock Tamson's Bairns, who you

made a study of, never could have made a living.[10] They couldn't
have made a living. I mean, they are all very good musicians and
they had a period of time in their own personal lives when they did
nothing else except play music. And then they all started to get families and that was all out the window. At that period of time, there
just wasn't enough money in the economy to support traditional
music. But there is now. There are a few more bands who can make
a living because things have changed.

What they have now is a skill that they use in a social context.
Their social life improves dramatically, having learned traditional
music, and they get hours of pleasure from it. Their children are now
being brought up in an atmosphere where there is live music and
ceilidhs going on in houses and people going to take their kids out
dancing with them. So, for me, it is much more about social and
community development than about making professional musicians, although there might be one or two that'll come through and
get really inspired.

SYMON: Were Tapsulteerie ever associated with ALP?

REEVES: As they stand now, I think four out of the six went to
ALP classes. Then they graduated and two or three of them have actually taught ALP classes. Sometimes we get people who change
from being a student to being a tutor. We get them to take the be-
ginners. . . .

SYMON: Did Burach come out of this at all?

REEVES: No, but there have been people in Burach that have been
involved as tutors. In every band in Scotland you can think of, there
would be people who have been tutors at some point for ALP. There
are around a hundred people on our list of tutors.

SYMON: To what extent is the training of the tutors an issue?

REEVES: Training of teachers is an issue because most people
haven't learned in a group. They've learned one to one or by picking
it up off their peers and older people by ear. They don't actually understand the dynamics of a musical group and how to be in it. So we
need to basically teach them group work skills, how to lead a group
of people through any kind of learning process and also how to structure a curriculum. Those are the two main things. A lot of tutors initially don't believe that they need to know that. . . . Then, after a while,
they either become unpopular tutors because they are not coming up
with the goods, and they leave, or they begin to ask questions about
working in a group, because it is very different to teaching one to one.

SYMON: Would you want to see that sort of thing taught in music colleges?

REEVES: Yes.

SYMON: Does it happen at all?

REEVES: No. Well, the Royal Scottish Academy of Music and Drama, the RSAMD, are now doing traditional music[11] and there's a bit in there where they learn about how to be teachers in groups. That's a good thing, because we're now a mobile population. The traditional way of passing on through, you know, an uncle teaching you, or the wee man down the road, or joining a pipe band or whatever, a lot of these ways are gone and they won't come back again. People will increasingly join together as groups and learn as groups, partly because it's economic. It's going to cost you between £12 and £15 an hour for a music lesson—it should cost you at least that—and it's not very sociable. . . . We have different levels of teaching right up to what we call "Advanced." Then we have "Workshops" where we get some of the key practitioners, the really good musicians from the Scottish tradition, to come in. They are very, very popular. We get folk who have never actually been through ALP who just come to the Workshops, because they're self-taught or they're in a Strathspey and Reel Society or something. But we don't encourage formal competition.

SYMON: Like the Fèisean movement?[12]

REEVES: Well, the Fèisean don't have a formal competition either. I think you don't need to. . . . Everybody knows what the hierarchy of music is. You can hear it. You can say, "That person is really good and that person is just a scraper." So, if you want to be like the really good person, you've got to work like billy-o. When we do the 'Fiddle '98,' for instance [in November 1998], we'll have forty performers there, and none of them will come on stage drunk, none of them will come on stage late—well, maybe a few exceptions!—because they know they're playing in front of their peers. There's going to be five hundred of the best fiddlers in Scotland there and they know that. So some of the performances that people put in are just the best, because they want peer approval. That's all you need. That'll bring out the competitive spirit. You don't need to then say, "OK, Iain MacFarlane's performance was very good, let's give him a wee Gold Medal." People will just say, "You remember Aidan O'Rourke last year? God, he was brilliant! He ripped the roof off the place." I mean, Chris Stout is a young man, he's quite a going-places sort of guy, and he just went on toward the end of the Friday night cabaret and gave it his best shot and he did very well. And you could sense that's what he was trying to do. But I think that's another whole discussion, about the role of competition in Scottish music.

CONCLUSION

SYMON: Do people in ALP talk about the politics of the Scottish experience or do these things not get expressed at all?

REEVES: It does get expressed. We've had assessments, where we've actually got groups of people together and said, "What have you got out of this?" People talk about. . . . Well, "It makes me feel proud of being Scots." We have people who are not Scots by birth who will come in and say, "It's made me understand more about Scotland, made me feel as if I belong, made me feel connected." The second most common thing is, it's fun. We really mustn't ever forget that, in educational terms and political terms. People are motivated by pleasure and if you can give them pleasure in the way you organize your education and in the way that we have been able to give them pleasure they will come back and they will learn. You're talking accelerated learning here, because there's accelerated pleasure.

SYMON: Where do you see the ALP Scots Music Group going?

REEVES: I think it'll grow but people will now have to create organizations or societies within the culture that are appropriate to the time. I'm not sure what they are. I'm toying with this idea of the "Ceilidh Club." . . . The good thing about the [Folk] Revival was the folk clubs. People learned a lot from each other, but as soon as they started to employ professional musicians, it stopped being a club. . . . We don't like to be organized anymore in mass groups, where we're obedient to a "dictator." People have moved away from that.

ACKNOWLEDGMENT

The research on which this chapter is based was funded by a grant from the Carnegie Trust for the Universities of Scotland and carried out during a visit to the International Social Sciences Institute at the University of Edinburgh in 1998. The views expressed in this chapter are those of the author and not necessarily those of the Carnegie Trust or the Directors of the International Social Sciences Institute.

NOTES

1. Runrig broadened their transnational Celtic appeal in 1999 by appointing a Canadian, Bruce Guthro, as replacement lead singer for departed founder member Donnie Munro.

2. Interestingly, the symbol of the Scots Music Group alludes to Celtic art. It is a stylized G ("treble") clef symbol wound through a musical staff in the manner of a Celtic knot although the musical staff and the ring bounding the clef symbol are actually links in a chain, rather than the endless thread motif of Celtic art.

3. These debates reflected the work of Franz Fanon—see for instance Reeves and Galloway 1995—and, in Britain, Michael Hechter (see Hechter 1975).

4. See Lockhart 1998.

5. The extremely unpopular Community Charge, also known as the Poll Tax because it required individuals to pay a fixed amount of tax for local services, was introduced by the Conservative government in Scotland in 1989 (one year before it was introduced in England). It was subsequently revoked.

6. The Scottish Constitutional Convention was set up to press for devolution, formulating The Claim of Right in 1988, which asserted the right of political self-determination for Scotland. Members of the Labour and Liberal Democrat parties sat on the Convention with other civic and political representatives (but not the Scottish National Party, which argued for Scottish independence rather than for devolution within the UK). The Convention's main demand was for the right of the Scottish people to elect a new Scottish Parliament or Assembly.

7. The Youth Gaitherin' was launched in Easter 1995 as a pilot project taking the music to secondary schools and recruiting young people aged 11–18 for a three-day school, along the lines of the Fèisean movement, on which, see Reeves and Galloway (1995) and note 12.

8. Bowie 1993.

9. She is pictured on a flyer for *Fiddle '97*. She was also presenting BBC Radio Scotland's *Celtic Connections* music program at the time of the interview.

10. Reeves refers to Symon 1997.

11. RSAMD launched their B.A. in Scottish Music in 1996.

12. *Fèisean* (the Gaelic word for festivals, singular *Fèis*) provide an opportunity for young people to come together in Gaelic arts tuition festivals,

with an element of performance, to learn skills in Gaelic arts, including singing, dancing, traditional musical instruments, and drama. Since the first Fèis was launched in 1981 on the Island of Barra, a series of Fèisean has grown up, which now take place throughout Scotland. There are currently more than 3,500 young people participating in 32 Fèisean annually, 2 of which offer tuition entirely through the medium of Gaelic, and over 450 tutor places are employed. The Fèisean movement is supported by Fèisean nan Gàidheal, the National Association of Gaelic Arts Youth Tuition Festivals (www.feisean.org).

BIBLIOGRAPHY

Bowie, Fiona. "Wales from Within: Conflicting Interpretations of Welsh Identity." In *Inside European Identities: Ethnography in Western Europe*, edited by Sharon Macdonald, 167–93. Oxford: Berg, 1993.

Hechter, Michael. *Internal Colonialism: The Celtic Fringe in British National Development*. London: Routledge, 1975.

Lockhart, G. Wallace. *Fiddles and Folk: A Celebration of the Re-emergence of Scotland's Musical Heritage*. Edinburgh: Luath Press, 1998.

Reeves, Stan, and Vernon Galloway. "If I Can't Dance It's Not My Revolution: Cultural Action in Scottish Communities." Paper presented at 4th International Conference on Adult Education and the Arts, St. Andrews, 10th–14th July, 1995.

Rose, Gillian. "Community Arts and the Remaking of Edinburgh's Geographies." *Scotlands* 3, no. 1 (1996): 88–99.

Symon, Peter. "Music and National Identity in Scotland: A Study of Jock Tamson's Bairns." *Popular Music* 16, no. 2 (1997): 203–16.

10

Afterword: Gaelicer Than Thou

Timothy D. Taylor

Every Saturday morning I drive across the George Washington Bridge in search of an Irish identity in New Jersey. Mike Rafferty lives there, in a little house on a hill on the outskirts of Hackensack. Mike is from the eastern part of Co. Galway and plays the flute in the classic undulating East Galway style, and he is teaching it to me.

The drive to Mike's house is short, but mine has been a long journey. Family legend has it that my mother, in labor with her first child, was warned by the doctor that I wouldn't arrive before midnight. "Oh yes he will," she said. "His grandfather is Irish and he'll be born on St. Patrick's Day." And I was: at 10:10 P.M., March 17, 1961.

I grew up thinking I was Irish, lucky to have a birthday on such an important day for Irish people, with the added bonus that in my public school system in Michigan, March 17 was usually a teacher in-service day and so we got the afternoon off.

One of my best friends, indeed, the only friend I had my own age who lived near us in rural Michigan, was Irish, too. His name was Smith. I'm Taylor. Neither of us were Murphy or O'Neill or Mc-Grattan, but we were both Irish.

Or so I thought. Cooper Smith was Catholic. This didn't mean much to me as a kid, except that on Sundays I went to a different church than Coop. In fact, he usually corrected me: He went to mass, I went to church. When we were the ninth grade, we were each confirmed into our respective congregations. Cooper got another name out of it, which struck me as odd; I was a little jealous, for I didn't seem to get much of anything; at least, nothing that tangible and fundamental.

It wasn't until I was a graduate student on an exchange/fellow-ship at the Queen's University of Belfast in the late 1980s that I finally got it. I might have thought I was an Irish American, but I wasn't really, for to be Irish was to be Catholic. My Irish forebears, the Taylors, left a small town in Co. Derry in 1846 ("Did they leave hungry?" asked one Catholic friend in Belfast, in the local way of obliquely inquiring if they—and thus, I—were Catholic) and settled in Ontario, as did many Irish, according to Johanne Trew in her fascinating chapter in this volume. My ancestors later moved to northern Ohio, where most of them, my cousins, still live. No, I was a Prod, a fuckin' Prod as they say. But being an American meant that this didn't matter to the good people of Belfast, Catholic and Protestant.

I still think of myself as Irish, sort of. Irish, but the "wrong kind." It helps that my first relative who came over brought a fiddle and a flute, both of which are still in the family. But I'm not really Irish, or, I suppose, "Celtic." No non-Irish Need Apply. Yet there is still a large number of Americans for whom "Celtic" is more than a basketball team, for whom it is a hugely popular label of identity. The term is vague, as Peter Symon notes in his chapter in this volume, vague enough so that just about any European American Christian can adopt it. "Got any Irish in yeh?"

Telling this autobiographical story is a way of warming up to a larger argument about commodification, both about race and ethnicity in America, and then, music. My search for my Irish identity was not just a personal quest, but one shared by other white Americans in a particular cultural and historical moment in the United States, made possible, in part, by the circulation and commodification of music.

Not given to magisterial pronouncements, I would like use my privileged position as the writer of the last words of this volume to make a modest contribution to the debate on commodification of Celtic music, Irish in particular. This discussion will necessarily also examine the commodification of race and ethnicity, and the role played by the evocation of place in ethnicized and racialized musics.

Let's address the question of the commodification of race and ethnicity first. This contemporary European American search for a racial or ethnic identity has its roots in the history of white dominance in the United States. The result of this hegemony historically has been that those in power naturalized the ideological structures of dominance so effectively that the members of the dominant culture believed that their own racial or ethnic heritage was out of sight, that they weren't "ethnic" (see Alba 1990, 3). So the presence of racial and ethnic minorities proclaiming and celebrating their heritage makes the members of the dominant culture feel as if they have no ethnicity, no way of identifying themselves.

This phenomenon was remarked upon by Fredric Jameson in his well-known analysis of *The Godfather*, in which he points out that the utopian fragment offered by that film is a "reference to an alien collectivity," a community based on ethnicity, and demonstrates the dominant white middle-class envy of ethnic and racial groups that they simultaneously oppress (Jameson 1979, 146).

Social scientists have documented this desire for community as well. The issue of dominant middle-class envy of racial and ethnic communities surfaced in *Habits of the Heart* (1985), in which the authors explicitly oppose the middle-class emphasis on individuality with lower-class concern for group solidarity and relationships. This contrast, the authors suggest, "is expressed by middle-class Americans themselves when they entertain envious fantasies about more 'meaningful community' among lower-class racial and ethnic groups" (Bellah, Madsen, Sullivan, Swidler, and Tipton 1985, 152).

In an earlier, more quantitative study of racial and ethnic identification, Jennifer Hurstfield (1971) surveyed white, black, and Chicano junior high school students (12–14 year olds) in Los Angeles in 1971, and showed that most white Americans identify themselves in ways other than race or ethnicity. In the analysis of her results, Hurstfield noted that 65 percent of the white sample defined themselves as unique individuals, as Bellah et al. later found, rather than with ethnic or racial designations. She also writes that twice as many whites referred to themselves in what she terms an "existential reference"—"I'm me," "I'm unique." Hurstfield also observed that, for the whites, their identities are more defined by what they buy, their "tastes," than for the blacks and Chicanos.

The role of consumption identified by Hurstfield is important here. Hurstfield was writing before a new shift in American consumer patterns, a shift that brought more and more goods and services under the umbrella of consumable goods (see especially Lee 1993 on this subject, as well as Cohen 2003; Cross 2000; Schor 2001; Slater 1997; Twitchell 1999). Americans today tend to create identities through what they buy, in what Douglas Holt has more generally called an "open-ended project of self-creation" (Holt 2000, 65);

this is no longer simply a phenomenon that can be ascribed to whites as in Hurstfield's study.

Race and ethnicity have become something that Americans can now consume. Howard F. Stein and Robert F. Hill (1977) forwarded a concept of "dime store ethnicity"—people can select a forebear with whom to identify, in effect shopping for an ethnicity (this idea plays an important role in Mary C. Waters's *Ethnic Options* [1990], in which she examines European Americans' selections of ethnicities available in their past).

So if Hurstfield's subjects defined themselves through goods, it appears that there is now more urgency in this identity construction for white Americans. While Hurstfield's subjects weren't necessarily purchasing overtly racialized or ethnicized goods with which to identify themselves, this practice has taken off since her study was published. Race and ethnicity in America are not simply consumed as abstractions, but have become something anyone can buy, own, adopt as a result of the commodification of racialized or ethnicized cultural forms. Perhaps the most salient example in an American context is the dominant culture's New Age movement. This movement was first concerned with exploring new kinds of spirituality, but discovering the cultural forms of other ethnic groups and cultures along the way, which now seems to be its most salient characteristic. Shoppers can buy books on eastern religions, Native American religions, health aids from other cultures and traditions, and more. Indeed, this example suggests that the commodification of race and ethnicity is not simply about white Americans' perception of a lack of such an identity, but that "having" such an identity has become a potent signifier about ethnic stereotypes, fantasies, and so on.

Ethnicized and racialized musics have not escaped commodification. Recordings of ethnic musics, music videos, concert tickets, fan books, biographies, plus the equipment necessary to make music all mark the entry of these once-marginal musics into the consumer culture mainstream of late capitalism. In the last decade, ethnic popular musics from outside the United States have become more popular than ever before; the new names for these genres—"world beat," "world music," Afro-pop—give an indication of their occasional commodification, uses in marketing, and growing popularity (see Taylor 1997). And on television ethnic musics are used in commodifying ways all the time. There are prominent African American rap and early rock 'n' roll musicians selling fast food and drink; a commercial for Life Savers features the South African group Ladysmith Black Mambazo singing the style of music they helped make, *isicathamiya*. And there is now fabricated world music used in commercials that evokes a generalized global Other (see Taylor 2000).

"Celtic" musics, most prominently Irish traditional music, have undergone a process of commodification as well, as a number of these authors in this book point out.[1] Editors Phil Bohlman and Martin Stokes rightly observe that commodification has produced complication on the musical landscape, "diverse sociomusical realities on the Celtic fringe." It has also shaped, as Scott Reiss and Fintan Valleley examine in their chapters, powerful differences among Irish musicians and aficionados about whether "Irish music" should be "traditional," or a potential vehicle for innovation.

It should be pointed out first, however, that the charge of "commodification" is frequently too easily made in the literature on popular music generally, and in this book. It is one of those terms that everyone has a general understanding of, even though the nature of the commodity is one of the most slippery and difficult concepts in all of social theory (see, of course, Marx 1967). And a thoroughgoing, theoretically sophisticated treatment of music as a commodity has yet to be written (see, however, Gramit 2002).[2]

It is not my goal to attempt that here. Instead, I begin by simply restating Arjun Appadurai's definition of a commodity as a starting point in the hopes of clarifying the issue: A commodity, he writes, is *any thing intended for exchange* (Appadurai 1986, 9; emphasis in original). This is a useful point, for not all musics, Celtic or otherwise, are intended for exchange. Many Irish musicians I know, including me, work hard to keep our music from becoming commodified, so that it remains in the realm of pleasure, not work, something seen as professional. But, of course, we nonetheless participate in Irish music as a commodified form in buying recordings, concert tickets, lessons, instruments, equipment. Online discussion groups about Irish music devote a good deal of bandwidth to discussions comparing and evaluating instruments by different makers to help prospective buyers. And a tip jar is pretty common sight at most sessions, despite the anticommodification stance of many musicians, me included.

The point is that Celtic music, or indeed any thing, has a life when it is sometimes a commodity and sometimes not. Celtic musics can be commodified, but they can also exist outside the realm of commodification, exchange. They can also be uncommodified: removed from the arena of exchange. Thus, they can also be products, artifacts, objects, goods, services. Jerry Cadden's chapter on Scottish pipe band competitions, for example, is a fascinating study of the flexible qualities of the thingness of music, caught up in a the phenomenon of the competitions in which, as Cadden writes, both sport and aesthetic criteria apply, contradictory commodifying and uncommodifying tendencies, maintaining tradition and moving away from it in new pipeband compositions.

In entering the debate on the commodification of Celtic musics I do not want to join the argument at the junction of "traditional" versus "innovation," however. Fintan Vallely—a great Belfast flute player, by the way—declares in a heading in his article that "'Tradition' and 'Innovation' Are Not Compatible." I have to disagree, respectfully. "Traditional" cultural forms, including musics, were always innovating, flexibly moving with their conditions of existence and those who made them (see Hall 1981; Williams 1983). Disagreeing with Vallely, however, is not intended to deny the prominence of his position in contemporary musicians' discourses and practices—mine included—and how it can serve as a lightning rod for larger debates around traditional music, as is clear from the articles just mentioned.

Rather, let's focus on what commodification accomplishes for "Celtic" music, and that music I know the most about in this context, Irish music (which some take to be the same thing as Celtic music, as several authors in this volume note). Irish music has escaped its original locality, first because of immigration, and later by commodification in the form of recordings and tunebooks, and the continuing movement of people. The last couple of decades have witnessed the rise of a "virtual community of Celtic music" in Scott Reiss's phrase. This is perhaps too convenient a characterization, for there are plenty of "real" communities of Irish musicians who also participate virtually. It would perhaps be more accurate to say that the "community" of Irish music is less place-based than ever, though it still has ties to place, and has cultural power to invoke place. Celtic music might exist in a mediascape flow (Reiss invokes Appadurai's ubiquitous "-scapes"), and people today might exist in an ethnoscape, but some of these people use Celtic, and other, musics to anchor themselves, to construct, however temporarily, a rooted sense of place using these commodified musics. Reiss sidles up to this point in a later passage when wondering if this kind of identity construction is a feature of what he sees as "postcolonial reality."[3]

Postcolonial or not, it is a feature of the contemporary moment that people use goods including ethnicized musical commodities to construct identities. It is not clear that this is a bad thing, though it is not without problems either. Generally, it would be difficult to argue that the commodification of music has been a uniformly negative process, though many have certainly done so.[4] First, because what is called "commodification" might not be; and, more to the point, commodification makes music available to people outside the immediate circle of those who made a particular music.

Even in an ethnoscape, a mediascape, a global flow, ethnicized musics possess the cultural power to evoke their places of origin. Several of the chapters in this volume offer useful and illuminating treatments of the movement of Celtic musics (Caroline Bithell on the Celts in Corsica, and Graeme Smith on the Irish in Australia), and musicians (Dai Griffiths on John Cale). Traveling does not mean that musics lose their ability to evoke place in listeners; travel may even enhance this power as the places of origin are signified in the music, and the commodification of music frequently plays a role in this process.

Place, origin, locality—all are another reason that ethnicized cultural forms have become increasingly popular. It is not, I think, simply a longing for an ethnic identity because others have them. There is also a longing for roots, rootedness, a sense of place. Contemporary Americans are so famously mobile—rootless—that I think a lot of "identity" politics is a way of "placing" ourselves: in Wales, Ireland, Scotland, Brittany. Or India, or China, or Puerto Rico, or wherever.

Place is a recurring theme in these chapters, for contained in the commodification of race, ethnicity, and music are conceptions of, significations of, place. Johanne Trew writes of the importance of placeness, the making of place through naming in the practices of Irish immigrants to Ontario. Immigrants from Ireland "replaced" Ireland in Ontario, and in the United States. Peter Symon, in his chapter on music in Scotland, includes extensive quotations from a conversation with Stan Reeves, community educator and musician in Edinburgh. Scottish music, according to Reeves, is "connected to the place. It's connected to the history. It's connected to the whole broad identity."

Place matters. Desi Wilkinson—another great Belfast flute player—writes of how Bretons in Brittany affirm their identity in dancing, and how non-Bretons are permitted to participate, without question. Breton "identity" is thus made real, at the same time it is made flexible, transportable, away from its original, originary place. This phenomenon serves as an opening for Wilkinson to coin the useful term "Celtitude" to describe the wider world of the Celtic, populated not only by Bretons but also by new agers and others. (For more on place, and place and music, see Feld and Basso 1996; Leyshon, Matless, and Revill 1998; and Stokes 1994).

In offering this discussion of commodification and the importance of place, I have been talking not just about the commodification of music, but the commodification of ethnicity as well. The two can't be easily separated in this context. But the main point is to argue that it is rare for any music to be simply "commodified." Rather, music, especially "Celtic" or Irish or Scottish or Welsh or Breton or what have you that spans different music industry categories (folk, traditional, world, New Age, rock) and has many local practitioners, is caught up in myriad commodifying, noncommodifying, and uncommodifying practices at any one time and in any particular place.

So the question is not simply whether commodification of Celtic musics is "good" or "bad," but what do the people who consume commodified musics do with them? The commodification of ethnicized goods such as music can, I am suggesting, permit consumers to find a moment of stability in the otherwise fragmenting nature of today's hustle bustle world, to find an identity, however temporarily, that offers a sense of self rooted in both place and community marked by ethnicity or race. As these authors show in so many ways, Celtic musics, commodified or not, are real musics made by and listened to by real people caught up in real practices in real places.

NOTES

1. See also Taylor (1997) for a discussion of the success of "Celtic" music in the "world music" category of the music industry.

2. Yes, we have Theodor Adorno. But Adorno's discussions of the commodified nature of music are usually the form of assertions and assumptions: Popular music and jazz are commodities that are not "heard" or "listened to"

by listeners, but are consumed (see Adorno 2002B). "Serious" music is generally exempt from this view but serious music, for Adorno, runs the risk of being commodified and fetishized through mass media repetitions (Adorno 2002A) or pedagogy that enshrines listening for surface details rather than structural ones. Adorno never wrote a comprehensive analysis of the nature of the music commodity in a theoretical sense.

3. See also Limón (1994) for a compelling discussion of the role that music plays in working-class Chicanos in finding a temporary sense of stability in a fragmenting postmodern world, a phenomenon not unlike the Bretons studied by Desi Wilkinson in this volume.

4. See also Neil Nehring (1997) who does not view the commodification of rock music as wholly negative.

BIBLIOGRAPHY

Adorno, Theodor. "Analytical Study of the NBC *Music Appreciation Hour.*" *Musical Quarterly* 78 (summer 1994): 325–77.

Adorno, Theodor. "On the Fetish Character in Music and the Regression of Listening." In *Essays on Music*, edited by R. Leppert, translated by S. H. Gillespie, 288–317. Berkeley: University of California Press, 2002A.

Adorno, Theodor. "On the Social Situation of Music." In *Essays on Music*, edited by R. Leppert, translated by S. H. Gillespie, 391–436. Berkeley: University of California Press, 2002B.

Alba, Richard D. *Ethnic Identity: The Transformation of White America.* New Haven: Yale University Press, 1990.

Appadurai, Arjun. "Introduction." *The Social Life of Things*, edited by A. Appadurai. New York: Cambridge University Press, 1986.

Bellah, Robert N., Richard Madsen, William M. Sullivan, Ann Swidler, and Steven M. Tipton. *Habits of the Heart: Individualism and Commitment in American Life.* Berkeley: University of California Press, 1985.

Cohen, Lizabeth. A *Consumer's Republic: The Politics of Mass Comsumption in Postwar America.* New York: Knopf, 2003.

Cross, Gary. *An All-Consuming Century: Why Commercialism Won in Modern America.* New York: Columbia University Press, 2000.

Feld, Steven, and Keith H. Basso, eds. *Senses of Place.* Santa Fe, N.M.: School of American Research Press, 1996.

Gramit, David. "Music Scholarship, Musical Practice, and the Act of Listening." In *Music and Marx: Ideas, Practice, Politics*, edited by R. B. Qureshi, 3–22. New York: Routledge, 2002.

Hall, Stuart. "Notes on Deconstructing 'The Popular.'" In *People's History and Socialist Theory*, edited by R. Samuel, 227–39. Boston: Routledge and Kegan Paul, 1981.

Holt, Douglas. "Postmodern Markets." In *Do Americans Shop too Much?* Boston: Beacon, 2000.

Hurstfield, Jennifer. "'Internal' Colonialism: White, Black and Chicano Self-Conceptions." *Ethnic and Racial Studies* 1 (January 1978): 60–79.

Jameson, Fredric. "Reification and Utopia in Mass Culture." *Social Text* 1 (winter 1979): 130–48.

Lee, Martyn J. *Consumer Culture Reborn.* New York: Routledge, 1993.

Leyshon, Andrew, David Matless, and George Revill, eds. *The Place of Music.* New York: Guilford, 1998.

Limón, José E. *Dancing with the Devil: Society and Cultural Poetics in Mexican-American South Texas.* Madison: University of Wisconsin Press, 1994.

Marx, Karl. *Capital: A Critique of Political Economy.* Vol. I: *The Process of Capitalist Production.* New York: International, 1967.

Nehring, Neil. *Popular Music, Gender and Postmodernism: Anger Is an Energy.* Thousand Oaks, Calif.: Sage, 1997.

Schor, Juliet. *Do Americans Shop Too Much?* Boston: Beacon, 2001.

Slater, Don. *Consumer Culture and Modernity.* Malden, Mass.: Polity, 1997.

Stein, Howard F., and Robert F. Hill. *The Ethnic Imperative: Examining the New White Ethnic Movement.* University Park: Pennsylvania State University Press, 1977.

Stokes, Martin, ed. *Ethnicity, Identity, and Music: The Musical Construction of Place.* Providence, R.I.: Berg, 1994.

Taylor, Timothy D. *Global Pop: World Music, World Markets.* New York: Routledge, 1997.

Taylor, Timothy D. "World Music in Television Ads." *American Music* 18 (summer 2000): 162–92.

Twitchell, James B. *Lead Us into Temptation: The Triumph of American Materialism.* New York: Columbia University Press, 1999.

Waters, Mary C. *Ethnic Options: Choosing Identities in America.* Berkeley: University of California Press, 1990.

Williams, Raymond. *Keywords.* London: Fontana, 1983.

Index

105, 281; national, 2–6, 21n27, 53, 57, 63, 69n24, 69n26, 73–81, 84, 88–89, 112, 122, 167n4, 230, 257–58, 260
"invention of tradition." *See* Hobsbawm, Eric and Terence Ranger
Ireland: famine, 75, 95, 97, 113n1, 202, 203. *See also* Gaelic Athletic Association, Radio Telefis Eirann, *Riverdance*
Irish Traditional Music Archive, 153
The Irish World Music Center, 209
Isle of Man, 16

Jameson, Frederic, 277
Jock Tamson's Bairns, 259, 260, 269

kan ha diskan, 224, 229, 239, 251n8
Kiberd, Declan, 251n10, 266
Kilpatrick, Jim, 127–29, 133, 140n21

La Villemarque, Comte de, 7
Lagerphone, 76
Lennon, John, 190
Liberty and Co., 15–16
Lipsitz, George, 12, 229
Lomax, Alan, 17, 223
Lorient Festival Interceltique, 228–30
Lunny, Donal, 82, 158, 165, 211–12. *See also* Moving Hearts, Planxty

The Mabinogion, 7
MacPherson, 3, 7, 37, 38
Madoc, legend of, 4
Mathieson, Robert, 127–30, 132, 133–34, 135–36, 140n22, 141n29, 141n30
mazzerism, 34
McKennitt, Loreena, 9, 10, 166
Mediterranean culture, 8, 29, 33, 38, 46, 50
Moloney, Mick, 77

Moving Hearts, 165–166. *See also* Lunny, Donal

Nairn, Tom, 358
nationalism, 3–7, 21n27, 59, 69, 73–88, 96, 112. *See also* identity, national
New York City, 94, 172, 174, 176, 182

O'Neill, Francis, 5, 17, 18, 202, 215n1, 249
Ó Riada, Sean, 77, 152, 153, 154, 159, 167
Ó Súilleabháin, Mícheál, 153–56, 158, 166, 209, 211, 212, 216n7
"Old Time" fiddling, 94, 211, 265
Orange Order, 100–105
Ossian, 3, 7, 15, 37, 38

pays, 221–22
Petrie, George, 4, 5, 20n9, 149, 167n3
pipe bands, standard beating in, 120–26, 138n4
Pipers and Pipe Band Society of Ontario, 138n4
place (music and) 9, 16, 97, 98–99, 163, 184, 185, 186, 229, 276, 280, 281, 282
Planxty, 85, 152, 165
post-colonialism, 3, 166, 231
professionalization, 11, 20n17, 51, 62, 64, 68, 214, 234, 235–50, 254n22, 269–72, 279

Quebec, Celtic music in, 4, 40, 93, 100, 101, 104, 108
Quimper, Fête de Cornouaille in, 228
Quinn, Bob, 8, 88, 207, 216

race, 88, 276, 277, 278, 281, 282
racism/anti-racism, 173, 175

About the Contributors

Caroline Bithell is lecturer in ethnomusicology at the University of Wales, Bangor. Following on from research for her Ph.D. (University of Wales, 1997), she has presented papers and published articles on a number of different aspects of musical activity in Corsica. Broader areas of interest include music and politics, music and gender, music revivals, world music and professionalization, and polyphonic singing traditions. She continues to conduct fieldwork in Corsica and has also carried out comparative research in Sardinia and Malta. She is currently coeditor of the *British Journal of Ethnomusicology*.

Philip V. Bohlman is professor of music and Jewish studies at the University of Chicago. He has written widely on European folk music and the intersections of nationalism and racism with music in the modern world. His books include *World Music: A Very Short Introduction* (2002), *"Jüdlische Volksmusik": Eine mitteleuropäische Geistesgeschichte* (2004), and *The Music of European Nationalism: Cultural Identity and Modern History* (2003). The recipient of the 1997 Dent Metal of the Royal Music Academy, Bohlman is also artistic director of the Jewish cabaret ensemble, the New Budapest Orpheum Society, which has released the CD set *Dancing on the Edge of a Volcano* (2002).

Jerry Cadden is a musician and ethnomusicologist who lives and works in Boston, Massachusetts. By trade a professional tuba player, when he's not playing in orchestras and brass bands, he is active in the Scottish community in New England and in the vibrant Celtic music scene.

Dai Griffiths is principal lecturer in music at Oxford Brookes University. He has published articles on single songs by Anton Webern, Bruce Springsteen, Bob Dylan, and Michelle Shocked and on the analysis of words in pop songs. He has reviewed Welsh poetry and published on Welsh pop and on masculinity for Welsh-language journals.

Scott Reiss is founder and codirector of Hesperus, an early and traditional music ensemble. He was also a founding member and codirector of the Folger Consort from 1977 to 1998. His articles on recorder technique, improvisation, and traditional music have been published in *Continuo, American Recorder*, and *Early Music America* in this country and *Tibia* in Germany. He also directs SoundCatcher, a series of workshops teaching musicians the skills of playing by ear. His most recent solo recording is "The Banshee's Wail," with Tina Chancey, Zan McLeod, and Glen Velez. While enrolled in the doctoral program in ethnomusicology at the University of Maryland, College Park, in 1998, he received a grant from Earthwatch funding his research on Celtic music in Ireland.

Graeme Smith has written on Irish traditional music and migration, Irish dance music accordion playing, the Australian folk movement, Australian country music, and on musical constructions of nation and identity. Currently, he teaches at the School of Music, Monash University, Melbourne. His book *Playing Australian: Folk, Country, Multicultural Musics* will be published in 2003 by University of Queensland Press.

Martin Stokes is associate professor of music at the University of Chicago. His publications include *The Arabesk Debate: Music and Musicians in Modern Turkey* (1992) and *Ethnicity, Identity and Music: The Musical Construction of Place* (1997). His current work focuses on musical sentimentalism, with case studies drawn from long-standing interests in the music of the Middle East, South-East Asia, Latin America, and Ireland. A book on Abd al-Halim Hafiz, coauthored with Joel Gordon, is also in progress.

Peter Symon has published widely on music, culture, and politics in Scotland. His recent articles include: "From Blas to Bothy Culture: The Musical Re-making of Celtic Culture in a Hebridean Festival"

(2002); and (with M. Cloonan) "Playing Away: Popular Music, Policy and Devolution in Scotland" (2002).

Timothy D. Taylor teaches in the department of music at Columbia University in New York City. His publications include *Global Pop: World Music, World Markets* (1997), *Strange Sounds: Music, Technology, Culture* (2001), and numerous articles on various popular and classical musics.

Johanne Devlin Trew was born and raised in Montreal, Quebec, of Irish parents. Educated in French and in English, including Baccalauréat en Musique, Université d'Ottawa; M.A. (Musicology/Ethnomusicology), McGill University; MLIS (Library & Information Science), University of Western Ontario. She completed a Ph.D. in ethnomusicology at the University of Limerick, Ireland, in 1999, where she was also employed as music archivist/librarian. Current research explores the cultural traditions, primarily music and dance, of the predominantly Irish-settled Ottawa Valley on the Québec/Ontario border. She currently teaches at Newfoundland Memorial University.

Fintan Vallely is a widely travelled musician, editor of *The Companion to Irish Traditional Music* (1999), and lectures in Traditional Music at DKIT College, Dundalk, Ireland.

Desi Wilkinson is best known as a traditional Irish musician. He has toured widely throughout Europe and North America and is a founding member of the internationally renowned group Cran. He completed his Ph.D. on Breton music in 1999 at the University of Limerick. His main research interests to date include the song and instrumental traditions of Ireland and Brittany and the interface of the French and Irish diasporas.